Masters of Corporate Venture Capital

Masters of Corporate Venture Capital

Collective Wisdom from 50 VCs
Best Practices for Corporate Venturing
How to Access Startup Innovation
& How to Get Funded

Andrew Romans

ISBN: 1530088690

e-ISBN: 9781530088690
Library of Congress Control Number: 2016910041
CreateSpace Independent Publishing Platform
North Charleston, South Carolina

This publication is designed to provide accurate and authoritative information in regard to the subject matter covered. It is sold with the understanding that neither the author nor the publisher is engaged in rendering legal, accounting, or other professional service. If legal advice or other expert assistance is required, the services of a competent professional person should be sought.

—*From a Declaration of Principles Jointly Adopted by a Committee of the American Bar Association and a Committee of Publishers and Associations*

Under no circumstances should any material in this book be used or considered as an offer to sell or a solicitation of any offer to buy an interest in any individual company or investment fund managed by Andrew Romans, Rubicon Venture Capital or any of the companies or individuals in this book. Any such offer or solicitation will be separately made only by means of the Confidential Private Offering Memorandum relating to the particular fund to persons who, among other requirements, meet certain qualifications under federal securities laws and generally are sophisticated in financial matters, such that they are capable of evaluating the merits and risks of prospective investments.

The views and opinions expressed herein are those of only each author writing or being interviewed and do not necessarily reflect the views of their existing or former employers, their affiliates, their employees or the author.

Contents

Chapter 5 - Advice & Best Practices for Corporate Venturing Related to CVCs, Entrepreneurs & Financial VCs · **138**

Chapter 6 - War Stories from CEOs, Founders and VCs – The Good, the Bad & the Ugly · · · · · · · · · · · · · 170

This book is dedicated to the creators, entrepreneurs, investors and supporters of the entrepreneurial ecosystem that donate some of their precious time to help others without asking for anything in return.

This is the pay-it-forward culture that creates the magic.

Contributors & Interviewees

- **Gaurav Bhasin**, Managing Director, Technology Investment Banking, Pagemill Partners, a Division of Duff and Phelps Securities, LLC
- **Roel Bulthuis**, Founder & Head, Merck Serono Ventures
- **Armando Castro, Jr**, Partner, Pillsbury Winthrop Shaw Pittman LLP
- **David Cohen**, Founder & Managing Partner, TechStars and Disney TechStars Accelerator
- **Nikolay Dmitriev**, Former CVC Managing Director, OJSC "Rostelecom"; Partner VITA VENTURES
- **Tim Draper**, Cofounder, DFJ, Draper Associates and Draper University
- **Max Dufour**, Partner Technology & Strategy, Harmeda
- **Eric Elfman**, Founder & CEO, Onit
- **Saman Farid**, Vice President Investments & Director of Silicon Valley Office, Legend Star 联想之星 (Legend Holdings); Managing Director, Comet Labs
- **Brad Feld**, Author & Managing Director, Foundry Group; author, "Venture Deals" and five other Venture Capital books
- **J. Skyler Fernandes**, Founder & Managing Director, Simon Venture Group (SVG)
- **Tom Fogarty**, Inventor of the Balloon Catheter and 165 Medical Patents; Founder, Fogarty Institute for Innovation; prolific investor
- **John Frankel**, Cofounder & Partner, ff Venture Capital

- **Anil Hansjee**, Former Head Google's European & Israeli Strategic Investment and Corporate Development Programs; Former CVC, IDG Ventures, MTG Sverige Modern Times Group; Partner & Co-Investor, Mojo Capital Fund of Funds
- **Michael Harries**, Cofounder & Chief Technologist, Citrix Startup Accelerator
- **Kenny Hawk**, CEO, Mojio; CVC-backed Serial Entrepreneur
- **David Horowitz**, Former Partner, Comcast Ventures; Founder & CEO, Touchdown Ventures
- **Villi Iltchev**, Partner, August Capital; Former Director & CoFounder, SalesForce Ventures; SVP Strategy & Corporate Development, Box
- **William Kilmer**, Former Head of Intel Capital EMEA; Operating Partner, Mercato Partners; Founder & CEO, Public Engines
- **Mitch Kitamura**, Cofounder & Managing Director, Draper Nexus
- **Christina Ku**, Investment Director, DOCOMO Innovations (NTT Docomo subsidiary); former investment professional, Vodafone Incubation & Ventures, Intel Capital, TriplePoint Capital and Silicon Valley Bank venture debt group
- **Jonas Landstrom**, USA Managing Director, Volvo Ventures
- **Pär Lange**, Founder & Investment Officer, Swisscom Ventures
- **Rick Lazansky**, Cofounder & Managing Partner, Silicon Catalyst; Board Director, Sand Hill Angels
- **Jack Leeney**, US Head of Investing, Telefónica Ventures
- **Toby Lewis**, Editor, Global Corporate Venturing
- **Suresh Madhavan,** Investment Manager, Verizon Ventures
- **Curtis Mo**, Partner, DLA Piper
- **Blake Modersitzki**, Managing Director, Pelion Ventures; Cofounder & Managing Director, Novell Ventures
- **Claudia Fan Munce** – Cofounder & former Managing Director, IBM Capital Group; VP, IBM Corporate Development; Venture Advisor, New Enterprise Associates (NEA)
- **Matthew Myers**, Senior Executive, BNP Paribas Banking Group, responsible for international CVC transactions

- **Tom Nicholson**, CEO, Nicholson NY (acquired by IconMedialab AB), Chairman & CEO, LBi International; Founding Member, Angel Round Capital (ARC)
- **Victor Pascucci III**, Former Founder & Head, USAA Ventures and Head, Corporate Development
- **Jacob Bratting Pedersen,** Partner, Northcap AB
- **Mark Platshon**, Senior Advisor, BMW i-Ventures; Managing Director, Icebreaker Ventures
- **Frédéric Rombaut,** former Managing Director & Head of Corporate Development International, Cisco Systems; former Founder & Managing Director, Qualcomm Ventures Europe; former Apax Partners; Cofounder, Bouygues Telecom; Founder-in-Residence, Founders Factory
- **Peter Rule**, Chairman & CEO, OptiScan Biomedical, Inc.
- **Anand Sanwal**, CEO & Cofounder, CB Insights
- **Jonathan Sherry**, Cofounder, CB Insights
- **Igor Shoifot**, Partner, TMT Investments; Chairman, Happy Farm Incubator; Cofounder, Fotki; adjunct professor, UC Berkeley, UC San Francisco and NYU
- **Igor Sill**, Managing Director, Geneva Venture Group; Founder, Geneva Venture Partners; through his Family Office, Limited Partner in Goldman Sachs Investment Partners, Benchmark Capital, Norwest Ventures, Granite Ventures, The Endowment Fund and ICO Funds
- **Ozan Sonmez**, Head, New Ventures Startup Accelerator and Hikmah IP Accelerator, King Abdullah University of Science & Technology (KAUST) Saudi Arabia
- **Rahul Sood**, Founder, Microsoft Ventures and Microsoft's network of Accelerators; CEO, Unirkn
- **Masatoshi Ueno**, Senior Manager, AGC Ventures (Asahi Glass America)
- **Sita Vasan**, CEO, Ernst & Young SVG Solutions; former senior exec, Silicon Valley Bank; 12.5 year veteran Investment Director, Intel Capital
- **Alex Wang**, Vice President, Strategy & Corporate Development, VMware

- **Fred Wilson**, Founder & Managing Partner, Union Square Ventures and Flatiron Partners
- **Bart Würman**, CEO, DDF Ventures; former CEO, AM Pharma and Lanthio Pharma
- **Jack Young**, Head, Venture Capital, Deutsche Telekom Capital Partners; former Head, Qualcomm Life Fund; General Partner, dRx Capital AG
- **Patrick de Zeeuw**, Cofounder, Startupbootcamp Global; Cofounder, InnoLeaps.com, the Accelerator for Corporates
- **Anonymous**, Financial VC active in Silicon Valley
- **Anonymous**, Managing Director, large Japanese CVC active in Japan and Silicon Valley

Foreword

WILLIAM KILMER

When Andrew Romans approached me with his idea of writing a book on corporate venture capital, I thought the subject made perfect sense. More than ever before, there is a need for a "how to" book on corporate venture investing. And it certainly made sense for Andrew, author of *The Entrepreneurial Bible to Venture Capital*, the definitive guide on venture capital and an active Silicon Valley VC, to write it.

Why the need for this topic at this time? As this book nears publication, corporate venture capital (CVC) has had another banner year. In 2015 we saw the most money deployed by corporate ventures in the last 14 years, up 37% from the year before, to over $7.5 billion[1]. Corporate VCs are now in approximately one out of every five venture deals, and we regularly see big deals involving corporate VCs hitting the press.

However, if you listen closely enough, you will hear the naysayers out there. They will tell you that corporate venturing is an organizational whim, tied to outsized corporate profits and short memories of the dot-com bust. Or they call it "dumb money." Just as soon as the economy goes bad and profits retreat, they say, so will the CVC investors.

But it's not a stretch to say that things are different this time. The rapid speed of technological change, the hyper-competitiveness of markets, globalization, lower costs of market entry, and the emergence of

---

1 National Venture Capital Association Q4 2015 Corporate Venture Investing

micro markets that can be ridden to larger threats are making corporate venturing an imperative for virtually every enterprise.

Nevertheless, if corporations are to rely on their corporate venture capital groups to guide them through the uncharted waters of competitive markets, or expect them to pave the way to access new innovations or support their strategic initiatives, they will need their CVCs to execute very, very well. That execution is based on two factors: how much the CVC can deliver returns, both strategic and financial, to the corporation, as well as how much differentiated value the CVC can add to the companies in which they invest. Without the former, CVCs will fail their corporate mission. Without the latter, they will not get access to most interesting, hottest, most beneficial or otherwise strategically relevant investments.

That is why this book is so important and so worth reading. It brings together essential information on the how and why of corporate venturing that every corporate VC needs to know. In it, Andrew brings together three unique perspectives that CVCs need to understand: from the best CVCs, traditional VCs, and the startup founder who has worked with CVCs. In doing so Andrew captures the three voices that can help CVC investors understand how to optimize their organization for success and forge those rough, uncharted waters.

I come from a unique background: a former investor and managing director at Intel's CVC group, Intel Capital; a consultant that has advised major corporations in setting up their CVC groups; a venture investor; and the CEO of a company that received investment from a CVC. I have seen corporate venture capital upfront, from every angle and I believe that *Masters of Corporate Venture Capital* captures those perspectives in a way that will help you understand corporate venture investing at its best.

Whether you work in a corporation, a venture fund, or a startup, I hope you enjoy this book and benefit from the many insights of the dozens of people that have contributed to it. Enjoy the journey!

William Kilmer
London

William Kilmer is the former Head of Intel Capital Europe, a venture portfolio based in London, with over $400m in invested assets. Earlier, as Intel's Director of Strategic Investments at headquarters in Silicon Valley, he oversaw and managed multiple exits in the US, Europe, Asia and the Middle East. While at Intel he also formed a $50m fund focusing on investments in the MENA region. William enjoys a strong and varied track record as a successful entrepreneur, corporate venture capitalist, senior corporate executive and advisor to VC funds and startups, completing scores of equity investments, acquisitions, technology buyouts, and corporate spinouts. He was Chairman & CEO of Public Engines, a leading VC-backed provider of cloud-based predictive analytics and data visualization software for public safety, government and other organizations, acquired by Motorola in 2015. William also acted as CEO of VC-backed Avinti, which he grew and sold to M86 Security, a cyber security company where he acted as Chief Marketing Officer through its sale to Trustwave. William has served on the Boards of more than 15 companies. He completed a master's research degree with a dissertation on the Corporate Venture Capital (CVC) model and its impact on corporate knowledge and continuous and discontinuous innovation. william.kilmer@gmail.com @ wkilmer

Orientation

ANDREW ROMANS

What's Driving CVC? In ancient times (before the 1990's), innovation in technology required billion dollar R&D programs. Those were the days when innovation happened primarily inside large tech titans like IBM and HP. Over the past twenty years, the cost to launch and grow startups has declined rapidly. The ecosystem of early stage angel and micro-VC investors has also developed very quickly in places like Silicon Valley, New York, London, Israel and China, with investors lining up to invest in pre-seed and seed stage startups. In more developed ecosystems there is a funder for every stage of startup into the pre-IPO phenomenon stages with multi-billion dollar valuations. These changes have combined such that innovation today is more likely to occur at a startup than inside a huge corporation, even one with a big R&D budget. Many more patents now come from startups; soon the majority will. In a world where young people grow up hearing about Steve Jobs, Bill Gates and Mark Zuckerberg, graduates from top universities want to work at a startup rather than a big corporation, bank or consulting company. Today, IBM and HP are reaching outside their companies to find innovation and bring it inside. Corporate Venture Capital (CVC) is a primary tool for such institutions to do just that in today's world, a trend likely to increase.

As an entrepreneur turned venture capitalist myself, I find corporate venturing to be a fascinating topic worthy of study. Such investing can ultimately be harnessed to make startups more successful, to create wealth for entrepreneurs and investors and to bring huge value to large corporate entities. As you will see in these pages, the benefits can be immense. I believe all large companies should participate in corporate venturing at some level. I hope this compilation of research with top practitioners in the CVC ecosystem will benefit all of these players: startups, VCs and the CVCs themselves. As with my last book, I turned to my network of CVCs, VCs, entrepreneurs, bankers and lawyers, interviewing them to collect real world data, facts, experiences and lessons covering a period of decades. I provide my own commentary throughout, which you can take onboard or happily ignore. Having advised corporates on the formation of their own CVCs, I find it evident that there is no "one size fits all" model for corporate venturing. Each person is unique and so is each company. Therefore, the best strategy for each of us requires unique analysis. I hope this collective wisdom and discussion will provide you with a clear vision resulting in actionable decisions leading you to be more successful.

What Is the Difference between CVCs and VCs? This book is about corporate venture capital ("CVC") or, as some say, "corporate venturing." Most CVCs operate very differently from classic VC funds, which I will refer to now as "financial, independent or classic VCs". CVC refers to large corporations ("corporates"), like Intel, Qualcomm, IBM, Verizon or Novartis, investing into technology startups. These CVCs are different from the classic independent Silicon Valley VCs who typically raise capital from a diverse group of Limited Partners and then invest that capital seeking a pure financial return. Such VCs are also motivated and obligated to return capital to their Limited Partner investors within a reasonable number of years; therefore, most financial VCs are hoping to crystalize an exit with each startup via IPO, M&A or secondary sale of some or all of their private shares. Corporates are less motivated and normally not compelled to exit within such a specific time frame. Most independent VCs claim to be value added investors that seek to deliver strategic value to their portfolio startups beyond the dollars they invest, but that is really just part of their strategy to make their investments perform well and attract the best deal flow to make money eventually. I would say most VCs are 100% focused on making a financial return. At my own VC fund I view our LPs as our shareholders and our portfolio startups we invest in as our customers. CVCs are different. They typically make investments motivated by a mix of strategic return of value to their corporate, coupled with some motivation of financial return, or simply motivated to breakeven.

Some CVCs will tell you their CVC group is totally separate from their corporate development group, but in my experience of 20+ active years in the ecosystem, the CVC team is rather closely linked to the M&A team at the same corporate. Sometimes the same people perform both functions. Some CVCs you will meet in this book claim to be investing purely for strategic return with no interest in financial return. Other CVCs go to great lengths to claim they behave just like financial VCs. Most of these corporates are investing their own corporate cash off the balance sheet, not other people's money. In some cases CVCs are structured with a General Partner-Limited Partner (GP-LP) structure with a 2% annual management fee and 20% carried interest on the profit of the fund (2&20), but these are rare.

What Can CVCs Do that VCs Can't? Moving from motivations to capabilities, many of these corporates can do things that most independent VCs cannot. For example, a corporate may decide to become a customer of the startup. Once the corporate issues a huge purchase order, the startup's sales may increase by 100x. From an investor's perspective, that's a good buy signal. The corporate may decide to invest, buying 10% of that startup at the same time. Or a corporate can invest and then force their global sales team to resell the startup's product or service. Some corporates can help a company grow from their home market in the US, France or any country and, over a 24-month period, roll out in 100+ countries. Obviously a corporate can, in some cases, add enormous value to a startup. Independent VCs and entrepreneurs should know how to help make this happen. Making any of this work is certainly not simple for the CVC, the startup or the helpful financial VC. This book points out many of the classic obstacles that get in the way, we dive deep into these issues and attempt to find the latest thinking on solutions.

Corporates in the US, other rich countries and many emerging markets are sitting on record piles of cash. With interest rates at an all-time low, the cost of capital is cheap. Because I live in Silicon Valley and spend most of my time with growing startups seeking funding from all over the world, my perspective leads me to think that we are living in a golden age of startup creation; but according to *The Economist,* small firms are being created at the lowest rate since the 1970s. Consolidation has made most major industries in the US less competitive including airlines, cable TV, telecoms, food and health care. Giant tech firms are currently enjoying high market capitalizations (both publicly traded and privately held) and are sitting on 41% of all the cash held by non-financial institutions. (should you footnote the 41%)

How Big Is CVC? In 2015 CVCs were active in 19.3% of venture-backed deals, spreading $28.4bn in funding across 1,301 deals according to CB Insights. According to the National Venture Capital Association (NVCA), CVCs invested a total of $7.6bn into startups in 2015 out of a total of $58.8bn invested into these companies combined with all VCs. According to the NVCA the percentage of VC financings in the US including CVCs has grown from 13% to 21% during 2010-2015. This important trend jumps out at anyone operating in the startup-venture capital ecosystem. Specific statistics may vary, but make no mistake, CVC is playing a much bigger role in the venture capital ecosystem. All players need to better understand CVC and do a better job working with it. The experience of many with CVC is negative; this can be improved. We may be just at the beginning of a new era. CVCs may grow to take a significantly higher percentage of the best startups via direct CVC investing and via LP positions in financial VCs. I also expect CVC to be a leading force as venture capital grows in the Arab world, Africa, India, China and other emerging markets.

Why do CVC? Our world is in a rapid state of change. Continuous technological change, the Internet, smart phones (mobile miniaturized super-computers armed with broadband internet access and GPS trackers), big data, the Internet of Things, the industrial Internet of Everything, fintech, edtech, adtech, marketing tech, social networking, the shared economy, low cost rapid manufacturing, hyper-competitive markets, globalization and growth of emerging markets means that everything has changed and will continue to change even faster. The lower costs to launch a startup or a product means that it used to require a huge corporate with a massive R&D budget to make and launch great transformational products or services. Now these can be launched with far less capital and with so many VCs ready to fund them the threat to corporates from startups is far greater now than it was five, ten or fifteen years ago. As Mr. Andreessen once said, "Software will eat the world." As just two random examples, the shopping and automotive industries may change more in the next five years than they have in the last fifty years. CVC can help a large corporation cope with the dichotomy of the pressure to deliver short-term quarterly results that can reward or punish a publicly traded stock price with the need to focus on long-term smart decisions. I find many large corporates make many key decisions looking only three, six and twelve months ahead and are challenged to focus on two, three, five and ten years ahead. CVC puts the CEO back in the driver seat to manage long-term innovation, vision, strategy, leadership and investment in a sensible manner and if done right make financial returns along the way. You can tell your shareholders that investing in CVC will bring innovation into your company while at the same time generating profit. After becoming a profit center CVC can act as a zero cost portion of your external R&D forever. This is true, but you can also tell them that this protects the investment of those that want to hold your stock for the long term. This investment in CVC today and commitment to maintain the program protects the business in many ways looking forward on a 10, 20 or 30 year perspective. I would think certain Warren Buffet-style shareholders of your stock would like to hear that you have a plan to make this a great business this year and next, but also for future generations into the long-term. There is something known as generational capital and not just looking at the next one to five quarterly results. China has done well with five-year plans.

Who Should Do CVC? Today 50% of the Fortune 50 and 33% of the Fortune 500 have a corporate venturing program. I suspect that 90% if not 100% of those in the Fortune 500 that do NOT have a CVC program are scratching their heads wondering if they should join the club and start one. My personal opinion is that any company with $1bn+ in revenue should establish a CVC. For many tech companies the threshold can be much lower. Not only tech companies like Intel and Microsoft should have CVC programs, but also non- or low-tech companies. Taxi companies probably did not consider themselves to be tech companies, but look at Uber. Blockbuster Video might have done well to have had a CVC group and been an early investor into Netflix. We are seeing CVCs pop up in unexpected places like Campbell Soup and Sesame Street. When I first saw Jet Blue, the airline, launch its CVC group I wondered what their investment strategy would be. When I met them I could immediately see tons of opportunities to put offers onto the TV screens in front of captive audiences, on their boarding pass print outs, email confirmations, smart phones and SMS message inbox: they know where we live, where we are going, where we have been, where we will have a layover, what section of the airplane we are sitting in and our mobile phone numbers. I started to see huge opportunities to make money with our own portfolio companies and airlines. Clearly every airline should operate a CVC.

Many large companies are the dominant player in a declining business market sector. I believe that the CEO and CFO should work very closely with the head of strategy and other execs responsible for the core and peripheral business units to use CVC and corporate development (M&A) to avoid just sitting on a number one position in a declining market. CVC and M&A together can enable such companies to diversify their product and service portfolio and even create ecosystems of businesses that support strategic directives to support or create new recurring business lines. Sometimes it makes sense to invest in a group of startups to create a new ecosystem around your business or the launch of a new product. Many product companies would be wise to invest in new start-ups that provide the professional services for their products. This can enable the core product business to enjoy high growth and high margins by holding minority positions in their service consulting businesses that are lower margin and without unique technology, rather than using valu-able investment resources to wholly own such auxiliary services. In this sense CVC can be used for surgical air strikes on your competitors and change the competitive landscape, while clearing a path for a more diver-sified long-term business. If you are not hotwired into the startup scene in Silicon Valley, New York, London, China and other tech corridors around the world, how do you expect to be at the leading edge of innovation? Venture capital can be used as a weapon and big corporates should know how to use it effectively for both offense and defense.

Got a lot of employees? Any company with a large number of employees, based on that alone, should have a CVC group to make their company more efficient and competitive while creating a positive impact on the lives of their employees. When I meet corporates with 15,000+ employees who tell me they are not interested in technology, I just think of how much they spend on technology today or how much they would benefit from bringing some tech into their internal operations. If these corporates access innovation via CVC, start to pilot technology, and as a result give huge purchase orders to the innovating startups, they can generate an annuity profit center that makes more legal "inside trading" investments than Gordon Gekko ever dreamed of making. If you are a corporate and about to make it rain for a startup, juicing their revenues, why not get in on the action and own some equity? CVC is full of double, triple and more bottom lines. I believe CVC creates win-win-wins when done properly.

What Makes CVC a Success vs Failure? Corporate venture capital is full of dead bodies and failures, but also has a number of shining success stories. Many of us in the industry have witnessed companies announce the launch of their new CVC program only to watch it become paralyzed and fail to make investments, upset the financial VCs and entrepreneurs, or be fully cancelled just a few years after launch. Historically the life span of the average CVC program has been 2.5 years; it is currently trending at 5 years. With new CVCs being formed every week, one should expect many to abandon corporate venturing with the next economic downturn, reorganization or change of CEO. Entrepreneurs and financial VCs have good reason to be cautious and suspicious about taking corporate capital. At the same time a few players like Intel Capital have proven their long-term commitment to corporate venturing and have stayed in the game for the duration, making venture capital an integral part of their innovative business on a continuous basis. Corporates beginning their CVCs must address long term vs short term goals, funding levels, compensation, portfolio management, lines of authority and reporting relationships, all potential opportunities or land mines. This book examines numerous CVC weaknesses and mistakes that can be avoided.

If you are a founder, you should know how and when to raise CVC funding or avoid it. If you are a VC hoping to turn one of your fragile startups into a multi-billion dollar monster, you should know how to harness the power of CVC while steering clear of the land mines. If you are a CVC, you should avoid laying your own land mines or stepping on the classic ones.

Why? What? How? Outcomes? In this book I first cover why corporates are motivated to form CVCs, then what they do to structure their steps toward venturing, how they structure, manage and measure these structures, and what sort of outcomes result. But in every interview I first asked the CVC the same questions: Why do you even bother with CVC? What are your core and lesser objectives? Why are you doing this? Chapter 1 lists and explores a broad variety of these CVCs' motivations for making investments into tech startups. Only then do we move onto what, how and so what. Every new or existing CVC should review the compendium of real goals outlined in Chapter 1 and then articulate their own goals. These goals become their founding constitution; all other decisions should point back to achieving those canonized goals.

Grounded in the Chapter 1 goals, I then share the insights and conclusions of roughly 50 interviews with leading CVCs. Here you will learn how CVCs are structured, how they decided to organize, report and measure themselves, and a myriad other decisions needed to make to become operational. If you are a CVC you can draw a baseline from this book on how other corporates made decisions. These interviews may help guide your own decisions on how to launch, structure and operate your CVC. All these decisions tie back to Chapter 1 goals. Your CVC should be structured to achieve your corporate's primary and secondary goals. When in doubt, go back to your own founding constitution: your articulated goals.

This sizable set of case studies and interviews begins to show some patterns and repeating issues. Here your true path will begin to emerge. This book examines options for corporates to get into the startup world ranging from accelerators, other open innovation programs, seed investing and late seed, to Series A, B, C, growth, and Fund of Funds (FoF) and investing in independent VCs. All are real world case studies from the big boys and girls, with some insights from me sprinkled throughout. CVC and corporate development are compared and contrasted, tied together or divorced. These big picture case studies illustrate how CVC can truly move the needle for "the Bigs."

What About the non-CVCs Among Us? A few top players in the business contributed to a chapter focused on advising entrepreneurs how to raise capital from CVCs. If you are an entrepreneurial CEO that has already raised or plans to raise CVC funding, I expect this chapter will also be worth your time. If you are about to go into a meeting with a specific CVC, this book may outline their investment decision-making process; I'd add that to your reading list. I conclude with some advice on how to operate or set up what I believe is the optimal corporate venturing program, with a set of options to customize for differing situations. Corporate venturing is so complicated with so many moving parts that in many cases it is broken and simply does not work. Many prominent independent VCs and founders have publicly vowed never to work with a CVC ever again. In this book I point out many of the problems and offer solutions in an attempt to fix these specific issues or at a minimum help the reader spot problems before it's too late. The prospect of making a startup massively successful truly excites me. Big corporates can help startups be successful; however, sometimes they do more harm than good. This book aims to achieve a win-win-win where the startup hits the big time, the corporate achieves multi-faceted levels of strategic and financial value and the independent VCs achieve unheard of financial success.

Here is the audience I had in mind when writing this book:

Execs at corporates thinking about starting a CVC program

Execs at existing CVCs You are either one of the contributors to this book or you probably already know a few of those that did contribute. This book is essential reading to form a baseline of how other CVCs are set up, to understand key opportunities and challenges and to come away with new wisdom on best practices. You may make some meaningful changes to your own CVC program or leave and join a new corporate with better CVC practices or start a new CVC within another corporate.

Independent financial VCs With corporates increasing their activity in VC, it makes sense to understand what makes them tick and learn how to best work with them. Opportunity to raise LP dollars from corporates and persuade them to invest in your VC funds is large and growing. This book may help you raise capital from corporates and even make your independent VC more competitive.

CEOs and founders of tech startups If you are going to play your best game as an entrepreneur, then it helps to understand how best to raise funds and derive strategic value from CVCs. Learn what motivates CVCs and figure out not just how to raise dollars, a commodity, but how to strike partnerships with huge global monolithic corporates that can do more to increase your sales than most mortal individual VCs in the Silicon Valley. These corporates are also good candidates to acquire your startup. Even with an open IPO market, M&A is the most statistically likely positive outcome for a tech startup. Taking meetings with a CVC is a great way for a startup to run your partnership ideas up the flagpole. You can possibly get on the radar of a major business unit at a corporate that would otherwise be very costly and time consuming to pursue. The CVC group should, in theory, be able to identify the correct folks within the corporate to examine a partnership. This is more than a CEO can hope for with the usual VC suspects on Sand Hill Road. Taking money from a CVC may change your startup forever in a way you cannot reverse. Investing some of your time to better understand the risks, details and pitfalls of dealing with corporates may pay back high returns. Reading this book can help you raise capital from CVCs, partner with them, and be acquired. Chapter 7 focuses on how to raise capital from CVCs. If you are feeling impatient feel free to skim through the first few chapters and jump directly to Chapter 7. There is a lot of relevant advice for entrepreneurs peppered throughout the book. I suggest reading this book with a fast forward mentality rather than just skipping to Chapter 7. If you see something that bores you, just speed read and skim to get to the nuggets more relevant to you. That's what startups do.

Other players in the ecosystem M&A investment bankers, corporate securities lawyers, LP investors in VC funds, headhunters, accelerator mentors and anyone giving advice to startups and their investors will pick up collective wisdom from these fifty or interviews and case studies. You may also benefit from my own experience gleaned from hundreds of CVCs and other players that have done deals with CVCs.

Anyone interested in getting a job As an entrepreneur, CVC, VC, angel investor, banker, or other ecosystem player: Read on!

One

Motivation & Goals - Why Corporates Establish CVC Groups

"In business, what's dangerous is not to evolve."

- JEFF BEZOS, FOUNDER & CEO, AMAZON.COM

Driving forces motivating large and mid-sized corporates to establish and operate CVC programs are as varied as the corporates themselves. Many of their motivations are explored in their own words in the 50+ Case Studies and War Stories that follow. But here is a cheat sheet of some common goals that appear over and over. Achieving any one of these goals could justify a corporate's entire investment to create or maintain a CVC program. Think of this list of "Chapter 1 Goals" as a mind-jogger to start your own thoughts spinning to clarify your own goals in entering the corporate venturing world. So, in no particular order:

- Reach outside the corporate to bring innovation into the corporate from those innovating more successfully outside.
- Access business intelligence and innovation in order to understand technologies, business models and trends that impact core and peripheral businesses. Many corporates call this technology scouting. This activity can be viewed both as offense and defense.

- Identify partnerships with technology startups where the corporate can become a customer of the startup, partner with the startup to put the startup's products or services in the hands of the corporate's sales force, find out if the corporate's customers are interested in what the startup has to offer and bring more value to those customers. This all spells "drive overall revenue."
- Strengthen strategy decisions with Silicon Valley and global innovation intelligence.
- License technology.
- Create a pipeline of investment opportunities for the corporate via mature or nascent corporate venturing programs allowing for direct investments that present strategic and financial return.
- Create a pipeline of acquisitions for the corporate development group with a long-term goal of creating new lines of business that will generate billion dollar recurring revenue streams, while diversifying the corporate's product and service portfolio for long-term survival.
- Play defense. Divide "hedge" investment opportunities into technologies and businesses that threaten the corporate's core or peripheral businesses. Such hedges can protect a corporate from declining business lines and protect the corporate from becoming obsolete, impacted by trends such as the Internet, smartphones, IoT and the shared economy. Protect your core & peripheral business from disruption (Taxi industry from Uber, Blockbuster from Netflix, Yahoo! from Google and Facebook).
- Create opportunities for the corporate to benefit from equity ownership in early stage and/or growth stage startups, where the corporate will enable these startups to grow their sales rapidly and become very valuable companies. If the corporate enables a company to grow to tens or hundreds of millions of dollars in revenue as a result of partnering with a corporate, that corporate may as well own a significant equity position and take part of the financial gain it helps to create.

- Bring the entrepreneurial culture and dynamic energy from the startup and venture world back into the corporate culture.
- Develop new entrepreneurial skill sets in executives that can join internal CVC programs to foster intrapreneurship, commercialize internally developed technology and spinout new businesses.
- Create a single repository to capture all internal startup ideas and connect the CVC group to senior management and back to heads of Business Units.
- Create a PR image for the public, demonstrating that the corporate is innovative and hip to work for, buy from or do business with.
- Access human capital. Many of the best graduates from top schools do not want to work at a big corporate and go into start-ups. Use CVC to access this part of the talent pool and the growing percentage of patents registered by this cross section of the human market.
- Influence your HR group to better know which kind of people to hire.
- Increase the quality of life for the corporate's employees.
- Lower attrition rates and the cost of hiring and training new replacements.
- Increase the corporate's revenues.
- Increase the corporate's efficiency and lower costs by adopting technology or becoming a customer of some of your portfolio companies.
- Increase the corporate's competitiveness.
- Enter new markets or defend existing markets.
- Use cash from revenues in foreign currencies to invest in those countries, capitalize on local tax schemes; or negotiate new favorable tax deals with local governments. Improve your PR image in those countries.
- Use CVC as a method of establishing offices and operations in different countries and tech corridors, driving globalization of the corporate as an organization.
- Access innovation from key tech corridors like Silicon Valley, Israel, New York, London, China and beyond. Do not miss what's

happening in these hot zones, but find innovation in additional locations.

- Expand product and service offerings.
- Focus on long-term product and service innovation. Use CVC to combat the short-term quarterly results mindset that plagues publicly traded companies.
- Leverage distribution networks to sell more or add new revenue streams.
- Fit into a "build, partner, buy" strategy.
- Replace or augment the corporate's R&D. Invest some of the R&D budget in a portfolio of startups alongside top VCs, with the expectation of making a profit after a few years, making this a "zero cost R&D program."
- Consider some innovation to be internal and some to be external. CVC and corporate development access external innovation.
- Outsource part of your R&D program, breaking free of its limitations. It's hard to think outside of the box when you are in a cubicle.
- Value being part of the VC-entrepreneurship-startup ecosystem.
- Develop ecosystems around products or platforms operated by the corporate. E.g., SalesForce.com investing in startups that use Force.com.
- Exploit domain expertise to make smart investments E.g., Yahoo! investing in Alibaba and Yahoo! Japan.
- Make a financial return to ensure the CVC program is sustainable.
- Increase Earnings Per Share (EPS).
- Make a financial return for the sake of making a financial return. If you create value for startups why not own some of them to benefit from success created by corporate. CVC done right can outperform most financial VCs.

I encourage every CVC or corporate considering forming a CVC to write your own list of top goals and objectives for playing in the corporate venturing space. Start by getting your CEO, CFO, Head of Corporate

Development, Head of Strategy and other top executives to sign their names to a document that outlines the top prioritized objectives. I can hear the screams of some of my readers at how hard this would be to achieve, but for some it is possible, especially if it is the CEO driving the CVC initiative. After you have agreed on this, use your list of written objectives to drive all decision-making on your strategy and structure for the CVC unit's operation. You may need to refer back to this list if you see things slipping off the rails. Most CVCs evolve rapidly and also suffer from high turnover of investment professionals. As you read through the rest of this book, try to tie your decisions back to this list of goals customized for your own use. Give special care to how you structure the interplay between CVC and corporate development (M&A).

CORPORATE R&D MUST BE REINVENTED AS CVC USHERING IN A NEW ERA FOR CORPORATE VENTURE CAPITAL - IGOR SILL - MANAGING DIRECTOR, GENEVA VENTURE GROUP

Igor Sill was kind enough to contribute this excellent overview of the case for corporates participating in the venture game. He coached me, conveying decades of experience as an angel, VC and Fund of Funds investor. Igor is not only Managing Director of Geneva Venture Group, he is also a Silicon Valley venture capitalist and founder of Geneva Venture Partners. Igor manages his own angel investment fund at Geneva Ventures and is also a Limited Partner in Goldman Sachs Investment Partners, Benchmark Capital, Norwest Ventures, Granite Ventures, The Endowment Fund and ICO Funds through his Family Office. After achieving extraordinary success in Silicon Valley you are most likely to find Igor on his terraced cabernet sauvignon vineyard in St Helena, Napa, California. In Igor's own words:

It would appear that US innovation has never been brighter. Global corporations are spending in excess of $650bn on R&D annually, most of it on technology advancements. The top technology R&D expenditures are from worldwide corporate giants including Samsung ($13.8bn), VW ($13.5bn), Intel ($10.6bn), Microsoft ($10.4bn), Roche ($10bn), Novartis

($9.9bn), Toyota ($9.1bn), Johnson & Johnson ($8.2bn), Google ($8bn), Merck ($7.5bn), IBM ($6.2bn), Cisco ($5.9bn), Oracle ($5.2bn), APPLE ($4.4bn) and HP ($3.5bn), representing a cumulative increase of $9bn over the previous year, according to *Fortune* magazine.

This outdated R&D model of the industrial organization that progresses through internal lab development has been eclipsed by the reality of new, venture capital backed startups that achieve far greater competitive advantage through rapid cycles of innovation, customer acceptance and global distribution. IBM accounted for $6.2bn of R&D, which ironically exceeded all of the annual venture capital industry's investments made. Over this past decade, the rate of technology innovation has rapidly accelerated, challenging those Corporations' ability to maintain a competitive edge. Corporate R&D executives lie awake at night worried that they may be blindsided by innovative technologies they're not aware exist. The technology innovations and investment returns are obvious, venture-backed technology companies have consistently exceeded every corporate R&D outcome.

Today's corporate R&D is no longer a simple matter of new product introduction, or merely adapting to the new technology realities. Instead, it has become a keenly strategic process that utilizes all available resources. Corporate R&D is realizing that they must partner with outside ventures in order to stay ahead of the game.

Corporate investments in tech startups are growing at an increased pace, according to the National Venture Capital Association. These corporations are eager to optimize Silicon Valley's technology, innovations and talents into their R&D ambitions.

I've noted an interesting trend in the number of multi-national corporations now opening up business development offices to capture access to the explosion of startups and the pace at which these deals are happening.

Of foremost interest to these corporations is venture capital's emergence as an exemplary financial engine for the explosive growth of advanced new technologies that are changing the world while creating entirely new industries. The reasons for venture capital's successes are many. The venture structure encourages innovation and gives entrepreneurs the tools they need to create, develop and launch their innovative ideas globally. In periods of low growth and high strategic uncertainty, venture investments can serve a very distinctively valuable business objective.

It can be a rich source of technological advantage and information about potential transformations in the companies' core businesses. The more established corporations are increasingly dependent on innovative new technologies in order to remain competitive, thus it would seem natural to incorporate a venture capital model for a portion of technology development. This approach exploits venture capital's efficiency in developing technology, its access to new advancements, its capacity to respond quickly to changing technology, its ability to leverage additional resources throughout the development cycle all while returning favorable financial returns. A corporate venture arm can also serve as an intelligence-gathering initiative, helping a company protect itself from emerging competitive threats. Also, these corporations use their venture capital network to explore sectors of longer-term strategic interest. Corporate venturing can provide both an inside look at new developments as well as access to possible ownership, joint ventures, licensing and use of new ideas, responding rapidly to market shifts and demands. As competition intensifies and uncertainty increases, corporate venture can open new strategic avenues and options.

Such an approach has proven successful for companies such as Apple, SalesForce, HP, Facebook, Oracle, Dell, EMC, Google, Cisco, as well as other technology-focused companies.

By combining its own capital with that of independent VCs, a corporate venture arm can magnify the impact of its investments. This is particularly beneficial when technological uncertainty is high. In the financial services sector for example, VISA elected to invest in Square, a mobile-payment startup whose technology transforms smartphones and tablets into credit card payment readers.

Another excellent example is Apple's iFund, supported by Apple and launched in 2008 by the venture capital fund, Kleiner Perkins Caufield &

Byers. The iFund provides a very unique leverage; it encourages development of technologies that rely on the Apple's platform, further increasing demand for its own products. As of September 2015, Apple has acquired over 70 companies while building a critical mass of innovative applications for its iPhone and iPad products. This approach, as well as Apple's demanding culture, helped it achieve one of the fastest growth trajectories and largest market capitalizations of any public traded company. Given this success, it is not surprising that others have initiated venture investments.

Getting in the venture investment game

The decision making process of forming a corporate venture arm, co-investing alongside venture firms or engaging a corporate venture investment partner is a critical one. For purposes of this book, I am assuming that many corporations have already recognized the many pitfalls of staffing a corporate venture arm, and have long since abandoned that path. Of course, I'll exclude Intel Capital, which stands out as an anomaly having developed a unique culture and successfully intertwined its venture relationships. Deciding between direct startup investment, venture capital fund investment, or the more conservative corporate venture partner path should entail a great deal of research and most importantly, compatibility with your long term strategy. Mature corporations are balancing their R&D exposure by funding some of their technology development through partnerships with venture capital teams.

Location, Location, Location

Though there are bright pockets of venture activity globally, the epicenter of premier technology innovation and talent continues to emerge from Silicon Valley. This is a unique place with a supportive ecosystem ready to back entrepreneurs' requirements for launching startups successfully. The weather is excellent, the lifestyle is wonderful, and the scenery exquisite. Stanford University, UC Berkeley, USF and University of Santa Clara provide an abundance of research and continually spin off new patents along with a steady flow of budding intellectual, entrepreneurially driven graduates. Hence, 80% of venture capital and angel investors operate in Silicon Valley; and, not surprisingly, 90% of the highest venture returns occur here.

Global companies bring a great deal of value to the startups they fund in the form of brand reputation, skills, and of course, deep resources—from a vast customer base, global distribution channels to armies of sales professionals. They also change the perception of how outside investors view startups' prospects. Institutional investors often anticipate that a corporate-backed startup will ultimately be acquired by that company, and generally at a much higher valuation, reflecting the strategic benefits that startups can offer its corporate investors.

There exists a massive market with a strong rising tide for optimizing this new corporate R&D paradigm, one with increased efficiencies and far better results. The opportunities of advanced innovations, globalization and the internet's disruptive nature make it a period of significant transformation that is creating extraordinary corporate value. Companies as diverse as BMW, Volvo, GE, GM, Novartis and General Mills are now complementing their traditional R&D by joining with other venture investors to fund promising, strategically aligned startups. The logic is indeed compelling. Given the benefits that venture investing provides, the real question is whether corporations can afford not to participate. In an economy where innovation spells the difference between success and failure, corporate venturing can secure its future competitiveness.

Two

Case Studies of Corporate VCs

"Even castles made of sand fall into the sea eventually."

- JIMI HENDRIX

CASE STUDY - MOTOROLA VENTURES - MATTHEW GROWNEY - FORMER COFOUNDER & MANAGING DIRECTOR; CEO, ISSABELLA PRODUCTS

Motorola Ventures is one of the first CVCs I came into contact with early in my career in the late 1990's. I thought it appropriate to begin these Case Studies with Matthew Growney's account of Motorola Ventures, an entrepreneurial story that tells of the creation of one of the first great CVCs. Here are his words:

I began my career at Motorola in 1994 in the Corporate Strategy Office. By 1997 when I was 25 years old my job was to hunt down unsolicited deal flow. As a company with $34bn to $40bn in revenue we would receive tons of inbound ideas and they would flow into the corp dev office. As the lowest analyst in the group in the first year I received about 2,000 proposals. We ended up investing in four and acquired one. There was no actual entity to receive, invest and act upon any of these opportunities.

I asked the head of corporate strategy if I could create an investment vehicle that would create one single place for the entire corporation to send these and be the repository. Bill Hambrecht became my mentor and he was flying into the golden days at H&Q at the time. You may remember these were the days of the Four Horsemen investment banks that were taking Internet and software companies public and the startup scene was booming before the consolidation of the banks and the first big dot-com crash. Bill had been advising both Texas Instruments and told me a lot about TI which was focused on semis and very different from Adobe. We had a lot of discussions in 1997 and 1998 about culture and what would be the most suitable for Moto which was a Chicago telecom vendor and very different from TI and Adobe.

Motorola Ventures become the de facto early stage investment arm for the company. No business units were going to do deals or hide deals. Anywhere an early stage business opportunity came from now had to come to Moto Ventures first. So I had to come up with the strategy and thesis and create support. For an entire year I went to the heads of 7 business units (BU's), up and down the organization and finally up to the CEO to get support for this. There was no budget or other examples. I explained that we would have beauty pageants and events where we could bring entrepreneurs to the BU's and save our BU's money where they did not need to go to outside events and spend money looking for things. In return they needed to give us a shopping list of the ten or fifteen technologies they were looking for. We knew we could find them better than they could.

We will bring you many beautiful things to look at but the quid pro quo is that they need to show us their shopping list and we will pay for it all by making investments. I still was given no budget. I moved to Palo Alto and started looking for deals. I was told that if I found a deal that was both strategic and financial I would have to pass the hat to get it funded.

The first deal I did was a $2m investment on a $20m pre called SnapTrack and we sold it to Qualcomm for $1bn 14 months later. Once this happened I got a $100m annual budget for Moto Ventures and we were up and running. We continued to invest in some pretty cool stuff. I invested in Online Anywhere, which got acquired by Yahoo! for $300m a year later.

Most corporates feel like they can get away with investing in companies with a 100% motivation for strategic and nothing financial. This is a huge flaw. Look, if you lose money there is nothing strategic about that. We succeeded because we had a 50-50 split that an investment must be strategic and it must be financial.

We grew it from me and one other guy to a team of eight. We then opened offices in Boston, Tel Aviv, London and Beijing. We were good at getting shopping lists from our BUs with the belief that even if Moto did not adopt any of these technologies, we would still benefit from IPO's and good M&A exits.

I remember once we invested in a company's Series A and B rounds. We later invested in the E round that wiped out our A and B rounds. That same company was later acquired for $300m. That's another example of keep an eye on financial returns, while staying focused on the shopping list.

Corporates considering CVC may not see value in financial returns, but if they don't balance strategic with financial the program will not survive.

There is a long list of financial losers in the CVC history books. Most of those no longer exist. When I left we had $400 of Assets Under Management (AUM).

I also started a Fund of Funds (FoF) program. The first deal we did was a domestic RMB fund in China. At Moto we had a ton of RMB currency. Most corporates would never want to keep the RMB. This enabled us to find local deal talent and learn the rules of the deal for domestic RMB China. We did end up making nine to ten investments directly in China, but we learned a lot by being LPs in a local VC fund first. We ended up investing in five different VC funds which gave us very specialized coverage in vertical markets and key geographies.

I also became the president of the Corporate Venturing Consortium at MIT. Ken Morris who was the head of the entrepreneurship program at Sloan asked me to set this up. I call this a "self-help" group for CVCs. We had Intel Capital, Nokia, Sony, Lucent, Ericsson Venture Partners and then a bunch that were contemplating setting up venture programs such as Proctor & Gamble. We met once per month and discussed all the ways to make CVC work.

By 2007 I left and did nothing for eighteen months and then started my own fund Rudyard Partners, which invests in early stage East Coast tech companies in consumer, but recently began to invest in some non-tech consumer-facing opportunities.

Most managers have their heads down looking at the present. CVC enables them to see the future. They get to outsource R&D. I think that's valid and viable. Why should I spend $50m to design a chip company when I could take this out for $18m and get team, IP and speed. I once heard the CFO of Moto say, "For every $1 of money spent in R&D we need to get $5 of revenue off of it." If I spend a dollar on venture and I get $20 or $30 back then that's pretty awesome. It's a very realistic rational for doing it.

I swung Earnings Per share (EPS) $0.02 per share which is huge for a very large corporate.

CASE STUDY - TELEFÓNICA VENTURES - JACK LEENEY - US HEAD OF INVESTING

I caught up with Jack Leeney, US Head of Investing at Telefónica Ventures in San Francisco and he explained the multi-faceted approach Telefónica is taking to corporate venturing.

Telefónica has been making venture type investments over a twenty-year period, but over the past five years their approach and structure has formalized how they capture external innovation and work with entrepreneurs.

Each time Telefónica Ventures makes an investment they consider how the investment will 1) benefit Telefónica strategically, 2) be a financially sound investment and return capital, and 3) how it will positively impact Telefónica's relationship with local regulators and local governments.

Telefónica is one of the largest telecom operators in the world, began in 1924 as the incumbent state owned telecom monopoly in Spain and has grown its business to become the largest, second or third largest operator in 23 different countries in Europe, North America, Latin America and Asia with a focus on fixed and wireless operations for voice, data and television with group-wide revenues of over $70bn and $10-12bn of EBITDA.

Telecom and television are highly regulated industries and Telefónica maintains strong relationships with local governments, which at times even present opportunities. In recent economic downturns some sizable office buildings across Europe and Latin America came under munici-pal ownership and Telefónica stepped in and turned some of these into shared workspace for startups, which resulted in job creation and became integrated into Telefónica's multi-faceted corporate venturing strategy. Telefónica controls the main telecom network assets in these countries; so it was rather simple for them to run broadband into these facilities and repurpose them for shared workspace for startups.

Telefónica Ventures has evolved around its Open Future Initiative (www.openfuture.org) where they have a number of pillars to their multi-faceted approach to CVC.

1) **Co-working spaces** - on the cashless side, Telefónica hosts hack-athons and co-working spaces, offering free work space to early stage startups which is viewed to be creating jobs, adding value to the ecosystem and being good citizens in the markets in which they operate.

2) **Accelerators** – Telefónica Ventures is behind Wayra, some would say the largest accelerator program in the world with 12 accelera-tors located in Europe and Latin America. Wayra has funded over 600 companies with typical investments today ranging from $60k to $100k per startup and runs them through a six-month program.

3) **Fund of Funds** – Telefónica Ventures has invested in five VC funds recently in Europe and Latin America usually acting as the anchor LP investor in each fund constituting 20% to 33% of the fund in most cases. Telefónica Ventures recently committed $200m to Coral Group, a new VC fund based in Israel dedicated to invest in telecom related infrastructure companies ranging from soft-ware and equipment topics related to telecom networks, data centers and surrounding areas of business. At the time I spoke to Jack, Telefónica was the main investor in the fund and the fund managers were still marketing the fund to other LP investors. The

Fund of Fund practice enables Telefónica Ventures access to the many deals that pass through these different independent VC funds and brings strong synergies with Telefónica Ventures' direct investment group.

4) **Telefónica Ventures direct investment group** – Telefónica Ventures makes direct investments into startups, but typically at mid to late stage Series C, D and later with typical check size of $5 to $10m as part of much larger financing rounds. Telefónica Ventures only invests in these cases when Telefónica will become a customer of the startup and these companies are truly at the phase of scaling their businesses. To complete an investment the startup needs to bring Telefónica near term value and significant impact. These are often US based well-funded technology start-ups that are doing well in the US market and can partner with Telefónica to globally scale their businesses in new markets in ways not previously considered. Telefónica itself can become an important revenue-generating customer for enterprise companies and can also leverage its 300m+ consumer customer base or small to super large enterprise customers that do business with Telefónica. To complete an investment the opportunity needs to be 1) financially sound in the sense that it will return capital to Telefónica Ventures and 2) will provide strategic benefit to Telefónica Group.

All four of these groups now sit inside of the Open Future Telefónica business unit, which reports directly to the Chief Strategy Officer who in turn reports directly to the CEO of Telefónica Group.

CASE STUDY - SWISSCOM VENTURES - PÄR LANGE - FOUNDER & INVESTMENT OFFICER

I had the opportunity to reconnect with Pär Lange to get his perspective on founding Swisscom Ventures and key lessons learned from a full decade of CVC. I first met Pär when he was a telecom entrepreneur before turning CVC. Here are his words:

Prior to founding Swisscom Ventures I had founded a few startups where I raised venture capital funding and so became familiar with all of this. I founded a mobile network operator in Sweden where I ultimately raised €1.3bn of funding and obtained a 3G radio license from Swedish authorities before making a successful and tax efficient exit securing more than 50x for investors. I raised funding from VCs such as The Carlyle Group and Investor AB as well as corporate investors NTL, the UK cable TV company, and Orange (France Telecom) who ultimately bought out all the other investors providing an excellent exit for all.

After this I also advised a number of Nordic VCs on deal sourcing, due diligence and completing investments further developing my VC experience.

When I was first approached by Swisscom to establish their CVC group I happily accepted the challenge and assumed that everything was in place and ready to get started. This was far from the case! At the time Dominique Mégret, who was then Head of Group Strategy for Swisscom was supporting the initiative and recruited me to set it up. Dominique is now the Head of Swisscom Ventures. He also had the support of the CEO. Despite this top-level support, for the first year we got nothing done.

They wanted us to work with the M&A corp dev guys on everything we did. These guys were former investment bankers who make all decisions from conclusions drawn from Excel spreadsheets and financial modeling. The financial plan of a startup is more of a directional guess than anything and the business of venture capital and entrepreneurship is without a doubt more art than science. Discussions on valuations with the M&A guys were totally foreign from my VC and entrepreneurial experience. Also these guys were accustomed to bringing in McKinsey type consultants before making any kind of decisions and taking weeks and months to conduct analysis before making a move. They were used to doing things via elaborate corporate processes with board approval and directly involving the CEO. We quickly realized we were not ready to get started and making investments until we fixed this and in fact we wanted to do the deals ourselves and not depend on the M&A guys.

At the time that I started Swisscom Ventures the corporate process we needed to go through to complete an investment was to get the written approval of the head of the following departments: M&A group, tax team, legal group, and then go to the Executive Board of Swisscom, then the CEO and then the CEO needed to go to the Board of Directors. And let me add that all of these committees and group heads are used to a certain level of polished presentations that in itself would render us paralyzed. When we tried to make investments we ran into trouble with the legal department, which was unfamiliar with all the terms in a term sheet. I also realized we need to address this issue to be successful.

I immediately went to work on establishing a lean corporate governance system that would enable us to get operational and start making investments. This was a victory when I got it done in just under one year of effort.

We worked less with the M&A guys. For investments below 5m CHF we only needed the approval of our new Investment Committee comprised of just the CFO and the Head of Strategy. Once this got in place we were in business and effective. At the moment we temporarily have no Head of Strategy and our CFO has gained more confidence on how we are operating. So for the moment we are operating with still only two people, but the Head of Network and IT and the head of one business unit. This lean form of corporate governance is essential to our ability to operate and the autonomy to make investments on the fly that are below 5m CHF. Over time our legal guys became seasoned corporate securities lawyers and now understand the legal terms as well as any law firm in the Silicon Valley and this part has also become efficient.

Sometimes we struggle with the question of why are we even doing this anyway? What is our purpose at Swisscom Ventures as part of Swisscom Group? Over the past ten years of running Swisscom Ventures from time to time we see consultants come in and they tend to usually focus on technology scouting and bringing the spirit of entrepreneurship into the Swisscom organization. I'm always happy to listen to what they have to say but in my view the ideal case for an investment is when we are able to invest in a company and get Swisscom to become a customer.

This means we are doing something good for Swisscom and obviously adding value to the startup.

Absent corporate venturing there is a reality within large companies of "no one ever gets fired for going with Big Blue – IBM." This is a serious issue and I think our CVC does a good job of addressing it. Often product managers and middle management executives at Swisscom are afraid to take a risk on using a startup's technology or solution. They think that if they go with IBM, HP, EMC, Broadcom or some other large well-known company and the project fails that they cannot be blamed for the failure, but the blame goes to that large company. And by the way, I have seen projects and technology from all of these large companies fail miserably. So failure does happen there. There is a concern for the middle management program manager that if they bet on a startup which might have better technology and probably is cheaper that if the project fails they will personally be blamed and they will suffer.

So how do you boost the confidence of the middle manager to take a risk and work with a startup? The key is to lower the barriers and create less resistance to work with small companies.

We spend a lot of our time fighting battles to get Swisscom to adopt the technology of the startup we invest in. The startups are hoping we will add value and so we need to fight this internal resistance to make it a win. I find that having the approval and endorsement of the Head of Network and IT and the CFO or head of a business unit gives that risky startup more credibility. The middle line manager can then hopefully conclude he will not personally be fired if the Head of Network has approved this vendor. Also high-level execs do not look at losing $500k or $2m into a startup as something that will upset the performance of a huge company like Swisscom. The middle manager is terrified of losing $500k or $2m and does not have the larger perspective.

So with this in mind we established an investment theme around investing into tech startups that can make Swisscom more efficient and where Swisscom can become a customer. We found that investing in companies that can result in Swisscom pushing out a new product or service to our customers does not work well in the real world. We have tried this many times and seen numerous failures. When it is technology that we can use it's easier. For example, we invested into a billing company called Matrixx. Normally telcos are terrified of making any changes to their billing systems. We took that risk and with effort we got Swisscom to adopt it and it enabled us to offer more flexible billing options to our residential and enterprise customers. We became the first customer for this startup and once we had things working (it did not work right away and took time to function smoothly) we were able to make introductions to Deutsche Telekom, Teléfonica, British Telecom and others. Bringing huge value to a startup and getting our organization to lower its resistance to better and cheaper technology has become our goal.

Sometimes we negotiate warrants or additional free shares if we can deliver Swisscom and other telcos as customers to the startup. If we are creating so much value for them we should be rewarded. Probably half the time we convince Swisscom to become a customer and half the time we fail to get internal Swisscom managers to adopt the technology. You can see this is where we are fighting the internal battles and need to position our organization to do this effectively.

Because we are the incumbent network operator in Switzerland we want to be seen as good corporate citizens and an innovative company that has evolved from the post office to a technology leader in the region. As such we also make seed investments into Swiss domiciled companies. There are very few seed stage VCs in Switzerland and so we fill in this gap. Part of this is justified as excellent PR where the image of Swisscom is tied to innovation, jobs, hope and fostering entrepreneurship and the future of our country. Mind you, we still strive to make money with each investment.

Swisscom Ventures is structured as an evergreen fund. That means that exit consideration is put back into our account and reinvested in startups. Achieving exits in venture capital can take time and so anyone entering this market needs to take a long-term perspective. Most CVCs getting started realize they need to invest for strategic objectives, but also run a profitable investment program so that they are not viewed as a cost center and risk the program being shut down. What many CVCs I know do not tune into is the importance of keeping a lean burn rate of the CVC group itself so that the capital deployed is returned and you also cover your operational expenses.

During the ten years I've been at Swisscom I have seen T-Venture, the CVC arm of Deutsche Telekom, reorganized more times than I can count. I believe Vodafone Ventures does not even exist anymore. Often what I see is that the telco or other corporate gets a huge budget from the leadership of the company, they make a big announcement and then the next time there is a downturn or outside consultants come along the CVC is the first victim of a reorg. When we first started Swisscom Ventures we took over the strategy group, but quickly decided to scale down. It is easy to end up with 45 to 65 people working in a new department and before you know it you are the least efficient VC in the world. So we have remained disciplined on this topic, although we recently have grown our group a bit. To survive reorgs a CVC needs to be profitable. We have learned how to use people from different business lines that know us and help us without getting con-solidated into our numbers and making us look unprofitable. Best practice is to get their ideas and help, but keep them as line managers outside of the CVC group. With each new reorg we make sure that we protect our lean governance model; that has so far yielded longevity for the program.

CASE STUDY - IBM VENTURE CAPITAL GROUP - CLAUDIA FAN MUNCE - RETIRED COFOUNDER & MANAGING DIRECTOR, IBM CAPITAL GROUP; VP, IBM CORPORATE DEVELOPMENT; VENTURE ADVISOR, NEW ENTERPRISE ASSOCIATES (NEA)

I met with Claudia Munce at The Sheraton Hotel in Palo Alto right before the NVCA – WAVC annual luncheon. Claudia struck me as very different from any other CVC I had ever done business with or even talked with while writing this book. A big difference was that Claudia had already worked directly with the CEO of IBM prior to forming the group. I sum-marize her words here:

Claudia had no issue with compensation. She was firmly in control with all the power, experience and conviction needed to run her corporate ven-turing program the way she wanted. She mentioned that most financial

VCs would gladly trade places with her when it came to compensation, an issue that plagues many CVCs who plan to make a move to a financial VC and make the same 2&20 compensation we financial VCs make. Most other CVCs are constantly surfing the delicate balance between strategic versus financial objectives. They are always playing their cards to make sure the program is profitable and survives amid all the fragile politics of a large corporation operating in a constant state of reorgs. Most other CVCs I know were either hired to establish the CVC or more commonly, were working in some other less senior role at the corporation. They had spent over a year lobbying the senior management to form the CVC. However in Claudia's case, she was already at one of the most senior roles in her organization. In her previous role at IBM she was in charge of IP licensing and commercialization for IBM Research Lab. With her fifteen years of running the IBM Venture Capital Group, Claudia had been at IBM for over thirty years. She retired from IBM and joined NEA as an advisor only a few weeks after our last meeting, as this book went to press. Different from some of the other CVCs that I know, IBM is also a very large and mature technology titan with operations on the scale of a medium sized country.

Claudia founded the IBM Venture Capital Group in 2000 at the request of then IBM CEO, Lou Gerstner. With Claudia's knowledge of internal R&D, the CEO figured that she was the one to identify startups to fill the gaps in IBM's portfolio and bring them internally within the company. Fifteen years later Claudia was firmly in the driver's seat as the Head of the IBM Venture Capital Group. Initially the group reported to Corporate Strategy, but quickly changed this to report to the Head of Corporate Development. Claudia explained that the most effective way to structure corporate venturing at IBM is to report to corporate development, and more specifically to the CFO of the entire corporation.

I challenged Claudia on the logic behind IBM Venture Capital Group reporting directly to corporate development. I had first heard Claudia explain this on stage at WiL's MOMENTS event at Stanford University on a panel moderated by Mitch Kitamura from Draper Nexus (also interviewed in this book). My first reaction hearing this as a financial VC at Rubicon Venture Capital, former VC advisor and a former entrepreneur who raised lots of VC and CVC funding, was that I would be very cautious of shar-ing information with a corporate investor that openly shares everything they hear with their corporate development team. To share information with this CVC is equivalent to alerting their M&A group on what you are doing. When a startup is seeking to raise capital from value added inves-tors it is most likely NOT the correct time to approach M&A groups of large prospective buyers. Some of these corporates could be the ones that the startup is actually disrupting. Furthermore, once you take their investment you are under the microscope of their corporate development group telling the CVC how to vote or influence the board level decisions at the startup. The CVC group may not be motivated to make your com-pany a success, but purely to drive the pipeline for their M&A group. This further broadens the conflict of interest a startup has with every other VC.

Claudia was very firm and convincing about her rationale that the CVC reporting into corporate development made the most sense:

This argument about corporate development not being aligned with corporate venturing, I think it's the opposite and that it's much better aligned. You want to make sure you are impacting the corporation's strat-egy. At the same time you want to know what you are driving is core to the overall strategy of the corporation.

Another difference about IBM Venture Capital compared to other CVC units is that we are 100% strategic. We seek to get our money back 1x, but do not consider financial return in the decision-making equation beyond 1x. If you get less than 1x then the company probably would not exist for very long and there is nothing strategic about that. Otherwise we are 100% strategic on purpose and open about it throughout the orga-nization. IBM Venture Capital Group has historically been a cost center. Rather than create new finance groups we leverage our dedicated corpo-rate development team and we still do dynamic provisioning and leverag-ing of resources that we need at any given time. We have big costs of our staff, although we do draw on many resources that are not on our P&L; so in reality we are spending even more.

For a company the size of IBM with 370,000 employees, with opera-tions in hundreds of countries, corporate venturing just cannot move the needle or make an impact on their business when operated in isolation. Trying to keep the operating costs of the CVC unit low to show a CEO or board positive unit economics was to miss the larger opportunity. Looking at the economics of how much of a startup a CVC can expect to own at the time of exit, cash on cash multiples or IRR and then considering the operating expenses of the CVC operation, I concluded that the impact would be negligible to the business and would never move the needle on IBM's large business. If, however, the CVC group were structured to create a truly meaningful acquisition pipeline, augmenting the corporate development team's effectiveness, that would be a meaningful way to move the needle on the business. M&A simply has more impact than investing off the balance sheet for minority positions.

Some of the startups IBM has acquired with the help of the IBM Venture team have gone on to generate tens of billions of dollars of lasting revenue and that makes a difference. Trying to limit the size of my team to balance the checkbook of cash invested to cash returned would mean missing the bigger opportunity.

Debating this issue with Claudia, I felt like I was talking to my late grandfather, a Navy Seabee in the Pacific during World War II. The Seabees ("Construction Battalion"), sailed LSTs, prepared for troop landings and managed supplies for US troops. First to land with the Marines, the Seabees saw real action, transported men and material, built what was needed where it was needed, and rested when they could. He used to tell stories about how he sometimes traded surplus jeeps for cots (or beer) for the Marines on small islands wherever they were landing or stationed. The resources my grandfather commanded in his young 20's during World War II were incredible.

Comparably, Claudia sounded like she was running the largest CVC operation I had come across with the knowledge that the mission was paying off in more than just being financially self-sufficient and sustainable. Her relationship with the CEO is what enabled this to work. I believe there are other CVCs investing larger dollar amounts on an annual basis and certainly making better returns, but you would be challenged to find another CVC running with the level of confidence as IBM Venture Capital. The correct path for each CVC will be different and for each individual or team attempting to launch an effective CVC, something worth noting. The theme of "strong support from the top" has been consistent throughout this book, but I would like to add a slightly different spin on the CEO level or corporate founder level support. Create a CVC that can operate with high confidence.

Strategy is a space where you provide insight and thought leadership. I did not want our CVC group to just throw things against the wall with strategy and see what would stick. Corporate development is where deals are done. That's where the money is invested and where the return needs to be reported. Reporting to corporate development makes us accountable for the outcome.

Sourcing good deals that will make money is the easy part. Identifying the correct companies that can be relevant to the core business of the corporate is also not the most challenging part. The devil is in the details after making the investment about how you drive that as a partnership, test solutions, implement pilots as part of your overall solution and eventually buy the company. The most significant heavy lifting happens after you find the right company and manage to get your money into it. Finding the right company is the easy part, but navigating the large corporation to unlock value - that is much harder to achieve successfully.

Do we build, buy or partner? This is part of the organic process of a corporation looking to revamp the portfolio of internal products and services.

In addition to her tenure running IBM's corporate venturing program, Claudia frequently meets with other large corporates that are customers of IBM advising them on how they can use corporate venturing to drive their growth:

Every large company should have some kind of venturing program. You need to pay attention to what is going on. Everything is disrupting so fast everywhere that there is no company that can keep up with everything that is happening from IoT, big data, to bitcoin or whatever. No company is equipped to monitor it all. The first movers who are seeing these changes are always the venture capitalists. Large companies need to understand the innovation coming from all sources, internal, external and academic. Venture and acquisition are the primary tools for large corporates to augment their own portfolio.

We acquired 82 VC-backed companies in the past decade that now represent multi-billion dollar new revenue sources to our bottom line. Now that has moved the needle. If my team generates more expenses than make our unit look profitable, I can point to the bottom line value we have delivered via successful M&A and market intelligence. This is much more relevant to our bottom line than paying attention to IRR. Venture is simply irrelevant compared to corporate development.

Another difference with our ability to be effective is that I sit at band B within IBM's hierarchal organization. Our CEO is at the band A. When I meet with other CVCs I always ask what kind of leadership position does the head of CVC have so, whenever there is an acquisition or big decision of engagement with the startup, I know how much power the head of CVC has to get something done. An ineffective CVC is limited in its ability to deliver on its mandate. I see some heads of CVC that are at the VP level. Some are not VPs, but have a Business Unit (BU). Some don't have an executive rank and are literally at the mercy of other execs to make their decisions. It is important to decide how much senior management wants this group to drive their business and articulate that by the level of people they place in charge of the corporate venturing group.

Is the CEO squarely behind this? In order to drive changes, in order to get pilots for the startups, transfer market intelligence and new knowhow, etc. you need to have senior execs running the CVC that already know the business and get things done. Even for us, we are only successful getting what we want for our startups in a minority of cases.

Where you report to and where you sit in the corporate hierarchy will have a lot to do with your effectiveness. A lot of corporate investments come from the CFO and corporate development can drive change from the cradle to the grave. Corporate development is an arm of the CFO office. The CFO's office is where all money comes in and comes out from every part of the business. The CFO sees large figures of cash coming in and out. This makes getting decent sized venture checks less of a hassle and easier to get buy in to support the CVC. If the CVC is docked in the strategy group or R&D group the numbers start to look bigger and support will hit friction. The CFO is the central command station for all money flowing in and out. This is the core of the business. If you can tightly integrate CVC into the CFO office then you are at the center of the business and that is where CVC needs to be in organization.

IBM is a very matrixed organization. Most large corporates only buy companies that they have done a partnership with or a pilot. However the people within the IBM Venture team not only understand the IBM strategy but also are looking at what other VCs like Rubicon are doing. They compare this knowledge and synthesize the external and internal insights to focus on which technologies can be commercialized.

When it comes to what technologies we are looking at right now, I'd say it's a vast list; a too limited shopping list for a CVC is probably a mistake.

When the dust settles, there is no way that we need that many micro payment startups or the many other overvalued 'me too' FOMO [Fear of Missing Out] startups. On the other hand, we are keenly interested in transformational technological shifts such as social profiling of unstructured data that is relevant to every industry from wealth management to retail. Acquisitions make sense for us when we can scale a company's solution with the distribution power of the large corporation. Other times we implement partnerships with companies like Apple, Twitter, Facebook and Microsoft. We want their data so that we can serve their clients.

I would conclude by saying that we are like the eHarmony guys. We profile the venture capital landscape including seeing what Rubicon Venture Capital and other financial VCs are looking at and we profile IBM. Then like eHarmony we make that match. That's what the venture team does in a nutshell.

CASE STUDY - SALESFORCE VENTURES - VILLI ILTCHEV - FORMER DIRECTOR & COFOUNDER; PARTNER, AUGUST CAPITAL; SVP STRATEGY & CORPORATE DEVELOPMENT, BOX

I sat down with Villi Iltchev at the Box HQ in Silicon Valley as they were overflowing their office space and ready to move into a new purpose built building in Redwood City. Villi recalled his experience of working at the

*HP strategy & corp dev team in 2008 when they were cleaning up the rem-
nants of their 1999 to 2000 investing spree, his experience of building the
CVC program at SalesForce.com and his perspective now at Box.*

CVCs should never lead deals. On the flip side, if a CVC will only follow
other VCs that lead the deals then why should a founder agree to take their
money? So as the CVC how do you get started and build an investment
program? Few CVCs have entrepreneurial experience. Most CVC investors
are neither smart enough to pick the good deals nor experienced enough
as investors and board members to advise the startups. For most CVCs
it's hard to make their VC program work. The corporate needs to be hot
enough to make it work. I predict most corporates that are entering the
CVC market will last a few years and flame out just like the last big boom
of 1999 to 2001. When I look at most CVCs that you hear of, and I mean
even the big name CVCs, I think that they are doing nothing to impact
their company's financial bottom line and are failing to deliver any strategic
value. I look at the investments they make across stages and fail to see a
clear strategic mandate. What's the point?

When I joined the strategy and corporate development group at
Hewlett-Packard we had a team calling up startups that HP had invested
in, asking what the status was. HP's CVC program had invested in hundreds of startups and eight years later had no one left from the original
team. HP had no idea if these companies were still in business, had exits,
gone bust or were growing into strong businesses. HP then canceled the
CVC program entirely; but I met an old colleague at HP last week who
told me they were planning to launch their CVC program again. I would
hope they do it differently this time, but I would guess history will repeat
itself.

I was part of the founding team at SalesForce Ventures. The original
SalesForce CVC program was very different from most other CVCs. When
we started we had four main pillars of our investment strategy.

1) **Invest in cloud related Systems Integrators (SI's).** There were
   no cloud SI's to implement and customize SalesForce. Rather than
   invest a few million dollars internally to grow a new business unit

and make a 20% margin on that business, we decided it was better to fund a bunch of these externally and help them get going. These businesses quickly became profitable and helped create an ecosystem around our core products. These SI's would help customers be successful with Salesforce and drive adoption of our products.

2) **Fund companies that are building on the Force.com platform.** We wanted to create an ecosystem again, but this time tech companies that would create their entire business and intellectual property on top of the powerful Force.com technology platform.

3) **Invest a small check into any company that we might acquire** at some point in the future – CVC with a purpose of feeding the M&A pipeline. For us CVC was tied at the hip to corp dev.

4) **Invest in demo day stage companies** with an average check size of around $75k alongside angels and micro-VCs, making a decision in a few hours on the spot at demo days, investing into seven to eight companies per batch. We mainly attended Y Combinator and TechStars demo days, relying to some extent on the entry screening for these accelerator programs. We did this typically in 1-day; the result was that we built great relationships with startups and founders who in turn introduced us to their friends. These relationships spun into a web of total deal flow coverage in the Valley and made this small capital and time investment totally worthwhile. I would imagine that, as a result of our strategy, SalesForce Ventures sees 100% of the high quality deal flow in the Valley today.

In all cases, the goal of the investment program was to deploy the smallest amount of capital into the widest set of companies that still enabled us to achieve our strategic goals. Notification rights and access to information allowed us to acquire extraordinary insight into key companies and trends that helped inform our strategy. Note how this is radically different from financial VCs who typically want to double down and invest more of their fund capital into their winners.

With this strategy we invested $150m into 130+ different companies in less than four years. Following these pillars, we at SalesForce Ventures invested into truly amazing companies. The key take away was to invest the smallest check possible that would give us access to notification rights, relationships and information. We maximized our optionality value with the smallest amount of capital. We were never trying to make a financial return, but at the same time were not donating money. We wanted to make good investments that would generate good returns across the portfolio; but returns were equally as important as advancing Salesforce's strategic mandate. It is in this context that I conclude a CVC should never lead a deal.

Clearly, since I left SalesForce and joined Box, the strategy at SalesForce Ventures has changed. Now they are leading deals and investing into many different types of opportunities. From the outside it is hard for me to identify a pattern of pillars they are focused on and they seem to be operating more like a financial investor. Clearly the scope of the investment program has expanded.

In almost all cases I think making a financial return for a corporate is less important than a strategic return. If you consider some company with a $10bn revenue run rate, then making a huge return on $50m or $100m per year being deployed will not move the needle on the overall business. In contrast, if their CVC program leads to one or two important M&A transactions, the Street may respond to those acquisitions and reward the stock price, which would pay for those acquisitions. A strong M&A program can move the needle on the business. If the CVC program is creating a true pipeline for the corp dev unit then the CVC program is moving the needle, but investments need to drive the ecosystem, partnerships, and M&A.

Regarding compensation, I think that it is a mistake to create a single LP fund like a Sapphire (SAP Ventures). Once you pay the CVC managers like a real VC, you lose the ability to get them to add strategic value to the corporate. Investing as an LP into independent financial VCs makes more sense on this level. In contrast, if you are a Nasdaq and want to see every piece of technology that can affect your business then it might make sense. Establishing a highly motivated team of CVCs that invest in EVERYTHING related to fintech can be justified. Again, even if you make no money from your CVC program and you end up making one or two acquisitions as a result, then it can all be justified. For other CVCs like Citi Ventures it is actually easy to make money. All they need to do is find out which startups Citibank IT is going to buy from and invest in those companies. The moment Citi becomes a customer then every other bank will become a customer, the startups they invest in will go up at least 4x in value and the CVC becomes an actual line of business that is very profitable for the bank. Why would they not take advantage of that and still get all the benefits of information. There will always be other businesses that are as influential as Citi Group that can invest when they become a customer and watch their investment increase in value by 4x on the spot. That can be justified to simply just make money.

When I joined Box, CEO Aaron Levie was open to exploring a CVC program. I knew that the timing was too early. A successful CVC program requires a platform strategy and clear strategic objectives. Today I focus on strategy and corporate development taking a long-term view on our strategy and roadmap.

From my experience in this game, I think corporates hoping to be the new entrants into the CVC space should consider a disciplined approach like the one we had at SalesForce Ventures. I predict most companies do not have the type of platform that we had at SalesForce and the most successful CVC programs will be those that can leverage a HOT corporate platform that many entrepreneurs would love to work with. This is not something everyone can pull off. In the end, the financial VCs are the ones that should lead and CVCs should be in this game for strategic reasons.

Note from Andrew Romans: since writing this piece, Villi joined August Capital, a leading financial VC, as a partner.

CASE STUDY - VMWARE - ALEX WANG - VICE PRESIDENT, STRATEGY & CORPORATE DEVELOPMENT

I got together with Alex Wang and discussed the timeless topics of how to make corporate venture capital meaningful and successful. Alex brings a career of relevant experience to the discussion having worked as a venture capitalist at Apax during the late 90's through the first big Internet bubble and crash and then focused on strategy, investments and acquisitions at both Cisco and NetApp. He is currently a Vice President at one of my favorite tech titans of the Silicon Valley - VMware – where he is responsible for strategy, investments and acquisitions. Alex shared how VMware is structured and advised on how to make CVC a success. (Full disclosure: very senior executives at VMware are LP investors in my fund, Rubicon Venture Capital.).

At VMware we are structured with two different teams that make venture type investments. The guys from our strategy group make small investments into startups, typically taking small positions where VMware does not own a significant percentage; they typically do not take board seats. That team is not 100% dedicated to making investments, they also act as our strategy group. This works very well as they see so many start-ups seeking funding that, as our strategy team is located in the heart of the Silicon Valley, VMware as a company sees a broad swath of the best deal flow and are tuned into the pulse of the latest developments in the tech world.

My corporate development team gets involved when the VMware investment takes a significant share of the startup, meaning over 20% or when we invest as a precursor to an acquisition or significant relationship with the startup. Although this is an active part of our job, we focus primarily on full-out acquisitions. So we have a fairly independent venturing group which doubles as our strategy team; our corp dev team makes the larger investments.

The early investments group is separate and does not need to obtain a business unit's sponsorship. Our group only invests when we do have a clear strategic fit with a VMware business unit and formal sponsorship from a BU. At VMware my team is the tip of the spear when it comes to acquisitions. We are the in-house investment bankers and our early investments team members are the in-house management consultants. Where we require a clear strategic fit to make a big bet, take a meaningful percentage of the company and typically a board seat, our small investments team operates very differently. Many of these investments are to gain knowledge and information of what's happening in our always-evolving complex ecosystem. Some of their small investments could be viewed as hedges, meaning they may invest in technologies that are directly competitive to what VMware is doing or even clashes with our technology roadmap.

EMC Ventures at our parent company operates completely differently than our two teams at VMware. Where we make bets that are extensions of our strategy, EMC Ventures operates totally independently and does not require business unit sponsorship. What I think is of key importance is that the EMC team's incentive is carry. If they make losing investments they feel it in their paycheck.

If they perform well they are paid a percentage of the upside. If the CVC team is financially motivated by carry, I believe they are more likely to make investments in startups whose technology matters, whose market adopts their solutions and whose business becomes valuable.

In an ideal world you want to incentivize financially and reward your CVC team for bringing both strategic investments and financial return to the corporate. The problem is that it is very hard to measure objectively the exact strategic value in dollar terms. By contrast, measuring financial return can be calculated down to the penny. Make no mistake - there is nothing strategic about investing in a startup that goes bankrupt. So incentivizing your CVC team to make a financial return and share in the profits provides a framework to direct the team to invest in companies that are making technology that our customers ultimately want to access.

EMC Ventures and EMC's corporate development group both report to EMC's CFO, Zane Rowe. The EMC Ventures team is structured to operate largely as an independent VC. Again, they don't need a business unit to sponsor any specific deal. Their CVC execs have carry, enabling them to share in the upside and theoretically to keep the team together on an ongoing basis; this has a positive impact on much of the behavior of the group. They are free to invest in companies that are potentially disruptive to EMC and diametrically opposed to what EMC is doing. They are free to move quickly and enter deals that might get away while seeking a business unit sponsor. Despite all of this freedom they are clearly tied to EMC's broader strategy.

At Cisco, investing was seen as a way to stay abreast of what was going on. Keep in mind I was at Cisco in the wake of the dot-com melt down and into 2003. When I joined Cisco the market was still recovering. Today Cisco is a much more active investor in hot venture deals and doing much more than just monitoring the market. Cisco also used FoF strategically investing in financial VCs. I don't think Cisco sees investing as something transformational to their business but rather an important tool in the war chest.

A key point is that the work of corporate venturing is done at a higher quality level when your personal paycheck is aligned with the objectives of the company. Again, there is no objective way to measure the soft strategic returns. If you provide compensation to the investing team, then they are less likely to make stupidly priced investments. From time to time I have seen VC financings completed at very high valuations where a corporate sees strategic value and the independent financial VCs decide not to invest at that higher valuation. That's what I mean by stupidly priced financings. Without an ROI on the returns you can't really tell if you are sharply bringing into focus your prioritization of anything to do with success measures. I think that every company out there should be watchful of what's going on in the market. There is no stronger instrument for achieving that than corporate venture capital. Sitting at a publicly traded high-technology company in the Silicon Valley with a valuation north of $20bn, and being a leader in the migration to software based networking and an evolving cloud computing world, it's a no brainer for VMware to be active venture capital investors and exploit that as a key tool in our toolbox. Even if you are a low-tech business, the moment you achieve significant revenues and a sizable number of employees, technology will touch your business. If technology does not drive your revenues, then, at a minimum, it will add efficiency and lower costs. I would think that we are not alone in this sense and that corporate venturing groups should exist at virtually all large companies.

Startups want access to your field. That means they want your sales team to promote their business. The last thing a corporate really wants is to provide a little startup or many startups with access to its field. On the other hand, when the corporate can see that its customers want access to a specific technology then the corporate should service its customers and collaborate with those startups and give the customer what it wants.

Every startup thinks we are giving them the VMware sales force as a resource to promote their technology and business. To truly do this the startup needs to sell why these deals makes sense. In some cases it may not make sense but they need to sell the story that this is a hedging investment. On the surface it may look like the startup's product competes with ours, but it may be a valuable tool for us to keep tabs on a new innovation. Who knows which direction that goes? This type of investment can be small enough so that the information is essentially cheaply purchased. The startup gets access to an investor with intimate domain expertise and knowledge of a complex ecosystem that most financial investors could not equally possess. Giving a startup access to our field and measuring a favorable response from our customers helps indicate if this is a company we should acquire.

M&A is a powerful tool. Absolutely getting the inside track on some of these companies is something corporate venturing can help with. In some ways making corporate venture capital investments can be understood as almost pre-diligence to an M&A target. Those investments therefore absolutely make a lot of sense. Do you have enough in there vs. having nothing in there and still be able to achieve the same result? Is it a big deal if you invest a few million dollars into a company and lose it or generate a return on that small dollar amount? For a company of our size it does not move the needle either way. If you have such a significant stake that you can get some detailed info and partnering opportunities, then that in itself can justify the investment, without concern for a financial return. Sometimes I question if we could still have obtained the information without the venturing investment. If Sequoia wants our corp dev team to consider acquiring one of their startups, we may still get the inside view without the venturing investment; however, it is indeed a luxury to invest in a startup, attempt to work with them as a partner and try before you buy.

Let's take another look at this again from the startup's perspective. When you take corporate money you - the startup - are changing. You may also be pre-bought. If you are OK aligning your fate with a specific big company then it's OK. If you are a rock star company you may not want to take that corporate money, because it may shut doors to other buyers. It kinda-sorta depends. I say that this way on purpose, because each financing event at each startup should be viewed on a deal-by-deal basis asking the questions of does this make sense for the startup and does this make sense for the corporate investor. If you get it right, the results for both startup and corporate are immense.

You can scatter shot and lose 80% and not worry about it. But if the job is to find the most innovative companies wherever they are, you need to incentivize the team. If you make money, that's a sure fire way of measuring how relevant these companies are. This ensures the level of discipline being conducted on the right companies.

Corporate venturing can be a powerful mechanism to see what the market is doing. At Cisco, NetApp and now VMware, I have witnessed CVC also used to drive meaningful corporate development and bring new dimensions to our ability to acquire the right companies at the right time as well as bring a unique perspective to strategy decisions. Corporate venturing is without a doubt a valuable tool to have in the war chest.

Note from Andrew Romans: since this interview Zane Rowe has become CFO of VMware.

CASE STUDY - DRAPER NEXUS - MITCH KITAMURA - COFOUNDER & MANAGING DIRECTOR

I have known Mitch Kitamura for years, hosting him a few months ago on the VC panel at our "Big in Japan" event in San Francisco. Mitch discussed the "multi-CVC" model. Mitch has been an active VC investor in the Valley since the year 2000. He is the former President and CEO of the JAIC America, a Silicon Valley subsidiary of Japan Asia Investment Co. (JAIC). Draper Nexus is a US-Japan cross border venture capital firm based in Tokyo and Silicon Valley, and is part of the global Draper Venture Network. Draper Nexus' first fund was a $50m fund followed by Fund II, which is over $150m. I wanted to get Kitamura-san's perspective because 80% of his LPs are Japanese corporates with an additional 10% of his LPs *being Japanese financial institutions. Draper Nexus is essentially what I would call a multi-CVC fund. Here are Kitamura-san's own words:*

Most of our investors are large Japanese corporations. Their number one objective is access to innovation and a plan to develop their network in the Silicon Valley. However, if we don't provide them with a financial return we risk not having them continue to work with us. My experience has also helped me understand the different perspectives of speed within the startup world compared to the corporate world and how to address this topic and make collaboration between the corporate and startups succeed.

We learned from Fund I that corporations do not intuitively know how to work with startups. So with Fund II we began training programs for our LPs on how to deal with startups in the US and learn what they are looking for. We focus on what the corporates want from the startups and what do the startups want from the corporates. The corporates are slow and the startups need to be fast. Much of what we do concerns training the corporates on this culture difference.

When corporates invest in our fund, that's a good start. The fact that they have invested in a VC fund like ours proves that there are already one or two guys willing to stand up and change the culture. Then we can begin to access and change the people below those senior supporters of our fund and our proposed collaboration with startups. Once you create one or two successful cases of working with startups things start to move faster.

LPs also leverage their domain knowledge and expertise. They often help us with diligence. This enables us to focus on making a financial return.

We have found corporate LPs can be very helpful in due diligence (DD) to provide perspective on whether a company can work or not. This is based on non-proprietary info - very helpful for us and the startup. We think we are discovering a different kind of VC model where working with the corporate is not just a "service to LPs" but they can actually help us make a financial return and create a win-win-win among the corporate, our VC fund and the startups. @drapernexus

CASE STUDY - SIMON VENTURE GROUP (SVG) - J. SKYLER FERNANDES - MANAGING DIRECTOR

Skyler Fernandes walked me through the founding of Simon Venture Group (SVG), the largest multi-stage venture capital group focused on retail, ranked by CB Insights as a top 5 corporate venture fund in the U.S. for retail, and the venture capital arm of Simon, an S&P 100 company and the largest retail real estate company in the world, with retail sales that are larger than Amazon.com and Apple.com combined.

I like Simon's style. When he was offered the job to create Simon's corporate venturing group, he clearly laid out the terms that Simon would need to agree to before he would take on the challenge. They agreed and this is how he operates. Here are Skyler's demands in his words:

1) **The CVC must be a separate legal entity.** This allows the Simon CVC to act more independently than the certainly slow moving corporate parent. The less influence from the corporate the better. Get more respect from entrepreneurs. Entrepreneurs are often scared of big corporate investors and independence strikes at this core issue.

2) **Operate like an independent financial VC.** Staff the CVC with former financial VCs and entrepreneurs and no one from the corporate. It's OK to have support from the corporate within the CVC but leadership must be professional VCs and entrepreneurs who speak the language and know the culture. There is too much subliminal knowledge to teach someone out of the corporate at inception. This is why most CVCs fail. BestBuy Ventures is an example of a failed CVC. They hired investment bankers to run their CVC. Don't repeat that mistake. Investment managers for a CVC or any VC need experience of shit hitting the fan. Most corporate folk are scared of failure and don't want to invest in companies that are sailing through rough waters. A good VC is at home sailing through rough waters. That's what breaks through to innovation and makes a success. It's also what entrepreneurs seek in a VC partner and lacks with most CVCs.

3) **The CVC must not be forced to get a champion from the corporate or a business unit (BU).** Many CVCs require a formal head of a BU to sign up before the CVC can complete an investment. None of that for Simon Venture Group! The CVC needs to be able to make its own investment decisions. Most commonly the head of a BU wants to invest in startups that can help them with their performance in the next quarter and not something that may take years to add to the bottom line. They certainly don't want to invest in something that can threaten their power base, disrupt their team or headcount. Most BU department heads want to maintain their allegiance to existing partners where they have relationships. This all goes against the mission of the CVC to innovate and disrupt. The CVC must be free of all of this weight.

4) **Go for normal VC terms.** No investing in uncapped notes or other nonsense that CVCs are famous for where they are focused on the strategic value and lose sight of rational financial terms. Operate just like a financial VC. There are always entrepreneurs that try to complete their financing rounds with corporates where the financial VCs are too smart to jump in on those valuations. We operate like the financial guys. Ultimately when there is a change of leadership, as in a change of the CEO of the corporate HQ, the CVC will be graded on its financial performance. That better be in the top quartile of venture returns and certainly not in the negative IRR zone. A CVC should be graded on a balanced scale of financial and strategic return. Strategic is hard to measure. Financial is black and white. There you go.

5) **Compensate the team in line with the financial VCs.** No 2&20 but an operating budget to cover salaries and expenses and something close to a 20% carry. If you don't have this, the CVC will fail to recruit and maintain the best talent in the game. It's all about people and the wrong people kill all of this. 90% of CVCs mess this up. CVCs should be compensated for delivering strategic value to the corporate, but it's pretty much impossible to measure this. You also don't want the CVC to become confused

with being part of the R&D group. If you are looking for a strategic benefit it will come from the deals with the highest return. (Remember the quote from the founder of Intel Capital, "There is nothing strategic about investing in a company that went bankrupt last year.") The longevity of the CVC group is contingent upon it distributing more capital than it invests.

6) **Have a committed pool of capital.** Even if it's just a press release that the corporate will commit $10m, $50m or $100m per year to CVC. That's a must have. You will destroy yourself if you just say that you have unlimited capital. It may be true, but you don't want the future to be endless. Commit to a specific number and get specific about how much reserves you have for existing investments. It's hard to operate with the discipline of a financial VC if you don't understand what you have to work with. This is also important for the entrepreneurs and web of VCs to understand how to work with you. Each investment must be able to return 25-33% of the entire fund. This is an industry rule of thumb and I insist that our CVC operate by this doctrine. If you don't know the size of the fund how can you stick to this rule and operate a profitable vehicle? You need to stick to the best practices of venture capital, which includes minimum equity stakes to make an investment worthwhile. Otherwise the model breaks. In CVC that's usually 5-10%, as you are often sharing the remaining equity of a round with the lead VC. If investment decisions are made at the corporate level by those who are risk-averse, they can destroy the venture strategy. For example if someone in senior management of a corporate pushes for a lower check size, which will equate to an insignificant equity stake for the venture strategy, you are going down a path of total invested capital > capital returned, as the winners will never be significant enough to make up for the losers. They may say you'll make it up by increasing the number of companies the CVC invests in, but that becomes quite challenging (changing the strategy from a 40-50 portfolio company strategy to 80-100 portfolio companies) and will decrease the quality of the companies being invested in. Given most corporates don't

want to lose any capital even more than traditional VCs, following the strategy of a seed fund (with many more portfolio companies and more individual losers), this will likely be something they won't be able to deal with emotionally. Corporates are often too emotional on short-term metrics, and instead should be obsessed with making a long-term financial return, accepting early losses when they happen, trying to save companies when possible with additional capital and strategic support, and doubling down on the winners.

7) **Be risk tolerant.** Be willing to lose $500k or more on a startup. This will not sink our ship. The risk of investing into startups is adjusted by the portfolio diversification and the balance sheet of the corporate. Take that in and become prepared to put capital at risk. Many CEOs of big corporates are successful entrepreneurs that obviously crossed the chasm and are afraid of risk now that they are safe. Get them used to this risk again. It's just the nature of war.

Simon Venture Group reports to an investment committee where the CEO has veto power. This makes our corporate venturing group very independent but also hot-wired to the top to unlock all the value adds of operating a CVC that hopes to leverage synergies with the parent corporate body. Simon is a monster-sized business and our corporate venturing group is just getting started.

CASE STUDY - TOO MANY PITCHERS AND NOT ENOUGH CATCHERS - AGC VENTURES (ASAHI GLASS AMERICA) - MASATOSHI UENO - SENIOR MANAGER

I had a chance to catch up with Masatoshi Ueno for lunch in San Francisco and learned from his 20 years' experience of corporate venture capital. AGC was established in 1907 affiliated with Mitsubishi, generated $11bn in sales in 2014, employs over 50,000 people globally and has number one market share in building glass and automobile glass markets, with a number two market share in display glass. AGC is also a major multi-billion dollar player in other high tech areas of electronics, chemicals, and ceramics, with a strong customer and employee footprint in Europe, North America and, of course, Asia.

AGC Ventures is funded by the R&D budget of AGC's HQ and reports directly into the office of the CTO. Sometimes R&D makes internal investments and sometimes the investments are external in which case it goes to startups either directly via AGC Ventures or into independent VC funds via AGC Ventures again. AGC in some cases can buy the startup, put some money into their cap table, refer them to one of the VCs in which AGC has an LP investment or create a JV, a Joint Development Agreement (JDA), or other partnering program. These investments of external R&D are viewed as outsourced R&D and are generally accepted throughout the company.

AGC made its first entry into the venture capital space in 1997 with an investment into the VC fund Advent International based in Boston. The following year AGC sent a senior executive to Boston to work out of the VC office and scout for technology opportunities for AGC to invest in, partner with or learn from. This began what has been a common practice among Japanese corporates to rotate executives through different programs including spending time with a VC. AGC continued its program of making LP investments into VCs consistently over two decades with a goal of accessing innovation and opened an office in Silicon Valley in 2005 when it became clear that Silicon Valley was more relevant to the VC sector than Boston. In 2008 AGC Ventures made its first direct investment into a startup. Masatoshi-san explained that the most sensible strategy for AGC was to start by making LP investments into a series of VCs over a period of years, partner with VCs that were willing to accept an executive from AGC to rent a desk within the office of the VC and begin to learn and experience a "training" séjour that the executive could then take back to the corporate.

Advantages of this "rotation" of execs from the corporate to the VC fund are that the corporate can access information and innovation via their own employee while picking up the very different culture of the VC itself and the constant flow of startup meetings passing through the VC's office and overall dynamic startup ecosystem culture.

When AGC Ventures established their office in Silicon Valley the practice became to send a senior executive to spend three to four years with AGC Ventures and then return home to Japan. Masatoshi-san pointed out to me that this practice is less than ideal, because after 3 years these individuals are just beginning to develop personal networks of contacts in the ecosystem. They are learning how things work so that they can begin to add value to the VC process. Just when the training and networks are kicking in, AGC Ventures loses this person back to the corporate and then begin training the next executive on loan from the corporate. The networks that these rotating execs develop do not transfer to the new executive that arrives next. These executives typically return home to a big promotion and they benefit personally, but AGC Ventures faces consistency issues. Masatoshi-san suggested that a better model for this Japanese practice of executive rotation would be to send younger executives from the corporate that are more malleable and quicker to pick up on their training.

Secondly Masatoshi-san suggested that the rotation be restricted to one year. Another Japanese monolithic corporation with $18bn in revenue has developed a syllabus and curriculum that rotating executives get while on loan to their CVC group. Masatoshi-san suggested this as the model to replicate. He then made a metaphor to American baseball of having too many pitchers and not enough catchers in the old CVC model and recommends a new model with more catchers. In some cases the rotating executive could start at the corporate, spend one year with the CVC getting trained, return to the corporate acting as a "catcher" and then in some cases return to the CVC joining as a partner or managing director with a goal to spend their career as a CVC that knows how to navigate opportunities back into the corporate.

He explained that the individual working at the CVC often finds a startup and technology and "pitches" that opportunity to the corporate. The corporate does not have a "catcher" in the HQ ready to receive and respond positively to these opportunities "pitched" by the remote CVC. This new idea of shorter cycle times in returning a young executive back to the corporate places these newly VC trained execs throughout the corporate to become "catchers" of the opportunities being "pitched" by the CVC team. They essentially can act as double agents working at the corporate, but receptive to the CVC. Masatoshi-san explained that the ratio of pitchers to catchers should be many more catchers than pitchers. At any large corporate there is a grass roots natural resistance to new ideas being pitched by the CVC. Not Invented Here (NIH) is the natural enemy of a CVC being able to navigate a large corporate and unlock opportunities. Corporates often think in three-month cycles and the CVC is thinking in more of a three to five and sometimes ten-year cycle. There is also a fundamental problem that the corporate does not have a clear technology or product road map. There should be a coherent idea of what the company should do that is somehow shared throughout the corporate and their hopefully relatively independent CVC group. Everyone wants to make products and services that make money and make their shareholders and other stakeholders happy. To do this one can try to develop 100% of everything in-house, but most would agree that is not the answer. The answer is to reach outside the company and bring innovation inside via CVC, licensing, partnering and other forms of collaborating with startups located worldwide. This then becomes a sensible overall corporate development strategy.

Masatoshi-san cautioned that the hard part is to sell the story of outside innovation inside of the corporate. Planting a steady stream of catchers to receive and respond to the pitches from the CVC is one way to address this issue and ensure that the CVC knows what is happening at the corporate's HQ.

CASE STUDY - INTEL CAPITAL - WILLIAM KILMER - FORMER HEAD, INTEL CAPITAL EMEA; OPERATING PARTNER, MERCATO PARTNERS; FOUNDER & CEO, PUBLIC ENGINES

- *Why do you think that corporate venture capital is here to stay?*

At one time corporate venturing may have been considered a passing fad for the Fortune 100 that had more cash than investment sense. And certainly CVC investments have been and will continue to move in step with the economy. But so is innovation overall. When the economy is booming and companies are flush with cash, they will always have a tendency to invest more, and that will include corporate venturing.

External corporate venturing in startups is a reality of the survival in the new hyper-competitive, global markets we deal with. Innovators like Uber and AirBnB have proven that a young company can come out of nowhere to challenge incumbents almost overnight. Others like Domo and Facebook are creating billion dollar markets that didn't exist a few years before. It has become a corporate imperative to simultaneously innovate and defend, and access to new innovative companies provides both.

What is driving the current wave of corporate venturing? An excess of cash on corporate balance sheets for one thing, but access to innovation is the real driver. With more funding sources than ever, startups are reaching into every market. Even non-tech markets are threatened by new innovation, especially with the new wave of Internet of Things (IoT) innovation.

- *Do you believe that corporate venture capital is just part of the boom and bust cycle and will collapse as it did previously?*

The current boom in corporate venturing will certainly end in a contraction at some point. Every corporation is not equally committed and when earnings start to fall in an economic downturn some of those companies will get burned because they invested at the peak of the market.

At Intel, corporate venturing has long been a strategic pillar of the company, supported by the executive staff and board. It's in the Intel DNA. They have learned to not swing too far with the economic pendulum—don't over-react by investing too much when the market is hot, or pulling out when the market is down. Some of the best deals we did were when the market had contracted and we invested in early waves of innovation that took off in the next economic upturn.

- *What about team member hiring?*

Hiring a great CVC investor is difficult. It requires a unique set of skills that is difficult to find. The biggest mistake most companies make is to pull someone out of the business unit, who only knows the world through the corporate lenses.

Looking back, I think the best hires I made when hiring new corporate venture investors were those that could master the basics of the technology, that had been in a startup business or business group before and understood what a good business opportunity looked like, could find and accept the risks with the business, could structure business development deals, and were overall creative thinkers.

One of the keys for a good corporate investor is to have a sense of independence. If you can't work a bit outside of the business unit in your vision and investment scope, you are not doing the company any favors. If you constantly work with the corporate blinders on in terms of what is happening in the market and how it will impact your organization, you are kidding yourself and not benefiting the company.

The individual CVC doesn't play the same role as a partner in a venture capital firm, but they are your brand. You have to think about what kind of person you want representing your fund and meeting with CEOs on a daily basis. Who is going to best represent your business unit and your strategy, and who is going to get you into the competitive investment with that hot company? At the end of the day, any CVC investment group is only going to be as good as their individual investors.

- *What about BU (business unit) access to innovation?*

There is nothing worse for a CVC organization than a corporate investor who doesn't have the respect of the business unit or who isn't willing to push them a bit. As a CEO, I once tried to get into a corporate business unit through the investor of their well-established corporate venture arm. We weren't looking for an investment but thought we'd be a good partner and looked for customer access through their business unit. After several tries, I was told by the CVC investor supporting that group that he wouldn't introduce me because he had already introduced a competitor of ours and they would potentially look to take investment money from his group. He was willing to sacrifice a good business relationship for his own personal investment portfolio! To make a long story short, two years later we were acquired by that same group and the CVC investor supporting them was gone. The business group had missed two years of working with us because this CVC investor cared more about just making an investment rather than what was best for the company.

Sometimes as a CVC investor you need to recognize that the business unit looks at the world through their own glasses, and be willing to push ideas and even investments that are contrarian. While at Intel Capital I brought in a company that had developed some very interesting process- ing capabilities in software that we predicted would be important. When I brought it to a particular group, I was told that it was, "covered on our roadmap already," meaning they would develop it in-house. After trying several times I decided to run it by our advanced research organization, Intel Labs. I spoke with one researcher who evaluated the technology and also knew the company roadmap. His conclusion, the business unit didn't have anything like what the startup had developed and was at serious risk of not being able to fulfill their roadmap needs."

After confirming the technical superiority of the startup's develop- ment and their overall business, which was ramping quickly, we made an investment in the startup against the business unit's recommendation. Just about 18 months later, we acquired the company for the very tech- nology the business unit had dismissed. That was an exception to the rule, but as a CVC investor, you have to make those kinds of calls and have the independence to do it.

The individual CVC investor plays a critical role as the go between for the startup and the business unit. You have to play an independent role. As an investor, you have an obligation to make that company suc- cessful and to make sure the corporate business unit does no harm. As a corporate investor, you have to maintain the objective of helping the corporation see some benefit from the relationship. That balance is where all successful investors need to play.

One of the best modifications Intel Capital made to its typical business unit supported deal requirements was the "Eyes and Ears" investment classification. It was incorporated during Les Vasdez' time, and was a staple of our strategy. Les Vasdez was the founder of Intel Capital and the third employee of Intel. If an investor found a deal that was outside the business unit's scope of vision, or even outside of Intel's scope or potentially disruptive to us, we could raise the "Eyes and Ears" flag and push it forward without strategic support. There was always a high burden of proof that it would eventually be important and we even looked to the business group to support the logic of why it would intercept us down the road, but it didn't require an agreement with a business unit to get it through. Some of those deals became very important two or three years later.

- *Board seats?*

There are some real issues, in my opinion, with taking board seats as a corporate investor. The first are the legal ramifications of taking such an active role as well as the potential conflict as a board member between shareholder and corporate obligations. Aside from those conflicts there is an obligation that you have as a board member to coach, mentor, and manage the executive team of startup. I don't think many CVC investors are qualified for that role.

At Intel Capital we pushed corporate Intel for years to take board seats, and finally got what we wanted. I was one of the first investors to lead a round and take a board seat. That was a trial by fire—in that company we ended up removing the CEO, only to have him lead an effort to terminate the new CEO and reinstate himself later on through a very political fight. Having an obligation to take such direct, hands-on effort with the company was a real learning experience as it took a lot of time and energy.

- *How do you balance strategic vs. financial?*

Strategic vs. financial objectives are not an either/or decision. They are not orthogonal to each other and they are two endpoints on the same continuum. In my opinion, you need to look at both together and they both need to be positive. If you don't expect a positive financial return for your investment, you should not invest. Period. Find another way to structure a deal with the startup. And if you are a purely financially driven investor that is just looking for return, you shouldn't be investing under the corporate moniker or off the balance sheet. You have no value to add as a generic investor and eventually you will see returns like the other generic investors.

- *Trust and the individual CVC?*

At the end of the day, all good CVC investing is based on balanced trust. CEOs and other venture investors need to trust that you will add value to the company. Business units and executive management need to trust that you will give them access to both near-term and long-term innovative companies. An individual CVC group may be able to work under its corporate brand for a while, but eventually its success will be based on how much their individual investors are respected and trusted.

In reality, trust in a CVC group is dependent on two things they can control: financial returns and value add. At one time, I was given responsibility to manage a team that had a poor reputation because they provided neither. They invested in things no one in the company really cared about, and their investments were not financially successful; so VCs had no respect for them. So, we started with the basics: investing in solid companies that were eventually successful, and implementing more innovative business agreements with the business units that showed we could be of value. Eventually the strategy paid off and we built a group where VCs brought us deals and the business units picked up the phone when we had something to show them.

- *Place of Value-add?*

Every VC claims to be a value-add investor. The reality of value-add for VCs is completely subjective, and varies greatly not only by venture capital firm, but by the individual investor. In the CVC world, there can be no doubt that you are a value-creating organization, or else you will fail. The essence of corporate venture capital's differentiation is that you bring value to the table that no one else can.

There is little reason for a start up to take your money if you aren't adding value. Sometimes it can be for the cache of your moniker, but that only goes so far. As a guiding principal for our organization, every investment we made was accompanied by a tear sheet we called "Gives and Gets," which defined what we expected to give the company, and what we expected to get from the investment. This was the lodestar of our relationship, and helped to define the strategic success or failure of the investment. Our portfolio reviews always included a discussion of the Gives and Gets progress so we could assess whether both parties were getting enough from the relationship. It was also a good barometer of whether the relationship was too lopsided one way or the other. @wkilmer

CASE STUDY - INTEL CAPITAL - KEYS TO SETTING UP A SUCCESSFUL CVC - SITA VASAN - FORMER MANAGING DIRECTOR; MANAGING DIRECTOR, SILICON VALLEY BANK; VP, BANQUE INDOSUEZ PARIS; VP, BANK OF TOKYO

To set up your CVC for success, build the best team with a clear mission focused on financial return, strategic objectives and a streamlined operation. It takes time for a CVC to build its reputation within the marketplace and to hone its internal operations. Below are brief examples of Intel Capital, where I worked for 12 years, and a CVC consulting project.

I joined Intel Capital in 2000, at the height of the dot-com boom, quickly followed by the bust, when we were investing in tons of deals, building a well-diversified portfolio. Until we started to divest non-strategic positions, this deal-making emphasis left us all with limited bandwidth – at one time, I managed 25 investments! There wasn't enough time to manage our companies operationally then, like the best VC's, nor strategically as the best CVCs. I learned how experience really counts as a CVC, investing in over 75 companies. As Intel Capital grew, as we all became more experienced, and under new leadership, we took bigger positions, leading deals, building domain expertise, and driving strategic relationships. Our compensation plan was changed to a financial IRR basis, motivating us to be selective, strategic and successful. Great investment managers spent time learning their sectors, fighting for the best deals, networking with VC's and entrepreneurs, and building bridges between Intel's business units and their portfolio companies to drive strategic value. Poor investment managers focused more on their personal career within the company rather than doing the hard work of a CVC. Remember this entrepreneurs - like VC partners, you need to choose your investment managers carefully, as they can be your best advocates within their corporate enterprise (or can ignore you or not deal with you frankly); integrity, experience and network (both inside the corporate and with VC's and other strategic partners) are all key.

A strong CVC must also have effective governance with an efficient, but thorough decision-making process. Given VC deal velocity, deal decision-making must be streamlined to get into hot deals. This is difficult for corporates who choose bureaucratic, senior decision-making processes, so the CVC must be granted some autonomy to ensure its effectiveness.

CVCs actually have a triple bottom line: financial return, strategic return and internal political approval. Strategic return is difficult to quantify, and changes dynamically as corporate objectives change. How the CVC connects with the business units, works within the corporate culture, and markets itself both internally and externally is essential for its success. Ultimately, it is the leader of the CVC who needs to set these goals well, define the CVC's corporate mission, select and motivate the team, and he/she must have the credibility within the company and support all the way up to the CEO level.

Leadership and the best, most experienced team are both essential to CVC success. At Intel Capital, I witnessed 3 regimes: a) highly strategic leader close to the CEO, b) Business Unit head, and c) CFO-type leader. All have their benefits and weaknesses, but I believe that strategic vision (a) and financial rigor (c) are most important. Recently, this was made clear when I helped advise an insurance company set up a CVC to drive more innovation and growth by building new revenue streams. The CIO had terrific strategic vision, but a bad earnings miss surprised him right after he was appointed to CEO, sounding the death knell for his CVC project.

To create a successful CVC, tie in the corporate culture, focus strategically into as many deals as possible, and get the best team committed towards strong financial returns. Intel's best strategic deals were also financial successes; you can't have anything strategic of value if your portfolio company goes bankrupt! In summary, build a team with experience (both internal and external), ensure support from the top with buy-in from as many business units as possible, and set up effective governance and streamlined decision-making. @sitavasan

A DOLLAR IS WORTH A THOUSAND WORDS – ANDREW ROMANS

Intel Capital employees have been putting this into their email signature files lately. I thought it worth including at this point in our CVC explorations:

"Since 1991, Intel Capital has invested
more than $11bn
in 1,440 companies
in 57 countries.
We plan to continue investing at our historical rate,
$300m to $500m per year."

I read this and think – WOW! To put that in perspective, Dick Kramlich founded NEA in 1977 and was up to $18bn last time I looked. NEA is the largest VC firm in the world. Just imagine if I am right in my prediction that CVC is just getting started and will be international. What a massive positive impact on society that might prove to be.

CASE STUDIES - CISCO SYSTEMS AND QUALCOMM VENTURES - FRÉDÉRIC ROMBAUT - FORMER MANAGING DIRECTOR, HEAD OF CORPORATE DEVELOPMENT INTERNATIONAL; FOUNDER & FORMER MANAGING DIRECTOR, QUALCOMM VENTURES EUROPE; FORMER APAX PARTNERS; COFOUNDER, BOUYGUES TELECOM; FOUNDER IN RESIDENCE, FOUNDERS FACTORY

I had a chance to catch up with Frédéric Rombaut, the former Managing Director and Head of Corporate Development International at Cisco Systems, Inc. where he also led the investments team (2012-2016). He is founder of Qualcomm Ventures Europe (2006-2011), and former Partner at Apax Partners (1998-2004) where he worked closely with Alan Patricof, one of the early pioneers of the venture capital and private equity industries. Frédéric is currently a Managing Partner of the Founders Factory VC Investment arm, which he set up in March 2016.

> *I asked Frédéric: You were running Cisco's CVC and corporate development group until a few weeks ago before setting up your own investment business. What can you share about Cisco's recent CVC activities?*

On the M&A front, with 12-15 acquisitions a year, aggregating $3-5bn each year (almost as much as our $5bn R&D budget), Cisco is one of the most active technology buyers in the world. With more than 200 cumulated acquisitions since the beginning of Cisco, M&A really is in its DNA and a critical part of its innovation framework. Cisco is recognized as best in class in M&A on an international level, both in terms of strategic impact and integration. However, its acquisitions used to be very US centric. What we have seen recently is a dramatic change of the balance between US and Europe. Over the last four years, the share of acquisitions made in Europe grew from 5% to almost 50%.

Similarly, on the investment front, with a $2bn investment portfolio, Cisco is one of the most active corporate venture capital investors in the world, and ranked #2 by exits. Its investment portfolio is made up of about 100 companies, about 45 VC funds, and some large partnerships, such as that with VMware.

However, as with acquisitions, investments used to be almost exclusively US centric, and apart from a dozen seed stage investments made in Israel, Europe used to be practically absent from the Cisco investment agenda until four years ago. Here again we have seen recently a dramatic change of this balance between US and Europe. Over the last four years, and under my leadership (2012-2015), Cisco's investment strategy has been completely revised, and now allocates a much more important role to Europe:

- First of all, Cisco Investment was launched as a marketing program to promote Cisco's value-add as a CVC investor. Its aim was to try to bring more strategic thinking, marketing and R&D guidance to the boards we sit on. Networking proactively to promote the portfolio companies, including multiple executive briefings with Cisco's customers, Cisco leaders, the General Partners Cisco invested in, and the entrepreneurs of the portfolio. Inviting some of its portfolio companies to Cisco Live events across the world, as an opportunity for them to meet with Cisco's large customers. And improving its ability to partner with early stage companies for co-R&D or joint-development initiatives. This is therefore a new co-development model that Cisco is offering to its investment candidates.

- Secondly, Cisco added new possible sponsors to the internal investment process. In the past, Cisco used to have only one possible sort of sponsor for its CVC investments (e.g., one of its myriad Business Units). The implication of this is that they focused only on areas that can impact revenues in the medium term. A good example is 6wind, a company that is enabling Software Defined Network architecture thanks to their software accelerator. That can be a long cycle, but once in place it can really help accelerate the scaling of a business. Three years ago a dozen "emerging" investment themes were added, which focused on longer-term innovation, and adjacent/non-core areas of business. These led to investments like, for instance, Evrythng, an IoT platform for connected things, focused on the FMCG vertical, or Intersec, a fast big data platform. Here Cisco could make its decisions pretty quickly, but the challenge is the uncertainty of our value-add, as there is no Business Unit sponsoring the investment in that case.

- Finally, last year Cisco launched a new initiative, named the Country Digital Acceleration program. Starting in France, several significant commitments of investments were announced in several European countries: $1bn in the UK, $500m in Germany, $200m+ in France and $100m+ in Italy, with a goal to accelerate the digitalization of several vertical markets that Cisco can enable, being a horizontal software networking platform.

Tell us about Cisco's indirect investments as a Fund of Funds?

With a portfolio of about 45 VC funds, selecting, partnering, and co-investing with the best GPs in the world is something Cisco strives for. But what's more interesting is to understand the strategic dynamic behind Cisco's indirect investment strategy. In that respect, it is worth observing and considering the different periods:

- Until 2004, Cisco invested broadly in Fund of Funds (FoFs). It had to learn the hard way. With the internet bubble, many VC funds turned out to be unprofitable, and Cisco was lucky that some of them were profitable enough to compensate for the loss making funds. In Europe, Index Ventures was the only survivor of its portfolio from that period. In Asia, Softbank was the best contributor of success.
- From 2005-2014, Cisco's indirect investments focused on emerging and frontier countries, with Corporate Social Responsibility being the sponsor. A good example is in Brazil where my team was able to pick the two best GP teams - Monashees Capital (2012 and 2015), Redpoint eventures Brazil (2012); but we also invested in Russia, Jordan, Egypt, Palestine, Israel and others.

- Since 2015, Cisco has returned with an indirect investment strategy in Europe. Under my leadership, Cisco announced three new funds in the portfolio, namely Partech Ventures, Idinvest, and Invitalia. They were all sponsored by the Country Digitalization Acceleration program. Cisco also decided to make several investments in some of the best Internet of Things focused accelerators, like Startupbootcamp for instance, one of the leading accelerators in Europe.

All of that makes Cisco the best in class Corporate Venture Capital tech investor across the board - from Executives In Residence, startup accelerators, VC funds, direct investments in startups, late stage tech companies, large Joint Ventures, to small, medium size and very large M&A. It is also the second most profitable CVC in terms of exits, as a proof that strategic and financial goals can walk together.[2]

How is Cisco organized internally and what is the interplay between corporate development and Cisco Investment?

Cisco Investment is indeed part of Cisco Corporate Development. It is not a separate team. The main reason is that Cisco is operating under a well-defined Innovation framework, consisting of three complimentary processes: Build, Buy and Partner, that is to say R&D, M&A, and Partnership, the latter of which includes CVC investments. Any time that Cisco isn't able to innovate internally quickly enough, the business acquires, integrates, and scales – and Cisco Investment helps considerably to fuel a pipeline of possible acquisitions.

The recent important change was its willingness to accelerate the IoE (Internet of Everything) market development, which requires more investment in our ecosystem. Cisco concedes that the IoE will be made a myriad of vertical market segments (AdTech, FinTech, MedTech, Smart Retail, Smart-City, Smart Manufacturing, Smart-Transportation, Smart-Agriculture, Industrial Internet of things, etc), and that each of these

---

[2] (Source: CB Insights) https://www.cbinsights.com/blog/corporate-venture-capital-ipos/

verticals requires entrepreneurs to create new concepts, new use cases, and do the tweaking required with the customers until they find a business model that can scale. That is what Cisco wants to accelerate by partnering with key leaders of each vertical.

It is also complimentary to Cisco's vision of the "network as a platform", a concept where the networking infrastructure is offering hundreds of northbound APIs to application developers. Software applications are being enabled to leverage network infrastructure as a way to virtually access any device through any network, but also to benefit from additional processing power, storage, security, micro billing, location, etc. Interestingly, Huawei has recently communicated a similar strategic evolution, that is to say, "from Hardware-defined, then Software-defined, to Application developer-defined."

What are the main differences between Qualcomm and Cisco, especially in terms of Corporate Development strategy?

Qualcomm has one of the most fantastic wireless technology R&D platforms, investing $5.4bn (20% of its revenues) in R&D to fuel its future with plenty of science and Intellectual Property-based technology innovations. This includes wireless GBps, wireless mobile device and electric vehicle charging, wireless power transmission, virtual and augmented reality, proximity location, wireless payment, drone related technologies, multi-core processors, 4G femtocells, next gen displays, physiological sensors, etc. As a chipset and IP vendor, it develops businesses along the whole value chain, from the component to the mobile phone, the mobile operator and its network, and the mobile app. Its venture arm, Qualcomm Ventures, one of the best CVCs in the world, used to act largely independently to place some bold investments. It does not necessarily move the needle for the core business, but it generates strong financial return while accelerating the 4G ecosystem. Occasionally Qualcomm makes some acquisitions, such as Arteris or Nujira (two of my investment portfolio companies), or Cambridge UK-based CSR for $2.4bn, but generally they tend to prefer developing the technology internally, given their strong R&D and IP culture.

Cisco has a more commercial approach. They listen carefully to their customers, and their innovation is more sales driven than technology led, which does not prevent them from driving significant technological evolution, such as software-defined networks, virtualized and video infrastructure, open source based cyber security, Internet of Everything, etc., given their ~$5bn R&D budget. However, M&A has been in its DNA from the very beginning and they don't hesitate acquiring when they believe they can buy time to market, competitive advantage, or scale up revenues on top of an infrastructure software platform. The investment strategy is about driving innovation and diversifying its risk while fueling a pipeline of M&A. This mainly explains why Corporate Development includes both M&A and Cisco Investments.

CASE STUDY - QUALCOMM LIFE FUND - JACK YOUNG - FORMER HEAD; HEAD OF VENTURE CAPITAL, DEUTSCHE TELEKOM CAPITAL PARTNERS; GENERAL PARTNER, DRX CAPITAL AG

Qualcomm Ventures ranks in the top three CVCs by most league tables along with Intel Capital and GV (Google Ventures). In my estimation they are tiptop for longevity in a game of weak hearts that fail to stay the course. Qualcomm Ventures has been at it since 2000 making them 16 years old as I write. (Full disclosure: Qualcomm Ventures is actually on the same floor in the same San Francisco building as Rubicon Venture Capital and is a co-investor with Rubicon Venture Capital in Navdy.) Here's my interview with Jack Young, former Head of Qualcomm Life Fund from 2008, who has recently become Head of Venture Capital at Deutsche Telekom Capital Partners; at the time of this interview, Jack was General Partner at dRx Capital AG:

dRx Capital AG is a joint venture investment company launched by Novartis and Qualcomm with a capital commitment up to $100m (50-50). We strive to catalyze the success of digital medicine products, services and business models by investing in early-stage companies and leveraging our extensive networks in Pharma, Mobile/IT, and the investment community.

Qualcomm Ventures is a truly global CVC poised to capture innovation where innovation is happening. We have offices in San Diego, Silicon Valley, Boston, London, Israel, India, China, Korea and Brazil.

Across these offices Qualcomm Ventures employs a team of 20 full time employees that invest from seed to late stage

Qualcomm's investment philosophy is underpinned by 1) make a strategic contribution to Qualcomm and 2) invest in financially viable projects.

We want to know what are the latest technologies and business models. We only invest when we know we can add value to the startup. We would not be in business after fifteen years if we were not financially profitable. Qualcomm Ventures is very profitable. Most CVCs fail for lack of balance between strategic and financial. This is a timeless tradeoff for CVCs and striking the correct balance is the secret. I view our mission to be forward looking. Qualcomm Ventures invests in the future. We are a forward looking group and we make money doing what we do while adding strategic value to our parent company and our portfolio companies. Compared to the trend of many other CVCs that are jumping into the game now I can assure you that Qualcomm Ventures will be here 10 or even 100 years from now and will continue to back innovation in places you never expected.

Our latest JV with Novartis is an example of things the world would not expect. I am very excited to be heading up dRx Capital AG.

CASE STUDY - VERIZON VENTURES - SURESH MADHAVAN - INVESTMENT MANAGER

I caught up with Suresh Madhavan, a manager at Verizon Ventures and he was kind enough to share best practices and discuss CVC with me. Like many large corporations trying to move the needle, investing in startups serves a dual purpose: to realize financial return, but often more importantly, to further the strategic direction of the parent company by either reinforcing its core business, or expanding the business in new directions. According to Suresh, Verizon's investments begin with the aim to fill a product gap or bring a value proposition that would be compelling to the company's customers.

I think the main reason for any corporation to establish a venture arm is primarily to stay abreast of potential disruption. It makes sense to maintain an active purview on startups operating at different stages that can disrupt your core or emerging businesses. Keeping track of change and trends, and being aware of new markets that are just forming can enable a large company like Verizon to establish new expansionary businesses. CVC also creates a strong pipeline for corporate development and for partnerships with emerging players. We have observed a lot of early stage innovation in the marketplace with respect to messaging services, enterprise offerings and artificial intelligence, which provide meaningful opportunities for collaboration.

Being able to share new ideas within the organization is also a core objective of corporate venturing. Some teams get so focused on bringing their own product to market that they can overlook things that could change the trajectory of what they are building. To be aware of this information internally is crucial. It may not create a new product opportunity, but it may convince you to pivot work on a current product, or abandon a product entirely that now looks likely to become obsolete in the future.

There is a regular cadence at Verizon Ventures of putting on events for the internal executive team. These often have themes around a particular sector - such as IoT - where we organize presentations from a select group of business partners, industry leaders, portfolio companies and other startups. We present market insights on innovation taking place in the sector and encourage open discussion of ideas, successes and challenges. We also produce insight reports and briefs that cover trends in key technology sectors, around CVC investing trends, or even on specific topics such as valuations in an area such as cybersecurity.

Verizon Ventures has been investing for about ten years and we typically average at least five to six new companies each year. Roughly 70-80% of our capital goes into new deals and 20-30% of our capital is deployed into existing portfolio companies as follow on investments, though these amounts vary in a given period based on available investment opportunities.

Verizon Ventures works with Product Team leaders throughout Verizon, who report directly to the CEO. As a CVC, it is interesting to work alongside internal business units to assist product managers or other heads of business units who are already working to strengthen existing or planned product offerings. It is important for us to know where our investments can bring value to the larger corporation and how a portfolio company can reinforce, strengthen or expand a product or business unit. Although priorities inevitably differ between product divisions and the investment team, navigating these relationships requires knowledge of the internal priorities, as well as a good handle on innovations happening external to the company to ensure successful and seamless collaboration across teams.

Stage-wise most of our investments tend to be Series B and beyond. We try to balance senior level input with each deal's specific priority level and company stage to make the best decision possible for the startup, and for Verizon. The investment process depends a lot on the startup's stage and preference, and we coordinate that with our Executive Committee, which in the end is the ultimate way to keep product leaders apprised on a deal-by-deal basis to make sure their teams are on board throughout the process.

Investing in Series B and later stage is really interesting because we're dealing with a startup in a position to ensure a solid business plan following their funding. Having said that, much disruption also happens at the earlier stages, so it is important we can access that also. And we do that primarily via indirect investment, which allows us to invest in select VC funds that bring us closer to younger companies in their portfolio. The active investment program is also an excellent way to generate highly qualified deal flow from GP fund managers we get to know and trust.

CASE STUDY - USAA VENTURES - VICTOR PASCUCCI III - FOUNDER & FORMER HEAD; CHAIRMAN, CORPORATE VENTURE GROUP EDUCATION COMMITTEE - NATIONAL VENTURE CAPITAL ASSOCIATION; HEAD OF CORPORATE DEVELOPMENT, USAA VENTURES

I have enjoyed working with Vic Pascucci in the past and look forward to continuing to work with him in the future. I asked him about the promise of CVC synergies to the corporate. Here are Vic's words on the story of USAA Ventures, taken over a series of lunch and dinner meetings:

The first question to answer is, are you a strategic investor or a financial investor? As a financial your primary goal is returns, similar to independent venture firms. As a strategic investor, your goal is to achieve the corporation's goals, increase their competitive advantages and accomplish their priorities. In the latter, a CVC must then clearly define what they mean by "strategic." This will determine what deals you do as well as your governance and approval processes. Strategic means different things to different CVCs as well as to entrepreneurs and co-investors. Does your definition of strategic mean that you invest in companies that are relevant to your industry or interesting to your corporation? Are you going to integrate the capabilities of the companies that you invest in?

Strategic can be defined as filling capabilities gaps, new product development, augmented or outsourced R&D, intellectual property development, access to new market geographies / sectors or access to innovation ("listening post" or "eyes and ears" deals that you will never integrate).

The reality is that you've been entrusted with capital, so even though you may be "strategic" either explicitly or implicitly you have financial performance expectations. For the longevity and survival of your practice, you must show some meaningful return. My experience is that if you stay true to your strategy and strategic value, the financial returns follow. USAA was able to generate top tier financial results in both IRR and Cash on Cash (CoC) returns. Multiple IPOs and successful acquisition exits were produced with the program's strategic focus.

Good entrepreneurs can raise capital from their choice of sources. As a CVC, the benefit and value-add you bring is integration and distribution with your parent company. The value-add is not just the commercial relationship but potentially more important is the time, advice, insight and mentorship the startup gets from your business partners (and hopefully from you).

Startups will have thousands or millions of customers, hundreds of investors and dozens of partners. When a company has an investor who is also a customer and partner, there is a level of alignment, insight, input, upside and risk mitigation that a corporate cannot achieve through any other means. You cannot be more aligned with the success of a company than when you put capital at risk with them. As a CVC you get insight not only to the startup's particular business, but visibility and perspective to their entire industry. Provided you have a positive relationship with your portfolio companies, you can have a certain amount of input on decisions that may affect your parent (provided you are appropriately balancing your fiduciary duties). Equity upside is best accomplished through direct investment. The upside is well due not just for putting money at risk or the commercial relationship but for the value added advice, insight and resources provided. Moreover, every corporation deals with third-party risk. That inherent third party risk is mitigated not only by the strengthening of the startup's balance sheet but also by the aforementioned alignment, input and insight. If your corporation is relying on a startup for critical strategic capabilities, it's in their best interest to get this level of alignment, insight, input, risk mitigation and upside.

At USAA, strategy is defined by the mission: to facilitate the financial security of the military community. As a strategic investor, USAA would look for those emerging trends, technology capabilities or disruptive models that will ensure USAA remains the financial services provider of choice for the military for the next 100 years as it has been the last 100 years. USAA would rely on the portfolio companies and investment to help provide a full suite of highly competitive products and services to the members.

What will most effectively define whether you are strategic or financial is how your deals get approved. If you can get deals approved absent business support, you're not a strategic. If you can get deals approved without expectation from the startup or your corporation that you will integrate, you're not a strategic. Regardless of who may be on your investment committee, if you can invest absent business consent and support, you are a financial investor.

If you are doing your job right as a CVC, you are combining the best of external innovation (startups) with the best of the internal innovation created by your corporation. By uniting the intellectual capital of all teams, R&D, incubation, product innovation, marketing and even compliance/regulatory areas, the end result is always better. As a CVC you should be bridging the gaps between both worlds and cultures for the benefit of everyone (what makes each other strong are often exact opposites).

As a CVC, you've got to appreciate you are part of a broader ecosystem of entrepreneurs, investors, incubators, accelerators, bankers, academic institutions and professional services providers. Ideally, you don't want to be just a deal team. You want to be a trusted advisor and facilitator for your business partners to this ecosystem. Internally you have to be seen as more than just a deal team. You must be the trusted advisor to your internal business clients on the entrepreneurial ecosystem. This broad network is a tremendous resource for your corporation as well as additional validation for your CVC efforts.

In order to be effective, a CVC group (especially a strategic who need to integrate the portfolio companies) needs to have extraordinary relationship skills. Without positive relationships across multiple lines of business, as well as the relevant control and administrative functions (and at all levels from admin to chairman), the CVC will not function. As a CVC, you are introducing disruptive technologies, emerging trends or even offerings that could be seen as competitive to your parent company. Such things can be viewed as intimidating change or an indictment against internal capabilities. Consequently, the best intended CVC initiatives can meet great resistance. Without the right amount of political skills, credibility, relationship equity, influence and true friendships across the corporate enterprise, CVC teams will be ineffective.

The challenge arises in balancing external obligations (board meetings, deal flow management, seminars, etc.) with the internal meetings and face time necessary to maintain the requisite corporate relationships.

In this vein, it's good to have a mix of internal and external hires. The internal will have the established relationships but not likely the external network and experience. This balances with the external team members who have the networks and experience. Your external hires must have the appreciation and customer service skills to work in a large corporation or they will be quickly marginalized and then rejected. The right balance creates a great team over time. As the internals gain experience, the externals establish the relationships.

CVCs should make as many contact points and resources available as possible to their portfolio companies. The reality of corporate life is that people, assignments, priorities, budgets, strategies and plans change. The more connection points the startup has within the corporation, the more support they can have and the higher likelihood they are to effectively navigate the inevitable change that happens.

Each deal should have its own independent investment thesis and value drivers that roll up to an overall strategy for the CVC group. The overall CVC strategy should clearly align to current corporate strategy and priorities. The thesis and value drivers should have quantitative and qualitative metrics that address both strategic and financial elements.

Before starting out you must decide:

- Why are you doing this? Strategic or financial?
- Decide the "why" you are doing CVC, then you can answer the "what" and the "how."
- What does strategic mean to you? Will you integrate?
- Have sufficient capital, (minimum $150m), to show your long-term commitment.
- Have the necessary process to get the parent comfortable yet the necessary agility to get deals done and compete.
- What's your compelling value prop to the entrepreneurial ecosystem?
- What's your internal message and campaign?

- Who are the necessary internal champions and coalitions necessary for the CVC to succeed?
- Know that this is a long-term commitment - can be 12 months+ to get your investments integrated and in market and then 7 -10 years for financial returns.
- What are your metrics going to be?
- How are your deals going to get decided, reported and tracked?
- What size of checks, stage and sectors?
- Will you lead deals?
- Will you take LP interests?
- Are you going to take board seats? Full or observer?
- How will you involve the corporate in setting CVC strategy?
- How will you integrate into the broader corporate processes, planning and strategies?

@victorpascucci3, victorpascucci3@me.com

Note from Andrew Romans: I had the opportunity to get to know the entire team at USAA Ventures first by sharing deal flow. Victor spent a good two years getting internal support within USAA to launch and then scale a serious CVC and recruited strong players to support him including Alexander Marquez, formerly of Intel Capital and Gopi Rangan, who had led venture capital and M&A for Silicon Valley chip-maker Altera, striking that healthy balance of internal and external hires for his team. They entered the market making real investments, seemed to truly get that strategic fit for the corporate and the startups and delivered very strong financial returns. They developed a portfolio of 21+ marquee companies (TRUECar, care.com, Personal Capital, Coinbase, Prosper, MX, Narrative Science, Snapsheet, ID.me and numerous others) and generated top tier financial results. Since Victor made his contributions to my book, the majority of the USAA Ventures team has moved on to other opportunities. USAA Ventures became another example of a prolific CVC reassessing what its place in venture world will be after its venture leadership has moved on. I'm sure the true reasons are more complicated, but providing the right long-term career environment for successful venture professionals in a corporate environment can be a challenge.

CASE STUDY - VOLVO VENTURES - JONAS LANDSTROM - MANAGING DIRECTOR USA

Jonas Landstrom was kind enough to share the story of Volvo Ventures. Many of my Volvo-driving readers may not know that the car division of Volvo was sold many years ago to Ford who then more recently sold the car division to GEELY, a Chinese company. So the Volvo you are driving today was made in Gothenburg, Sweden, but is owned by a Chinese company. The Volvo today that owns Volvo Ventures focuses on trucks, buses, construction equipment, motors and other industrial motor vehicles. Swedish Volvo used the roughly 300bn SEK ($34bn) from the sale of the car division to double down on trucks and acquired many other well-known brands such as Mac trucks. Jonas Landstrom's words:

Volvo Ventures was established in 1997 as an evergreen fund and is structured as a separate legal company that is entirely owned by Volvo, the Swedish group that focused on trucks, buses, etc. The automotive industry will change more in the next five to ten years than it has over the last 100 years. Some large companies may not think of their core business as a technology business, but virtually every company has technology all around it if not at its core. Automotive when you think about it has always been a technology business. Change in the automotive industry is now abundantly clear to everyone. It is hard in fact to find a part of the automotive industry that is not under threat of total transformation or a major arms race among competitors to lead these changes. Think connected car, autonomous self-driving cars, mechanical engineering, software engineering, design, customization, clean cars, telematics, how people will buy cars, rent, lease, share, trade, service and so on. We expect major changes in how people think, take and interact with public transportation and the idea of car ownership or the concept of a personal car.

After being operational for nearly twenty years Volvo Ventures has increased its pace and doubled the fund size, which is currently trending at $120m to $130m. As an evergreen fund this means that exit dollars go back into the fund providing capital to be reinvested into new startups. Today roughly one third of this capital is dry powder to be invested and two thirds is in the form of shares of privately held companies hopefully on track to eventual exits. The past year slowed down to only two new investments with the arrival of a new CEO at Volvo HQ.

Volvo Ventures is part of the strategy group and reports to the Head of Strategy. The group is staffed with six full time employees based in Gothenburg and two in Silicon Valley where Jonas resides.

I asked Jonas if it made sense to have 75% of the CVC team hunting for deals in the HQ, which is not known as the epicenter of technological innovation and only 25% of the team in Silicon Valley, the clear center of the innovation universe.

I would like to reverse these numbers but it's important to make sure the corporate venturing program is closely linked to the corporate to be effective. Volvo Ventures is structured with an external board which needs to approve every investment comprised of the Head of Strategy, the Head of Corporate Development (M&A) and one external executive who used to be the chairman of CapMan, a reputable late stage Scandinavian PE and VC fund.

In addition to the obvious objectives of bringing new innovation from outside of Volvo into the organization, Volvo Ventures focuses on three things.

1) Find and bring new talent into the organization
2) Identify and negotiate partnerships among startups and Volvo
3) Create a pipeline for the M&A team

Rather than focus on a specific shopping list, Volvo Ventures operates with a broad mandate to invest wherever technology meets transportation.

The group is stage agnostic investing from pre-seed to growth, but typically invests $1m to $10m per investment with a sweet spot of investing in Series A and B rounds where the startup has demonstrated product market fit. Volvo Ventures seeks to take board observer seats wherever possible. Looking back at nearly twenty years for the CVC program and operating as an independent entity with clear independent financials, it is very important to be financially sustainable. That said, Volvo Ventures only invests when there is a clear vision for collaboration between the startup and the corporation. This works best when Volvo can add value to the startup in the short-term and bring long-term strategic value to Volvo. This is the win-win that corporate venturing should achieve. Volvo Ventures is the central point that looks after all commercial deals between Volvo and the 65+ companies in the Volvo portfolio. Post investment the Volvo Ventures team becomes the champions within the corporate to remove resistance from various business units and ensure maximum collaboration.

It is pointless to operate a totally isolated CVC program. The CVC team must drive collaboration with the corporate. When you get down to the nitty-gritty details of corporate venturing, someone needs to identify the correct person at the corporate to do business with the portfolio companies. This is not always a top down, but often a bottoms-up exercise. The skill set for an effective corporate venture capitalist is essentially everything the independent financial VC has plus the ability to navigate the corporate effectively, patiently, politically and persistently.

CASE STUDY - BMW I-VENTURES - MARK PLATSHON - SENIOR ADVISOR; MANAGING DIRECTOR, ICEBREAKER VENTURES

I met with Mark for lunch in San Francisco. Here is what he had to say about CVC:

If your industry is going through massive disruption you might decide to do this: Hold up a flag and say we have capital, brains, market access, relevant sector know-how and huge resources to help a startup scale. That flag is called venture capital. BMW is a $100bn company that is celebrating its 100th birthday, but we believe tomorrow's competitors will be a whole new cast of characters including Apple, Google, Tesla, Invidia, Lyft and others you might not expect. At BMW we recognized that our industry is going through severe change. Electric cars, carbon fiber, self-driving cars, connected cars, automation and continuous servicing of cars. New business models like Uber and Lyft. Who owns the car? How is it purchased? Will urban city dwellers want to own or drive cars? Is Asia going to be the same or different from the US or European markets? You can study these changes by reading Gartner research reports and attending conferences or you can get your hands dirty and truly embrace these changes and immerse yourself in this disruptive change. That comes through actual investing in the best ones after meeting them all. Investing capital creates accountability. Putting cash on the line as well as someone's career reputation, the quality of your game is raised to a new level.

When we started iBMW Ventures six years ago there were no examples of bottoms up innovation at BMW. All strategic programs came from the top down. Innovation should flow into the CVC from all business units and then report that to the senior management at the HQ and then feed it to where it needs to go.

CVC should carefully consider where to dock the unit. It is a mistake to plant the CVC group inside of a specific business unit. You don't want long-term thinkers to be managed by short-term doers. You don't want ops guys managing strategy guys. For this reason I support the formation of a real fund with a GP-LP structure. The more independence the better. Let me offer a metaphor. Looking over the horizon icebreakers go over the polar ice clearing a path so the mother ship may follow. The head of the icebreaker cannot be held back by the mother ship. The icebreaker must be given sufficient autonomy or he will never find the path through the ice. The automotive industry is going through such extreme change you want to make sure your CVC unit can find more than just the easy and obvious startups to partner with. I've seen cases of dysfunctional CVC where the CVC investment professional needs to go to HQ for approval to pay for a flight to visit a portfolio company or attend a board meeting. If you start the next 475th CVC and staff it with internal hires that are not from the VC industry, you will fail to get access to the real deal flow and, even if you get access, you will fail to get into the financings you want to be in. In order to get the top VC talent running your CVC, you need to spin off with the GP-LP structure to solve your compensation problem. Offer 2&20 and you'll get an A team.

Ops and strategy BU heads often try to give the CVC a shopping list of topics to invest in. Had we accepted that list we would have missed Uber, Waze, the early days of connected car, sensors, industrial internet, etc. The ops guys would complain we are not sticking to the shopping list. More than just cars, CVC needs to be autonomous and self-driving. If you don't know what you're looking for, that's venture! @ MarkCPlatshon

CASE STUDIES - DOCOMO INNOVATIONS, VODAFONE INCUBATION & VENTURES - CHRISTINA KU - INVESTMENT DIRECTOR, DOCOMO INNOVATIONS (NTT DOCOMO SUBSIDIARY); FORMER INVESTMENT PROFESSIONAL, VODAFONE INCUBATION & VENTURES, INTEL CAPITAL, TRIPLEPOINT CAPITAL AND SILICON VALLEY BANK VENTURE DEBT GROUP

I caught up with Christina for sushi at one of my favorite Japanese restaurants just outside of Stanford University. Here are her lessons from a failed incubator/CVC and two successful CVCs.

Vodafone Ventures & Vodafone Xone

I have worked in an investing role for two successful CVCs and one failed CVC/incubator, all in the mobile, internet and telco space. Two of the CVCs were international telcos (Vodafone Xone/Ventures and Docomo

Innovations) entering the US venture ecosystem and one is a marquee, US based technology company expanding worldwide - Intel Capital.

From this perspective, I would like to offer a few lessons on best practices for what works and doesn't work for a corporate venture firm. I strongly believe that corporate venture firms have to invest for a financial return as a primary or secondary objective. CVCs are entrepreneurs within an organization, injecting innovation, new ideas and change.

When I met the founder of Vodafone Xone at their launch party in the Mission, I was intrigued by the idea of helping entrepreneurs develop a business in the mobile space with an international brand such as Vodafone. I joined Vodafone Xone and Fay Arjomandi's team in the fall of 2011, at a time when Vodafone had high hopes to expand beyond their venture activities in the Bay Area.

Vodafone Ventures was created in 2000 with a £100m fund with the average size of investments ranging between £2m and £10m targeted primarily at Series A to mid stage investments. Lead by Peter Barry, Vodafone Ventures before the Xone was getting a lot of recommendations from the top tier VCs and had great working relationships. In 2010, Vodafone Xone as an independent entity was one of the top 5 investors in mobile related startups globally. The top realized investments were MobileIron, Amobee and Evolution Robotics. All of the startups in the portfolio had the support of the business with commercial agreements and cash investments.

By 2012, Fay had taken over Vodafone Ventures and merged it with Vodafone Xone. Xone expanded into Redwood City with a modern office decked out with European furniture that matched the other Vodafone offices in Europe and a fresh flair of enthusiasm. Vodafone had decided to invest into a Silicon Valley presence extending from R&D and the Office of the CTO. Capital was spent to build an internal lab testing facility, which allowed developers to test their applications and hardware on Vodafone's global 2G, HSPA, and LTE networks from Redwood City with office space for entrepreneurs. Vodafone Xone was focused on identifying startups with potential and putting their ideas on the fast track to proof-of-concept trials. The target startups were mobility related and the stage was early from seed and pre-product to early customer. Vodafone Xone provided NRE (non-recurring engineering) funds of under $1m which was less dilutive than a venture round and essentially a consulting fee for the startup to provide engineering resources to adapt the product for Vodafone or a version of the product for one of Vodafone's markets. When the startup was raising a venture round, Vodafone's fund would then consider an investment in the company.

In order to do so, the center provides technical expertise, business advice and access to its lab to ensure that products are compatible with Vodafone's global 2G, HSPA, and LTE networks. Xone's goal is to "accelerate market delivery" of products that can benefit Vodafone's 26 operating companies in different regions. These products may be for consumers, enterprise use, or infrastructure, but the plan is to get the fruits of the center's labor into users' hands for real-world trials in six to nine months. Vodafone Xone was a showcase center for startup technology for Vodafone executives as they traveled to the Bay Area and centralized Vodafone Venture's fund activities.

By 2013, Vodafone Xone was not finding enough innovation, products, IP or projects that Vodafone could work with and by 2014, Vodafone Xone and the combined Ventures was dismantled and Fay Arjomandi left the firm. In roughly 18 months, Vodafone Xone had hired like a growing Series A startup, merged with Vodafone Ventures and then slowly dissolved both activities of incubation and ventures. Identified below are several lessons from the Vodafone Xone start in Redwood City:

1. Wrong structure with startups: Vodafone wanted to offer NRE (non-recurring engineering resources) to startups in exchange for rights to the co-created IP for use by Vodafone. This was the

wrong structure to bring innovation into a corporation. Adverse selection is a primary problem for CVCs in sourcing startups to create technical products, business partnerships or investments. The best US and Silicon Valley based startups have many options for capital and do not require their IP to be encumbered going into a Series A financing at such an early stage of their product development. Be realistic in what you can provide a startup and what a startup can offer in exchange. Work with the best start-ups you can rather than any startup willing to accept your painful strings attached terms.

2. Find the right structure to work with startups: the CVC must support working with startups at all levels and have startup friendly commercial agreements. Standard big company commercial agreements do not work.

3. Lack of good deal flow from key players in the Silicon Valley ecosystem: Vodafone Xone did not work with the local Silicon Valley technology ecosystem. The primary deal sourcing was done by reacting to startups referred to us from the Business Units of Vodafone, Fay's network and Vodafone Ventures. We did not work with the top Venture Capitalists nor incubators such as Y Combinator or 500 Startups to invest in the existing seed stage network. We wanted to recreate the wheel and identify top seed stage startups on our own but this was an extreme oversight of the maturity of the ecosystem of Silicon Valley startups and funding. Work within the existing Silicon Valley infrastructure.

4. Light guidance: we told the startups what products to build. Fay was an entrepreneur and tried to tell the startups what products to build. To fully leverage the innovative mindset of a startup you need to let them provide the ideas and solutions with light guidance. Without equity or skin in the game from the startup, as employees of Vodafone we were advisors at best but not

product managers of the startup's product nor their sole customer. We spent many hours working with the startups to find product market fit and create new products that may interest a Vodafone business unit to adapt as part of their business. They should build their own product and find their product market fit. After there is adoption and usage models for the product, then a CVC can determine how the innovation can fit into their organization.

5. The venture business and startups require patience: the CVC must be patient with startups and work in a win-win manner, especially global players like Vodafone. It is unrealistic to launch globally in a short period of time unless you are dealing with a very mature startup. On the other hand, early stage startups do not have the resources to service a full commercial deal with a large corporation. So understand the strategy and objective of both constituencies.

6. Leadership and philosophy of Vodafone Xone was not from Silicon Valley nor senior in the organization: the leadership of Vodafone Xone, philosophy, operations and goals of Vodafone Xone were separate from the Silicon Valley ecosystem. In an interview by Silicon Beat, the journalist asked the most important question of Fay and Vodafone Xone's purpose with this question, "Vodafone's based in the UK and most of your prior career was in Canada. What's it been like to operate in Silicon Valley?" Fay's response encapsulated the way that the Xone operated, "I honestly don't see any difference in operating in Silicon Valley compared to other regions." Silicon Valley is like no other region in the world. Albeit on the surface it may appear to be globally minded and international, there are established communities of entrepreneurs and venture capitalists. The Valley is changing every day and is open to new players disrupting the system, but there is an ecosystem and successful players operating in Silicon Valley. Vodafone did not work within

this ecosystem but rather spent millions of dollars creating a small ecosystem located just outside of this ecosystem believing that good things will happen by just having a presence by the 101 freeway. The lead of the venture fund must be very senior in the company and be located in the HQ to champion the effort through the political landscape of a big company and create the internal relationships that can smooth the path for startups seeking commercial relationships with the business and investment.

In conclusion, do not mix incubation and venture capital. The venture capital team has to be able to make judgments as to whether what is coming through incubation is worth the investment and is the best in class in their field. The venture capital team has to have a financial background and access the startup with the same criteria as a financial investor for pure financial return.

You need to be able to try innovations in the market quickly and break down the barriers to do this. The biggest issue some startups have is how long it takes to get to trial and prove the innovation in the network or with customers. I do not think the Xone or Vodafone Ventures had the right model. The quickest time to market came from identifying a problem/market need of the business and finding a startup that immediately meets this need with the right pedigree. Our investment and commercial support of Mobile Iron was one of these – about a 10x return.

Startups are born out of risk and require capital to sustain their ideas. This does not correspond with the goals of a large corporation that focuses on the short term. Be clear that you can provide: 1) capital, 2) introductions to business units, 3) defined partnership path or 4) market entry into a specific market but not a blanket set of skills. They don't need you to create their product or find their product market fit, they need you to fund them, find them a customer or bring them to a new market. Leave the seed stage investing and incubation to the successful incubators.

Docomo Innovations and Docomo Capital

By 2012, I had joined the team at Docomo Innovations and Docomo Capital. The philosophy and leadership of Docomo Innovations was completely different than Vodafone Xone. Docomo Innovations was headed up by Takayuki Inagawa and was a part of Docomo's R&D Group at the time I joined. The main leadership started with an influential executive from the HQ in Tokyo who reported directly to the CTO of Docomo. Neil Sadaranganey managed the Docomo Capital $100m portfolio and I was hired to assist with business development and investments.

Business development is helping startups enter the Japanese market. This is value add for startups when they are ready to enter the highest ASP market for consumer mobile applications. When expanding internationally in the mobile sector, Europe and Asia are the largest total addressable markets (TAM) with the two largest markets being China and Japan. For Japan, entering the market with one local partner provides an advantage. The value proposition for startups is very clear and singular.

Neil was formerly a GP at Bay Partners and had invested in companies like Cornerstone and was a Stanford MBA. He was from Silicon Valley, had relationships with at least one partner at every top venture firm, sat on boards and invested in local startups. This local knowledge of the venture business and key people in the Valley helps Docomo Capital with collaboration in the venture ecosystem, find top trends and gain access to better deal flow.

The Docomo team has a mix of ex-pats from HQ who have relationships with executives and the Business Units and local hires, such as myself. We are a football team where I bring a startup to the 50-yard line and the ex-pats bring the startup to the end goal of working with a Business Unit in Tokyo. The synergies with an investment create a symbiotic relationship between the startup and Docomo to pursue multiple commercial or product partnerships. The Docomo Innovations team was created to enforce this internal business development within the corporation.

General Lessons from CVC: Vodafone Ventures, Docomo Capital and Intel Capital

1. Clear, specific goals: market entry with one telco in one country.
2. Clear, mutually beneficial relationship: we offer market entry for the startup, the startup provides us with a share of their equity in their investment round.
3. Work within the Silicon Valley ecosystem.
4. Do your homework on what will be best in class in a field and do not invest in first off the rank. Due diligence has to equal that of a financial VC if the venture capital effort is going to succeed in identifying the best innovations and those most likely become the leader in their field.
5. Any corporation wanting to enter venture capital must be patient - the reward comes after five to ten years of investing and deploying startups. The venture capital industry requires consistency in order to build trust and relationships that will lead to early insight into the next generation of innovations and innovators. You cannot dabble for two years and then expect outstanding results.
6. Must give the venture team the ability to invest ahead of the current thinking in the business – perhaps say 20% of the fund. Vodafone Ventures was not able to invest in the emerging stages of Twitter, YouTube and Facebook because the senior management did not see the relevance in those early stages despite the recommendations from the venture team.
7. The corporate venture capital fund must make a good return on investment, be self-funding, and have a reasonably high success rate. This means that the companies that are being invested in and that have commercial agreements with the corporation are successful in the market place. If all your companies fail, then the business is not gaining a benefit from supporting those startups. Unlike a financial VC a corporate VC that is trying to create commercial and strategic relationships with startups cannot afford to have just one success that carries the fund. This will not be seen as a success by the business as there is a high internal cost for all the failures. This will mean the fund is weighted a little later stage, but for a large corporation this

is not a bad thing as long as you have some funds set aside for more speculative investments. This is exactly what the VCs do. They have their early and later stage funds to balance risk. Being self-funding enables the CVC to survive in the long term as senior management changes – e.g. new CEO, etc. I strongly believe that corporate venture firms have to invest for a financial return as a primary objective.

8. It is not just about the investing, it is also about highlighting new trends that launch new initiatives within the corporation even if a startup does not ultimately become a part of the mix. A classic example of this is M2M. Vodafone launched a new M2M/IOT business after Vodafone Ventures showcased Jasper Wireless and highlighted how our prior analysis of this space had underestimated the size of the prize. Consequently Vodafone was an early leader in the Global M2M business, which is one of its fastest growing revenue streams. @TechVentureGirl

Hearing Christina's experiences at Vodafone investing non-capital "in-kind resources" prompted me to extend her comments on this topic with some thoughts of my own.

THOUGHTS ON STRINGS-ATTACHED FUNDING & INVESTING IN-KIND RESOURCES - ANDREW ROMANS

One of the largest television networks in Europe opened a CVC office in Silicon Valley. It was one of the dominant TV networks in Germany, Austria and Switzerland (DACH). Rather than invest purely cash into startups they tried to get into deals by investing a combination of advertising time in DACH and a little bit or zero cash into the round. So if a startup was raising a Series B, C or D round of expansion capital, they could strike a deal with this TV company: rather than the startup pay cash to buy advertising time to promote their business in Europe, they could pay for that with equity, selling it at the same price that they sold equity to other investors. This was a total failure and I believe all of those investment execs have since returned to Germany. Another mistake they made was sending internal TV execs from Germany to Silicon Valley with no local relationships. I have heard other TV execs talk about the same brilliant idea and I warn them of the reasons it will fail. The best startup CEOs can raise capital from their choice of investors and avoid "strings-attached" capital. I can see how the TV guys were thinking they could get into CVC and grow their revenue directly, but the best, good and even worst startups would not chose to do this. Just don't do this.

When I raised funding and vendor finance from Lucent Technologies in the 1990's and 2000's I learned that much of the financing was spent not on telecom switches and network devices that I wanted, but on services that I learned I needed. I relived this experience at Rubicon when we invested in numerous startups alongside Foxconn and Flextronics. These two companies often offer a mix of cash and services and then offer to do small production runs of a startup's first or early hardware manufacturing. These transactions often look like a combination of cash and services, but normally end up being nearly 100% services. This is still a good deal for the startup to be able to partner with a multi-billion dollar world class sophisticated electronics manufacturer that is willing to bring their best of class and economically optimal cost of production company to partner with a startup that is doing production runs that are too small to attract most tier III partners in Asia. Rubicon likes to invest alongside both of these guys. More manufacturing companies should start these types of programs, but I would encourage them to buy their way into better deals by offering not just purely services for equity, but also by adding some actual cash. They would also be wise to invest alongside the top VC names to use them as a filter to help select the best ones to back. If you get a full scholarship from Harvard and no scholarship from Stanford, you will probably go to Harvard.

Startups often work with offshore or near-shore contract software development shops where they pay hourly rates or fixed rates to make web and app design, software, etc. Even the best teams augment their full time employees with some outside contractors. Over the years the good agencies see a lot of revenue growth charging the clients more than they pay their employees and after watching some of their clients exit for hundreds of millions of dollars they decide to start investing cash into their own clients or (they all have this thought at some point) to invest development resources for equity. Normally they end up offering startups a combination of paying 70-80% of the bill in cash and put the remaining 30-20% of the dollar amount owed in exchange for stock or convertible note on the next financing round.

This makes a lot of sense aligning interests and helping the company essentially access more capital faster; however, it usually goes wrong when I notice the hourly rates of these hybrid development/investor shops are about 20-50% more expensive than alternative outsourcing shops. If you are not careful these hybrid investors are really just tacking on some equity on top of being paid their normal hourly rates.

My takeaway here is that cash is king and in-kind services can generally take a hike, because they start to look like "strings-attached" investors. The good ones like Microsoft just give you full access to the candy store once they have invested cash in you. They use the drug dealer model of giving you free access to their software and web hosting services to prevent you from getting started on Amazon Web Services and competing software platforms.

Another side of this is the corporate attaching too many strings when investing into financial VC funds (FoF). It is important to strike a balance between the financial VC fund and the corporate becoming an LP in the VC fund. General Partners (the top VCs) should be careful not to be blown in the wind and change their strategy to accommodate "strings-attached" demands by the corporate LP investor. Normally, the GP can overlap enough strategy with the wishes of the corporate to find something that works for all, thus creating the win-win-win.

CASE STUDY - OJSC "ROSTELECOM" - NIKOLAY DMITRIEV - FORMER CVC MANAGING DIRECTOR; PARTNER, VITA VENTURES

I met Nikolay for lunch on a lovely day in June on a rooftop restaurant in Moscow and learned of his experiences of running the CVC group of

Rostelecom prior to setting up his own financial VC. Here are Nikolay's words:

We closed a $100m fund CommIT Capital as the CVC fund of OJSC "Rostelecom", the largest telecom operator in Russia with revenues in the range of $10bn. We established the fund from scratch in two years. We used the benefits of our anchor investor to add value to the fund. We developed an investment strategy based on strategic aims of Rostelecom synchronizing long-term strategy of Rostelecom with our CVC investment strategy. It gives to us four priority blocks - import substitution, synergy, pre-M&A and syndication with VC funds, including LP investments in other funds based on a FoF model. As far as deal flow generation acceleration is concerned we agreed on a partnership with IIDF (Internet Initiative Development Fund) that invests at earlier stages and has an accelerator program that provides additional proven deal flow. With regards to forming the team we hired investment professionals from the market with a vast track record in the VC market, fund management and key managers that also had experience in the corporate development group at Rostelecom. We set up a separate structure for the fund to speed up the decision-making process and implement best market practices in business processes for the fund. @Rostelecom_News

CASE STUDY – LEGEND HOLDINGS – SAMAN FARID, FORMER VICE PRESIDENT INVESTMENTS & DIRECTOR OF SILICON VALLEY OFFICE, LEGEND STAR 联想之星; MANAGING DIRECTOR, COMET LABS

I sat down with Saman Farid in our San Francisco office to discuss how Legend Holdings is structured and their well known business model of "strategic investments + financial investments." Saman grew up, studied and worked internationally in the US and China, has a track record of three startups, became a manager of the early stage investment group of Legend Holdings called Legend Star, and has now spun off a recently formed VC fund to focus on investing in and helping robotics and intelligent machine startups in the US and China. Legend Star is one of the top rated and most prolific early stage tech-investors in China. (Full disclosure: Legend Holdings via Legend Star is an LP investor in Rubicon Venture Capital.) Here are Samans' words:

I first took investment from Legend Holdings as an entrepreneur at one of their portfolio companies and later joined their investment team at Legend Star, leading their Silicon Valley office. Legend Holdings is structured in two key divisions: 1) strategic investments and 2) financial investment. Legend Star is part of the financial investment group where we cover early stage investing. Legend Capital and Hony Capital make later stage growth and private equity investments.

Our strategic investments group is well known for its controlling ownership position in Lenovo, the world's largest computer maker, as well as large real-estate holdings, one of China's largest auto rental companies and generally key investments into six key sectors: IT, financial services, modern services, agriculture and food, real estate, and chemicals and energy materials.

As of the end of 2015, the revenue of Legend was RMB 309.8bn ($46.25bn USD), total assets were roughly RMB 306.2bn ($45.7bn USD), and the conglomerate employed 75,000 people. Additional investors in Legend's VC and private equity funds include numerous American and Canadian pension funds, the Bill & Melinda Gates Foundation, Goldman Sachs, and China's national social insurance fund. Legend today is one of the largest diversified investment groups in China. It built up an innovative business model of "strategic investments + financial investments" with synergy between our two businesses to increase the value of our investment portfolio. Our strategic investments group is more motivated by strategic returns and unlocking synergies than a pure financial return. In contrast, our financial investments group is driven by financial returns. What makes Legend different is the way we seek opportunities to create synergies between these two units.

A good example of this is a recent investment into WeWork, the shared office company. Hony Capital, as part of our financial investment group, made a large investment into WeWork and took a board seat. Our strategic investments group also made a matching investment and took a board seat. Our strategic group owns a real-estate company that was successful obtaining land from the Chinese government on very favorable terms with the aim of brining high tech startups into that development project. Beyond our own technology investment group from seed VC to late stage PE our investment into WeWork paved a road to bring even more startups into this project. For Legend this investment is strategic and will grow the value of their real-estate holdings. For Hony it's purely financial and brings WeWork something other financial investors could never deliver and so Hony differentiated itself from other sources of growth capital for WeWork and won its way into that investment opportunity.

From my perspective both as an entrepreneur who has raised VC funding and from my perspective as a venture capitalist, I think most CVCs do not get the same high quality deal flow as financial VCs. Our company Lenovo recently announced in May 2016 the launch of a $500m VC fund with half in USD and half in RMB. I am sure they will attract high quality investment projects, but I am also certain that some of the hottest startups in the Silicon Valley will not want to take funding from a CVC because they think it comes with strings attached. It will limit their ability to do business with the competitors of that CVC. There could be lingering conflicts of interests for acquisitions and pricing of the M&A. And finally, CVCs are notorious for being slow to wire the funding. Simply put, a financial VC like Legend Star, Legend Capital or Hony on a net net basis will attract better deal flow than a classic CVC. I think of what Legend is doing still as a great experiment. They are in my view marrying together the best characteristics of strategic investment with the best characteristics of financial investment. It is my belief that the most competitive deals where the startup has a choice of which investor to take funding from will go for the financial VC over the CVC. So if Lenovo wants to access these best in class technology companies they are wise to do so via Legend Holdings or another financial independent VC via their Fund of Funds (FoF) program. They can have both and eat their cake too!

My new VC fund is a spinout from Legend Star with Legend as an anchor LP and part owner in our GP. We are the first VC to focus on investing in and incubating B2B robotic and artificial intelligence startups in China and the US. We invested in 25 portfolio companies from our first fund and will be able to announce the closing of our second fund shortly on the back of Legend Holdings, our anchor LP investor (http://cometlabsio/). We look forward to continuing to work closely with Rubicon Venture Capital and the many other VCs in our network to fund and accelerate the best transformational companies in the world.

CASE STUDIES - TELECOM ITALIA & FININVEST - MAURO PRETOLANI - SENIOR INVESTMENT ADVISOR, FONDO ITALIANO D'INVESTIMENT, A VENTURE CAPITAL FUND OF FUNDS

I had a chance to catch up with my old friend Mauro Pretolani on the topic of CVC over breakfast in London. He shared some insights about Fund of Funds and direct CVC investing at the corporate level. Mauro is a Senior Investment Advisor to the Venture Capital Fund of Funds at Fondo Italiano d'Investimento and also a cofounder of TLcom Capital Partners where he and his partners raised and invested roughly €225m directly into startups. Mauro has been an advisor to me for over ten years, but also advised Telecom Italia and Fininvest on their launch and early travails into corporate venturing in the second half of the 1990's. Telecom Italia is, of course, the incumbent telecom network operator in Italy, and Fininvest Group is composed of a number of large companies, whose main focus is media, most relevant ones being Mondadori, Italy's leading publishing companies, and Mediaset, the largest private TV entertainment player in Italy (both companies have also significant business outside Italy). Fininvest is a financial holding company controlled by Silvio Berlusconi's family and managed by Silvio Berlusconi's eldest daughter Marina Berlusconi. Here is Mauro's contribution in his own words:

Under the counsel of a team of whom I was part, both Telecom Italia and Fininvest started off acting as if they were a Fund of Funds (FoF). In fact they invested into VC funds in the USA and Israel. They both also established their own CVC operations making direct investments into startups. If you look at the financial results they did well investing into VC funds, but had mixed results when making direct investments into start-ups and differing results achieving strategic goals.

Telecom Italia launched Telecom Italia Ventures and a second fund named Media Euro Ventures. From inception in 1996 to 2000 things went very well for Telecom Italia and a big part of this success was the fact that the transfer of knowhow from startups to Telecom Italia worked so well during this period. Without any question during these years Italy leaped ahead of France when it came to anything related to the internet. France was in catch up position during these years, a situation that is a far cry from today's world, with France ahead of Italy in practically all metrics related to the internet. In recent years both Telecom Italia and Fininvest group have started working again on the CVC front, after a long break that has not been beneficial to the two companies' capability to innovate.

I can contribute two key points of advice to readers of your book on corporate venturing, Andrew: 1) In order to obtain results, corporates must make a long-term commitment to corporate venture capital. In contrast to their nature of short-term goals and decisions, CVC must be structured in a manner to last ten years and a view to go much longer. 2) Corporates need to implement specific organizational structuring to ensure the transfer of what the CVC unit learns to the senior level of the corporate body. By this I mean the CEO, CTO, CFO, etc.

At Telecom Italia we had information shared from the CVC to the C suite and almost more importantly operational Managing Directors who had the ability to make use of this information to make bold choices, like acquisitions, international partnerships and investments in new areas. This was very effective and the entire program was viewed as a success, even if the CVC group was disbanded following the group LBO that reduced the resources available for long-term investment.

Fininvest made a critical mistake. The CVC reported to the CEO of the holding company. This all sounded like the correct thing to do at the time of formation, but it became clear over time that this did not work. The operating companies (op-co's) of Fininvest did not have direct access to the CVC and resisted ideas pushed on them from the holding company management into whom the CVC reported. CVC would have been much more effective if they could have had direct access to the core op-co's, especially Mondadori and Mediaset. Fininvest also failed to incentivize the op-co's to support the startups the CVC unit invested in. When the group launched an ambitious portal project, we recommended an ownership structure with a majority of the capital in the hands of the operating companies, according to their capability to contribute to the business - across the op-co's. Unfortunately they did the opposite. The majority control was in the hands of the financial holding and not of the operating companies. It was built with almost entirely new personnel and as a consequence the startups failed to achieve the synergies with the operating companies that had been a pillar of the plan to be successful.

Andrew, you asked me how to facilitate good communication between the CVC and the corporate. I have seen a number of different models work and others fail to work. One model which sounds like a nightmare that I have seen work is to establish an "innovation transfer board" for the CVC and have it populated by several tens of managers from all the different departments of the corporate. The ordinary thought is that you only need execs from the R&D group, or the strategic marketing group, but that is not true. It is key to get as many different business units represented and in particular HR. If the human resources group becomes active in communication with the CVC they can get better insights on what type of people they should hire within the corporate. The know-how transfer can in itself justify the entire investment into CVC. In my experience, if the CVCs bring startups that are NOT of interest to the board of their own managers, they will tell you quickly.

I recently had the opportunity to ask a question of Jean Botti, CTO of EADS-Airbus, about his company's approach to CVC. He said that they have a newly established CVC fund, with an initial allocation of $100m, which will be managed by Tim Dombrowski, a partner recruited directly from the VC fund Andreessen Horowitz. What struck me is that the Airbus executive added "this is an experiment for us." It is possible that they were saying that they are risk takers and prepared to explore new models, but one may also think that it is dangerous for a startup to take funding from a new investor characterizing their investment business as "an experiment". Venture Capital as purely financial or purely strategic must be a long-term commitment and not an experiment. We have co-invested with Intel Capital and what was always good about Intel Capital is that they have stayed in corporate venturing for the long term. Many corporates came in and left or failed to keep their CVC practice going with a change of the CEO or economic downturn, but Intel Capital has proven that for them this is not an experiment and if you are the best CEO with a choice of VC investors fighting over who gets into your deal, Intel Capital remains a fine choice thanks to the clear track record of stability.

Another key point I would make from my twenty plus year view of the evolution of CVC and independent VC is that before a corporate gets "all in" into VC they should start with a Fund of Funds (FoF) investment strategy. VCs may know everything about venture capital with thousands of subliminally learned lessons, but most CFOs of multi-billion dollar companies do not have a clear understanding of venture capital. An initial period of Fund of Funds investing with strong communications among the VCs and the corporate is the best way to become wise on the VC world quickly. Then with this knowledge and set of relationships with GPs they have invested in the corporate can expect better results with their CVC program. @mauropretolani

CASE STUDY - MERCK VENTURES - ROEL BULTHUIS - SENIOR VICE PRESIDENT & MANAGING DIRECTOR

I met Roel Bulthuis for breakfast in London a few weeks before he launched his CVC. Roel is the founder and Managing Director of MS Ventures, the corporate venture fund Merck KGaA, based in Darmstadt, Germany. (Full disclosure: Roel was also on the board of advisors of my previous company - The Founders Club.) He answered several CVC questions:

Access to early-stage financing is the lifeblood of biotechnology innovation. In a very similar way, access to biotechnology innovation is a critical factor in modern-day pharma's ability to still its continuous hunger for new products. We established MS Ventures in 2009 to take an active role in this ecosystem. Originally set up as a €40m seed fund, MS Ventures now manages a €150m evergreen fund and is one of the most active early stage CVC investors in the pharma industry. MS Ventures is currently expanding its mandate to serve as the dedicated entity for any equity investment by the Merck KGaA Group, across seed investments, early stage strategic investments and spin-offs. Merck is a leading science and technology company in healthcare, life science and performance materials. Around 50,000 employees work to further develop technologies that improve and enhance life – from biopharmaceutical therapies to treat cancer or multiple sclerosis, cutting-edge systems for scientific research and production, to liquid crystals for smartphones and LCD televisions.

Will the highly selective current market environment lead to a more focused 'pipeline' of biotech companies?
The current market environment is highly selective for both biotech companies and VC firms. We expect that the challenges the industry has today will lead to a more focused "pipeline" of biotech-developed drugs and to more realistic (valuation, exit options, timelines) investment models driven by a selective group of VCs. Emerging biotech companies, in particular those with a focus on drug discovery and development, have the challenging task to match their ever changing risk profile and long development timelines to significant amounts of risk capital. In general

(for some niche indications this may be off) we see a natural divide at the stage of clinical POC (Proof of Concept). Before that point, the total amounts of financing required are manageable for a syndicate of VCs and the risk profile of the asset matches the return expectations of the VC asset class. Also, we generally believe that small biotech companies are much better positioned to drive innovation at this stage than large pharma. Beyond clinical POC, the required amounts of financing are typically beyond the means of VC investors and even if available, the cost of capital of the VC money for the company becomes too high in light of the remaining development risks (i.e. VC cost of capital does not match late stage clinical development risk). Also, at this point in its development we believe that for the first time in the life cycle of the drug, an established pharma company is better positioned than the biotech to lead further development.

Do the Biotech or VC models need more market realism?
We don't think that the biotech or the VC model "failed". We do see many examples of unrealistic expectations though. Many of the companies that we see, more so in Europe than in the US, are primarily driven by science. Although science is obviously fundamental to our business, in the end we need to create products that we can sell. As a Pharma company, we live the challenges of increased regulatory and payer pressure and a highly competitive commercial environment and work back from that to make R&D decisions that are aimed to position our drugs with a maximum amount of commercial differentiation. We often find that biotech companies work the other way around and that their basic science drives later development decisions. We also often see founding scientists in CEO positions based on their academic authority, not necessarily because of their strategic or leadership skills. Especially in countries with a more hierarchical culture, the "arrogance of science" is very strong. Another key symptom of this is that we find that CEOs and Boards tend to wait longer and invest less than we would expect to attract business development skills to their team (i.e. often the expectation is to hire a head of BD once the company is ready for a deal). If you take into account

that (1) the majority of products will require a partner, (2) the value of the program will be largely defined by commercial considerations, and (3) it takes a long time to build sponsorship with potential partners; this is a losing proposition.

Should business models be driven by the resource needs and risk profile of an asset, not by market trends?

We believe that there is a place for a number of different business models in biotech. It is important though that the chosen business model follows the resource needs of the asset the company develops. More concretely, a platform technology requires a full discovery research and early development setup whereas, on the other side of the spectrum, a one-product company can typically do with a small team and outsource a significant proportion of their work. At a deeper level, the indication and therapeutic modality will define whether quality external resources are available or that they need to be built up in house. The danger in the current market environment is that VCs are looking for new models to show their LPs a renewed opportunity (the VC model is dead, long live the new VC model) to make money and then impose their new (experimental) business model on their investee companies. We see many opportunities in the current market (asset-based financing, structuring of entities into holding companies) of single asset financings that require broader resources or multiple single asset financing vehicles that form a company together and are not managed effectively due to their complex structure. In the current market there is an increased role for corporate venture groups in the financing of biotech companies. We started MS Ventures six years ago to make strategic investments and with the objective to provide, in addition to funding, inputs in the development of products and technologies that would better position them for deals with us or other pharma. We currently see that, with a very selective group of CVCs and VCs we take up a significant role in new company creation. @MerckSerono_de

CASE STUDIES - GOOGLE VENTURES, IDG VENTURES & MTG - ANIL HANSJEE - FORMER HEAD, GOOGLE'S EUROPEAN & ISRAELI STRATEGIC INVESTMENT AND CORPORATE DEVELOPMENT PROGRAMS; FORMER CVC, IDG VENTURES AND MTG SVERIGE MODERN TIMES GROUP; COFOUNDER & INVESTOR, MOJO CAPITAL FUND OF FUNDS

I got together with my old friend Anil Hansjee who shared insights from working at three different CVCs. Here are his words:

My first experience as a CVC was working for Pat McGovern at IDG in the early 2000s. Print advertising was falling off a cliff and Pat had been diversifying through venture capital. Originally he had issues of repatriating revenue cash from China in the 80s; so that's part of why he got going in China so early through venture capital. At IDG we had no need to seal a business development deal to get an investment done, in fact the investment committee was the general partners plus Pat. IDG were primarily driven by financial diversification from new digital media business models and new emerging market access. However, what became clear to me was the risk of being dependent on a single LP. Once Pat personally moved onto other things or IDG prioritized capital allocation elsewhere, the long-term commitment waned.

I also spent a number of years from mid 2000s in London at Google responsible for both strategic investments and M&A for Europe, Africa and Israel. During those days approximately 50% of Google's revenues came from Europe, but most of the company's product development was in Mountain View, California, hence a need to keep an eye on the ground in EMEA via investments and M&A. Larry, Sergei and Eric were the investment committee originally with SVPs from product and engineering joining at various times, so decision making was very decisive and mostly driven by product or engineering. Investments at that time were highly strategic and typically focused on ecosystems/value chains where outright ownership did not make sense or was not needed, but influence and deep relationships were sought – such as in Internet access and telecoms, especially pre- and early Android days.

Google Capital and Google Ventures as formal structures both came later on. Capital was set up as the natural successor to the strategic investing we did with a focus on addressing the question of what other businesses, the soon to be, Alphabet might develop – banking, transportation etc. and as such was a late stage investor. Google Ventures was set up to behave just like a financial VC based on a recognition that the wealth of deal-flow Google saw and some of the core business/product building skills it had in its own people could both be viewed as unique asset to leverage in creating a new business model for Google in generating financial returns from investments. Google was at the center of all things Internet. We saw everything at an early stage. We started with focus and broadened the focus step-by-step. In a good market the entrepreneur has choice and the CVC or any VC must demonstrate the value they bring to the startup and syndicate of investors. If you have an inherent domain expertise and platforms to leverage startups should want to come to you. This is especially true in complex ecosystems. You should become the first port of call, which is the inherent advantage in venture for meaningful corporates if they can leverage this cleanly.

Over time Google in EMEA achieved more geographic decentralization with more people on the ground in Europe, especially product and engineering. As the EMEA startup scene improved over time, M&A sourced regionally. This also became more meaningful for Google on a global basis – Global IP Solutions, Waze and Deepmind are good examples. With this improvement in the startup ecosystem, with more and more, and larger, successful startups coming from Europe and with an increasing desire to show commitment in being part of nurturing this eco-system, Google became more active in the startup community. I initiated the first Google Campus that was opened globally, in London in conjunction with the London Olympics; eventually Google Ventures put people on the ground in Europe too. Although Ventures was independent, generally speaking if we put more money into the game with investments we got more chances at M&A. We had a view of increasing our chances at M&A with more people knowing Google via venture capital. Nest is a good example of venture invest, nurture, engagement all leading to acquisition. Although when the purpose of a global business unit like Ventures is non-strategic, there will always be potential regional conflicts between prioritization of asset allocation for the best deals vs. asset allocation to develop a market which led recently to the removal of a local European dedicated fund.

With the benefit of hindsight, the path towards the Alphabet structure was a natural one in creating ultimate diversification. Google leveraged its core assets of people, capital, and platforms to create multiple business units under Alphabet; acquisition and investment were core to that journey.

I later established the digital M&A and CVC arm of MTG, a publicly traded Swedish television broadcaster. They were very concerned with what was happening with falling linear TV viewing, especially from younger demographics due to businesses such as YouTube (a Google company). At the same time they were very scared of cannibalizing their established revenues. For example, they had a very innovative OTT VOD platform (developed long before Netflix and with great content from cross licensing from PayTV); but it was always given as a retention tool as an add-on to PayTV, rather than monetizing it as a standalone business with great content. Ultimately this led to a late start in pushing digital meaningfully.

So my focus became what would quickly and meaningfully shift the revenue dial to digital. M&A can do this, but without a systematic CVC program it becomes a case of constant catch-up through M&A in a world of fast moving innovation (and probably a need to overpay). It is key to look for innovation before you fall off a cliff.

We did manage to develop some digital revenues streams. The MTG development is a success story now both in terms of acquiring meaningful YouTube based multi-channel networks and in becoming the leading e-Sports production business globally, but we should have started earlier. The list of missed opportunities is long for a business like MTG that understands video and entertainment content and advertising: ad-tech, digital sales, betting, music, and interactive video are just some of the areas for which a CVC business could have advantageously positioned the mother ship. Broadcasting is a very complex ecosystem and the bulk of ad dollars are still offline. Startups need media partners to navigate and survive. The financial VCs should have welcomed the opportunity to work with us and MTG could also have invested in VCs to develop these relationships, as we have seen other media companies (Pro7Sat1, Burda, Sky) do.

Another classic mistake I see is the European corporate looking for VCs only in their home market. If you're sitting in Scandinavia you need geographical diversification. Investing in VC funds outside one's geography can help the corporate see trends and startups from Silicon Valley, New York and London earlier. In digital, businesses are global, unlike traditional TV broadcasting. M&A becomes easier once you put these networks in place and start to build relationships. Change happens quickly in technology but these relationships do require time to generate results.

Ultimately, for a CVC to work successfully with the best funds and the best entrepreneurs, you need to add industry and ecosystem partnership value, invest with no M&A strings attached and don't push M&A too hard because the opportunity will come and then you are best positioned. This multifaceted approach is the best approach. @ahansjee

CASE STUDIES - MIDDLE EAST, NORTH AFRICA & TURKEY (MENAT) - HOW CORPORATES, FAMILY OFFICES AND SOVEREIGN WEALTH FUNDS CREATE CVCS - OZAN SONMEZ - STARTUP ACCELERATORS HEAD, KING ABDULLAH UNIVERSITY OF SCIENCE & TECHNOLOGY (KAUST) SAUDI ARABIA

I caught up with Ozan Sonmez, who is based in Saudi Arabia where he leads a number of startup accelerator programs and is very active with the main startup events and programs across the MENAT region including Startup Istanbul, Arabnet, MIT EF Pan Arab, Startup Mena, Step Conference and Enpact. Here are his words:

I feel the need to start with a couple of points to give you a context of the business world in the MENAT region to understand the emergence of CVCs here. Although being geographically in the Middle East, I am excluding Israel from this analysis. Israel is ahead of the US in VC backed startups per capita, VC dollars deployed per capita and ahead of all other developed countries in building startups that IPO in the US.

There are not many exits for startups in MENAT and as a result the number of financial VCs and angels in the region are low in numbers compared to equally wealthy countries. So the way startup innovation has begun to take off has largely been driven by corporations committed to the region; therefore, CVC is in fact central to the development of the startup innovation economy here. Very often a large business is owned by a single family and so, rather than the family office network funding financial VCs as one sees in the west, the family offices here are often tied to a single corporate; their interests are more in line with CVC where strategic return trumps financial returns, so again it is really just corporate venturing.

The countries of the MENAT region have been ever changing, especially in the last twenty to thirty years. Turkey endorsed a liberal western wealth creation based economic model after the 1980's. The Gulf States embarked in developing similar free market models with varying degrees of success over the last two decades. North African countries are building vibrant economic hubs with ever growing potential for cooperation and trade especially with Europe. All these political developments led to the emergence of two different types of wealth and resource creation models. One is mostly family owned local holdings that grew and became the main drivers of these respective economies. The second is directly state owned but privately managed large corporations.

A few examples of the first type of companies are Koç and Sabanci group companies in Turkey, Abdulatif Jameel (ALJ) Group in Saudi Arabia, Oger group companies in Lebanon, and Zain group companies in Kuwait, where a small number of mostly still privately owned family holdings produce large private economic outcomes and also improve their national GDP. They mostly developed their wealth from consumption base economy elements such as banking, manufacturing, construction and Fast Moving Consumer Goods (FMCG). These few large conglomerates and family owned holdings are at a prime position to lead innovation with all their assets of established supply chains, brand names, infrastructure and talent they employ every year.

Good examples of the second type of companies are Tüpraş and Turk Telekom from Turkey (prior to privatizations) and Saudi Aramco from Saudi Arabia. These companies are in heavy infrastructure businesses where the state needed to finance the capacity building and use the excess value creation to build more capacity and grow wider. However slow moving in decision-making, these companies that operate on natural resource extraction as well as telecommunications industries are most impacted from innovations and rapid changes in their fields. Much like the private family owned companies these state owned companies also have the financial, technological and human resources available at their disposal to engage in innovation.

In summary, there is enough wealth and resources in slow moving, mostly noncompetitive, private and state owned large institutions in MENAT. Both types of companies mentioned have been involved in the startup, innovation & investment ecosystems of their countries with different initiatives and different motivations. Below is a short case-by-case analysis of the unique models born in MENAT to tackle the unique challenges of the region.

Opportunistic motivations: going for the low hanging fruit.
The lack of established growth financing options for SMEs [small medium enterprises] where bank loans are expensive and historically not highly reputed and the lack of an attractive public market where IPOs are very rare and limited in quantity have created an opportunity for cash-rich conglomerates to pick up the startup opportunity. These acquisitions are usually triggered from the company itself and do not involve minority shares but full buy-outs. However attractive to provide growth through acquisitions, these M&As are usually driven not by new innovative technology, but by providing channels to new markets, by economies of scale benefits and, sometimes, by diversification opportunities. That is why I will separate the mergers and acquisition discussion from venture financings.

There are mainly two approaches I want to highlight, that have more strategic thought and consideration driving the investment appetite of these large institutions. An important point worth mentioning before getting into the details of the cases, is to state that the CVC and innovation based startup ecosystems are fairly nascent in MENAT. Although diverse in formation and structure, the initiatives are fairly at their infancy periods and most have yet to prove impact. These activities should be seen by the reader as the initial ground breaking where the high rising startups will emerge with the emergence of CVCs and VCs.

1) Fully owned and operated startup accelerators – focused on early stage startups
2) Fully owned and operated Corporate Venture Capital companies – focused on late stage startups

There are many reasons why CVCs in MENAT are created.

1) To hedge against black swans and protect the old economy model through new technology investments.
2) To use the existing infrastructure and know how that is not easily replicable by startups.
3) To build a diversified portfolio of services to existing customers.
4) To be perceived as a leader in innovation and thus attract more talent.
5) To create national wealth and utilize resources.
6) To help implement government policy especially job creation and reversing brain drain.
7) To provide financial returns.

Though it may sound bizarre, I believe the CVCs in MENAT are usually not built primarily with the traditional financial return expectations. One reason is that the family companies are already LPs in large PE investments usually outside their own country with above market rate financial return expectations. The other reason is the limited IPO markets in the operating countries where they would not be able to exit within a predictable timeframe, creating a barrier for exit-oriented transactions. Thus I believe a mix of the first six motivations mentioned above drives CVCs in MENAT. Usually in the formation of the investment thesis of CVCs, all these motivations play a role, but in my experience one of them is more dominant. Below is my take on the dominant motivation and cases based on this understanding.

Case study - family university-affiliated CVCs' investment thesis: access to new technology
One tool the private holding groups in MENAT have used to access to innovation is to build legacy by name-bearing private universities. These universities had been the entry point of the large conglomerates to more technology heavy innovation and startups. The state in Turkey has very generous tax incentive packages once any R&D in the university is developed and funded through an industry and university collaboration, thus the holdings are fond of creating these jointly operated structures. Therefore the corporate venture arms of these companies are by no surprise embedded, hosted and operated very closely to the universities. Although limited in number and size of deals, there are double digits of startups emerging out of these universities that are backed by the local CVCs. Sabancı Group and Koç Group are examples of CVCs operated closely within their name bearing private universities and invest in innovation and intellectual property coming out of these universities. Sabancı University's Inovent is fully owned by the university, not by the holding company, therefore it is technically an independent university seed fund, not a CVC. It has a broader mandate to invest in startups other than the ones coming directly from the university. Koç University on the other hand, has created a joint venture directly with the holding, which qualifies them as the first innovation/IP focused CVC of Turkey. The primary motive for investment is not exit drive but opportunity drive. These investments are usually very tightly knit to the mother companies' subsidiaries and acts as a cost effective way to access new innovations that would

have direct impact on the traditional businesses owned by the holdings. Automotive and manufacturing industries and heavy family companies have benefited from this direct involvement. Usually the startups become fully or partially owned subsidiaries since the CVC terms are designed to primarily benefit the mother company. The appetite for trade and IP portfolio sales is also strong with these CVCs.

An example of another university led initiative from the region is Berytech in Beirut, Lebanon. Born as a collaboration and innovation eco-system completely out of the University of Saint Joseph, Berytech has extended the reach and depth of activities and added a for profit VC fund to the structure getting support from the Circular 331 initiative that will be separately mentioned in the sovereign fund case. They have an impact first, revenue later approach, and aim to create more innovation based startups to create opportunities for the young and multi-cultural Lebanese (who usually speak Arabic, French and English fluently) in an attempt to avoid the brain drain.

Case study – Family companies leveraging economies of scale to drive emerging new businesses
The family companies that are fundamentally engaged in international markets are also attracted to be involved in CVC formation and direct investment into startups. The case of Farplas and Zorlu Group's Vestel Ventures from Turkey are good examples to this model. Vestel Ventures operate fully strategically attached to the mother company whose main business is to export TVs, white household major and small appliances mainly to Europe. The company has a dominate market position and has grown also via international M&A. Vestel Ventures, the CVC arm of Vestel, has been scouting for new economy expansion towards mobile and digital in the last five years and has also been a preferred domestic partner to the education initiatives of the Turkish government. While the hardware capabilities of the company are world class, they scouted new startups to integrate into their software value add portfolio. The primary motivation is to engage with startups to embed them into their existing infrastructure and other deals. Farplas on the other hand chose a more diversified

approach with the establishment of F+ Ventures where they focused on a larger set of startups that are in the broader mobility space since their customers are usually automotive manufacturers.

Case study – Telcos leveraging economies of scale to drive emerging new businesses

There are institutions that did not built their universities but are either forming their accelerators or working closely with accelerators. We see this trend picking up especially in the telecommunications (telco) sector with Saudi Telecom's (STC) Inspire U, Mobily Ventures, Turkcell's partnership with a university based accelerator, Zain's ZINC initiative, and Turkish Telekom's Pilott programs. These organizations can loosely be called CVCs since their involvement as investment partners are different in every case, but in at least half of the cases cash for equity transactions are occurring.

Turkish Telecom's Pilott is an example that has been formed primarily to address the long new product development cycles existing within the company that is not compatible with the fast changing needs of mainly mobile consumers. They built and still operate the accelerator without an equity engagement but with revenue share models. Turkcell has been the primary supporter of a university accelerator in Turkey with a hope of accessing the new startups without going through lengthy investment procedures within the company. Zain has created Zain Innovation Center (ZINC) and is operating as a partial co-working and startup hub not like a formal equity based accelerator.

Saudi Telecom Company is a unique case which we will mention twice, both in the early stage fully-owned and operated accelerator model, and also in the traditional financial reward-seeking CVC model. STC has chosen to create its own accelerator InspireU, with the traditional cash for equity model. They are more involved in the startups to embed the existing new value based service offerings to STC customers. The current cohort was taken in 2015 and they are deeply integrated into the technical and managerial structures of the corporate parent.

Apart from the fully operated InspireU of STC, many Telco's in the region have stepped into the startup and CVC game with a safer bet by creating partnerships. Mobily from Saudi Arabia (owned partially by Etisalat of United Arab Emirates) and Umniah from Jordan (owned by Batelco of Bahrain) have both chosen to operate an accelerator with the traditional cash for equity model, through a partnership with a US-based investor/accelerator operator that aims to bring startups from the region to the US market. Qatar's Ooredoo has partnered with Rocket Internet Group, more as a traditional LP but with a focus on Asia-Pacific. Etisalat has also partnered with iMENA with a similar LP model but that also involves heavy strategic and operational involvement. These companies are not necessarily the first movers into the startup investment space, but are interested in benefitting from the emergence of fast growing startups that benefit from the region's highly engaged and connected youth. Although it will take time for the regional telco CVCs to reach double digit deals per year like their European and US counterparts, I believe their involvement with accelerators will help build a portfolio of good seed and early stage companies that will drive growth and new services to them.

One last notable example of such a partnership is from the Turkish Ecosystem MV holding, who has funded the European based StartupbootCamp's Istanbul branch through its dedicated CVC. The holding also built a hybrid model that includes a co-working space and a follow-on funding structure that cooperates with VCs in their early stage deals.

It should be noted that Turkey has the least number of CVCs in MENAT with the most developed ecosystem. Apart from telco/accelerator and university led structures, there is almost no other CVC in spite of the growth orientation of the country. The reason for this is the extreme ownership obsession and the delusional belief that the holdings have enough resources to build whatever they want. The generation born in a closed economy, now leading most of the family owned holdings in Turkey, still do not grasp the significance of the emergence of startups that only employ a few hundred people, grow double digit every month and then disrupt major businesses.

Case study – media companies leveraging economies of scale to drive emerging new businesses

Apart from the telco's that are mentioned who have invested directly in accelerators or partnered with accelerators, the media sector has also been very active in the startup scene. The two examples are Twofour54 (Abu Dhabi) and MBC Ventures (Dubai). Twofour54 has both invested in Flat6 Labs, a regional accelerator operator and also created its own CVC. Their investment portfolio is not limited to the Flat6Labs since they also invest in later seed/idea stage companies independently. MBC Ventures has entered the space without any affiliation to accelerators or incubators and financed three startups but seems to have slowed down in recent years.

Case study - STC Ventures & Hikma Ventures seeking diversification and financial return
Apart from the InspireU initiative, the STC group is active in their fully owned CVC. Operated in partnership with Iris Capital, STC Ventures has made at least nine investments within the region - the largest portfolio of its kind - into startups in various sectors such as education, e-commerce and enterprise SaaS. The focus of the fund is towards growth stage start-ups with post product and post revenue with proven business models in ITC and media fields.

Hikma Ventures out of Jordan is the newest and perhaps the most traditional type of CVC in the region. Hikma Group is the largest pharmaceutical company in the Middle East, which is active in fifty countries and through its partnerships, licensing operations and facilities has grown to IPO on the London Stock Exchange in 2005. The group has traditionally been more involved in M&A during the growth stage but now has opened up a fully funded CVC with $30m dedicated to focus on early stage digital health startups. The fundamental motivation is to benefit from the nascent scene in the Middle East and developing economies and create an alternative faster access to innovation with startups compared to the traditional long cycle of R&D in the pharmaceutical industry.

Case study - family offices leading later stage direct investments seeking financial returns

The large family offices owned and operated as integral parts of their main company are also getting closer to VC type direct investments apart from their LP positions in VC and private equity funds. There are more family owned VCs motivated with financial returns and diversification but not all of them are transparent about their investment portfolio. Although the numbers of transactions are probably much higher than these, the most significant recent deals that can be named include Al Tayyar Travel Group leading Careem's $10m Series B round and $67m Series C rounds (Uber's archrival in Middle East); Abdul Latif Jameel group investing in MarkaVIP's $30m B round (a prominent e-commerce platform); and Al Sanie Group in the $4m Series A round of Holiday.me. These examples (and numerous non-disclosed transactions) show the strong emergence of direct access to the deals once the risk level has dropped after the first angel and VC rounds. As documented by CB Insights for the US market, I believe the average deal sizes made by CVCs are significantly higher than the VC deals also in the Middle East. It is very difficult to track the investment thesis of this model without direct involvement with the actual partners and decision makers.

Case study - sovereign wealth funds & direct state funded structures seeking financial & social returns
Sovereign wealth funds, which are usual suspects for PE and large VC exposures, are also attracted individually to the emerging startups at later stages. Like Impulse (a subsidiary of Kuwait Investment Authority) participating in the C round of Careem there are many sovereign funds especially in the GCC Area that are dealing directly with startups. The Gulf Cooperation Council (GCC) is a regional political organization comprising the energy rich Gulf monarchies – Bahrain, Kuwait, Oman, Qatar, Saudi Arabia and the United Arab Emirates. Taqnia Ventures of the Kingdom of Saudi Arabia is another example of the sovereign wealth fund financing startups in the region.

A very important initiative to mention is definitely the King Abdullah Fund of Jordan. I had personally witnessed, the King Abdullah himself presenting the growth and future prospect of Startup Ecosystem in

Jordan, at a special networking event at UC Berkeley in 2014. The fund created by the royal decree, has supported one of the most diverse accelerators in the Region from Jordan: Oasis500 and also an early stage fund Silicon Badia.

Another recent development of importance is the government support via the Central Bank of Lebanon, Banque du Liban (BDL) Circular 331. BDL, by injecting an estimated $400m of funds, an unheard of amount for a small country like Lebanon, wants to play a decisive role in building the startup ecosystem. The fund guarantees 75% of the investments to the knowledge economy completed by the privately owned banks. The independent banks are now becoming LPs in the emerging VCs of Lebanon since their risk is highly mitigated by the BDL, rather than trying to adjust themselves to the uncharted territories of high risk early stage startups.

Another example of a government led initiative that resembles a CVC is the Dubai Silicon Oasis Authority - a 100% government-owned free zone that promotes modern technology based industries with a built-in community, infrastructure and in-house business services. A mix of incubation space and mentorship is provided to startups and the fund operated by the DSO takes equity positions in the early stage startups.

Case study - Saudi Aramco Energy Ventures (SAEV) seeking strategic value and financial returns
Andrew asked me to write about Saudi Aramco. The most well-known CVC born out of the region is for sure the Saudi Aramco Energy Ventures (SAEV). What makes SAEC particularly interesting is their focus on emerging technologies on certain fields, their multi-round and ticket size agnostic deals and their completely international investment mandate. With an estimated but not confirmed fund size of $500m to $1bn, SAEV enjoys the autonomy of having an independent entity and at the same time integrated connections to the company managing the world's largest crude oil reserves. The drive coming from the technical innovation edge needed in the chemicals and materials businesses pushes the corporate venture arm to be at the forefront of scouting startups around the world. The company has six offices in the US, UK, China, Korea, Japan and Norway

apart from their Dhahran Headquarters. The portfolio approach of SAEV also shows a broader understanding of the value chain with their big data startup investment of $26m into Manaa, and their wearables device investment of an $11.6m C round into 908Devices. The company lists fifteen direct investments into startups serving upstream and downstream oil and gas, petrochemicals, renewables, energy efficiency and water sectors and also three confirmed investments into funds at different locations investing in development to growth stage. Among the investment positions in funds, Tsing Capital is one of the first clean tech funds in China. The unique structure and format of SAEV makes it a significant player in the international CVC arena on materials and resources. The total portfolio of the company is estimated to be more than 100 companies in various stages of developments in the strategic sectors with the direct investment in addition to the startups funded by the three funds in which SAEV is an LP.

Case study - Saudi Aramco's Wa'ed seeking social impact & returns
The MENAT region has grown out of many obstacles especially over the last ten years. The continuous changes in the political landscape have hurt the youth of the region the most. Today youth unemployment is a critical time bomb for many countries where innovative solutions are needed to tackle this issue. In this context, it is not strange to see such items as "(we...) *Invest in companies with a unique value proposition that have reasonable probability of success and significant impact in terms of job creation and consolidation for the general workforce"* in investment thesis of a for profit cash for equity based CVC. The case of Wa'ed, Saudi Aramco's National focused CVC has so far invested between four and fourteen companies per year according to the company's website. The self-proclaimed driver of the activities of Wa'ed is not profit but impact as stated on their web site *"Wa'ed Equity advocates an approach that differs from typical Venture Capital functions that focus exclusively on one objective: profit. At Wa'ed Equity, the focus is not only on profit, but also on the creation of quality jobs and economic diversification in Saudi Arabia."* Therefore, it is a VC function with a national agenda.

As seen in these cases there are many unique CVC structures in MENAT to understand and learn from. Exit opportunities are limited due to lack of public offering markets and highly regulated foreign direct investments. Talent is relatively cheap and except for few countries like Turkey, local businesses in the Middle East rely mostly on expats from the first world to lead with local talent and manage third world country expats. New technology-based innovation is not backed by resources yet except in few places like King Abdullah University of Science and Technology and the Masdar Institute of Abu Dhabi. Brain drain drives most of the local born talent outside to study and remain in other countries building their successes outside the region. There are legal and cultural challenges in doing business as ranked by international reports. Lack of tolerance for failure and expectations of a stable structure due to family and culture presents a barrier for young people to start building their startups.

To tackle all these disadvantages and challenges for the regional players, hybrid models are emerging. From impact-focused initiatives like Berytech and Wa'ed, to King's that invest to build ecosystems to create job opportunities and stop brain drain, and family office extensions that invest directly in growth stage startups, the ecosystem is vibrant and active. With highly engaged, connected and young populations, all these countries are sitting on what can either be a gold mine or a time bomb.

The effectiveness of these "Born in Middle East" models of investing will determine if innovation and wealth will be created in the region for the region or if it will flow out of the region. It is my advice to the international players and GPs of funds in the startup-financing ecosystem to be able to see the region with new eyes and come here not only to seek LPs for their PE & VC funds but to build interconnected hybrid wealth and impact driven models. Remember that in MENAT, the startup pie is too small to compete for aggressively. The focus of local players is not always financial return maximization but a longer vision of ecosystem development through leap frogging older models and building unique MENAT structures. @mrozansonmez

CASE STUDY - MICROSOFT VENTURES & MICROSOFT ACCELERATORS - RAHUL SOOD - FOUNDER; CEO, UNIKRN

I caught up with Rahul to talk about CVC and he gave me the story of how Microsoft Ventures and Accelerator program came into being and the logical progression for him to found Unikrn. (Full disclosure: Rubicon Venture Capital is an investor in Unikrn.) Here are the takeaways of our chat in Rahul's words:

I was working at Microsoft and looking for something interesting to do. One of the things I was thinking about is how big companies innovate industries from within. Then I considered how startups innovate the same industries from the outside. What struck me is that Microsoft has a HUGE footprint of customer success in enterprise. Walk into any major enterprise in the US or even a government office in Vienna, Austria and you will see Windows running on every PC not to mention dominance of the server market. A group of us got together and built a plan that would position Microsoft as a leader in connecting large companies with startups. It hit me that we can offer startups access to customers like no other. Microsoft is unique and we can deliver customer revenue success and scale to startups. Now, how can we do this in the most effective way, while at the same time capturing innovation we can drag into Microsoft itself and also deliver that innovation to our enterprise customers? We viewed this challenge from the vantage point of three stakeholders: 1) MSFT, 2), our customers and 3) the startups we'd choose to work with.

Once I became excited by this challenge I then considered how to execute operationally on this dream. When you can harness the resources of Microsoft, you can allow yourself to think big. Joking aside, I was thinking a bit differently.

After some pulling and pushing with people you may have heard of in Microsoft senior management, we came up with a comprehensive plan for Microsoft's Global Startup program - Microsoft Ventures and the Microsoft Accelerator program. Some of the accelerators were already in operation, along with the Bing Fund, and we consolidated all of it under one umbrella and turned that into Microsoft Ventures.

From Day-1 we never focused on or gave a shit about making profitable investments. We were all about finding innovation and helping startups blossom. If we did that some good would flow back to Microsoft. It worked.

As the founder of Microsoft's Venture program I established the following core guidelines:

1) Help startups build and grow
2) Help Microsoft enterprise customers access innovation
3) Help Microsoft (I did not even make it about Microsoft accessing innovation, but of course we benefitted as well.)

By the time that we set up Microsoft Ventures the VC world had already shifted towards later stage investing; so we decided we needed to be early stage. We launched a network of seven Microsoft Accelerator programs around the world.

1) Seattle (partnered with American Family Insurance Company)
2) Tel Aviv, Israel
3) Bangalore, India
4) Berlin, Germany
5) Paris, France
6) Sao Paolo, Brazil
7) Beijing, China

To point to one success, after a few years the collective market cap of our Beijing companies exceeded $4.5bn. It is difficult to call our endeavor anything but a blockbuster success. Even if you take one point of success, for a company like Microsoft, this program was worth doing and a profit center.

Our accelerator program was a 3-4 month program. We never took equity unless we made capital investments, our primary focus was to just help build and grow companies. When I think of the options for other corporates to mimic what we did or take a different strategy I would caution that Microsoft had a unique set of circumstances working in our favor that do not exist for most large companies.

We had two things at Microsoft that most corporates do not have: 1) a totally unique footprint to enterprise customers and assets, 2) a well-developed platform of software assets and services that can be given for free, leased, or lent to a startup. And the stuff Microsoft has is stuff startups need. At Microsoft Ventures and Accelerator we always offered our startups the option to not build or use Microsoft products or services, but it was rare that one of our companies would go to Amazon or Rackspace for hosting when we offered best in class.

I think it must be hard for any single corporate to set up an accelerator program or VC program and get the good deal flow and value exchange. Any massive telecom operator trying to launch a platform for example would need to craft a strategy around the fact that they lack any proprietary software or secret tech sauce.

At Microsoft we had a platform to offer. Andrew has not provided me with enough words in his book to truly describe the platform that Microsfot has to offer, but I assure you that it is unique and moves the ball for startups. It is a combination of technology, customer access and culture injection.

Andrew asked me about financial objectives and IRR type stuff with Microsoft Ventures. That part never really entered our thinking. Microsoft is so big that strategic objectives always trumped financial goals. With our platform we were able to consistently project a profitable business unit and we had support all the way to the top of the company from Bill Gates.

At Microsoft Ventures we were very flexible about budgets and access to resources. We basically focused on Seed and Series A. We were open to pre- and post revenue startups when I ran the program. With the existing business of Microsoft being so massive we were wide open when it came to industry focus sector.

Andrew asked me to talk about my shift from corporate venture capitalist to entrepreneur. When I was at Microsoft I used to think of trends.

From my vantage point, most VCs had left Seed stage investing as their funds got increasingly larger and larger. We got our trends from angels and micro-VCs. One trend we could see was the growing importance of e-sports, gaming and in-game advertising. One company we got excited about was Pinion in Australia and we made the investment from Microsoft Ventures into Pinion and got to know the company even better.

When I left Microsoft I made a decision to get back into gaming since that's where my passion lies. I made the decision to acquire Pinion, and the CEO of Pinion became my partner in Unikrn. Another company on our radar was the large corporation Tabcorp. Tabcorp is a multi-billion dollar gaming company with large company challenges in accessing innovation. We took a page from my Microsoft Ventures experience of bridging disruptive startups with big companies and created a partnership between Tabcorp and Unikrn. We enabled real money gambling in markets like the UK and Australia where it's legal and then we enabled wagering for our own currency – Unikoins - which can be used to win merchandise like gaming laptop PCs. Playing for Unikoins is legal worldwide.

Today Unikrn is a gaming and entertainment company with a focus on eSports. We own a network of gaming communities that reach millions of gamers in over 100 countries worldwide. We provide eSports fans and newcomers alike a safe and legal place to gather, game, and bet on eSports. With games like League of Legends, Counter-Strike: Global Offensive, Dota 2 and more, there's always something to watch and bet on at Unikrn. We raised funding from Matt Michelsen (another Rubicon-backed founder), Rubicon Venture Capital and other value added investors and have since raised additional funding from well-known tech investors including Binary Capital, Mark Cuban and Ashton Kutcher. With $10m in capital raised, great technology and a strong position in an explosive market, we are currently managing hyper-growth. @rahulsood @MSFTVentures, @MSFTVenturesUK

Three

Accelerators & Incubators and Other Ecosystem Options for Corporates

"To improve is to change; to be perfect is to change often."

- WINSTON CHURCHILL

A nother option for corporations to bring innovation from the outside into their business is to engage with accelerators. Some corporates launch and operate their own accelerator branded as the "<your corporate name> Accelerator" such as the Microsoft Accelerator or Citrix Accelerator. Other corporates partner with an established independent accelerator like TechStars or Startupbootcamp, e.g., the Disney and Barclays accelerators "powered by TechStars." Other options are to invest capital into an accelerator or not invest at all and simply assign employees to be mentors to one or more independent accelerators. I know a lawyer with a US law firm that is a mentor at seven different London accelerators with a goal of flipping the British and European startups to US Delaware C corps, then capturing more of those startups' legal work. Accessing this level of innovation can be done inexpensively or very expensively with reputation risk if it fails. If not done properly I think it is rather easy to fail. Early stage startups require a lot of heavy lifting and with thousands of accelerators currently operating in the San Francisco Bay Area, it's amazing that there are hundreds more about to be launched, covering a myriad of topics ranging from robotics to mobile digital health. Accelerators are also very different and changing all the time. Y Combinator (YC) seems to have transitioned from a hands-on accelerator to an investment fund with a great network for its portfolio companies, but no shared work space for the startups; it is more of an admissions program, a distributed set of volunteer "mentors" and the best attended investor demo day in the world.

My personal opinion on this may change, but I think in most cases a large corporate launching its own accelerator will suffer from adverse deal flow and therefore fail to achieve the goals outlined in Chapter 1. The best startup in the world is more likely to go to YC, 500Startups or TechStars than Microsoft Ventures. That's just my humble opinion, but I don't think the really good ones would tie themselves to Microsoft Windows, Azure and Kinect that early. Then again a startup can do multiple accelerators. A startup might benefit from going through 500Startups and YC. Sphero went to the Disney Accelerator powered by TechStars after having secured sizable VC funding, which proved to be a transformational success for the company and the corporate, resulting in the new BB-8 droid in the new *Star Wars* movie. For sure, the pack of VCs on Sand Hill Road invests in later stages than in the past. The average size of a Series A financing in the Silicon Valley is currently trending around $10m. Those startups scoring a Series A typically have already built their initial products, launched the products in the market, gotten to first revenues and even seeing revenues trending up and to the right by the time the Series A happens. I would go so far to say that 90% of the most important entrepreneurial decisions have been made before the Series A investors come on the scene. So if a corporate's goal is to access early innovation they need a strategy to go even earlier. Accelerators can be a good choice for that.

Corporates have choices on how to engage at the accelerator stage. They can invest in one or more accelerators, possibly only sponsoring a program at an accelerator or simply assigning full time employees of a corporate to be active mentors at multiple accelerators. Corporates launching their own accelerator solo or with a partner like Startupbootcamp or

TechStars can also be done at the same time or in steps. I would only caution the corporate to, as all things with venture capital, move out of the short term perspective of eyeing the share price and earnings per share ratios on a quarterly basis and take a 7 to 10 year if not a 20 year perspective to measure success and results. If done properly, the capital investment should be profitable within 3 to 7 years at the longest. That's really true for venture capital, but for accelerator investing investments may take longer or may never actually be fully returned. Profitability and self-funding for this initiative will take longer than with a VC and many accelerators, in my opinion, have negative unit economics and will never turn a profit without getting lucky. One should also clearly understand the difference between an accelerator, an incubator, a shared workspace and a VC fund. Many are one and position themselves to be another. There are a few corporate innovation programs that charge large corporates $25k to $250k annually for access to corporate innovation programs. Patrick de Zeeuw, cofounder of Startupbootcamp runs one of the best ones if not THE best one - InnoLeaps.com - and Duncan Logan, CEO of RocketSpace in San Francisco offers a good program, but I view most of these as only positive if the corporate has failed to get into actual investing by making an LP investment or making direct investments into startups. I'm not a big believer in corporate innovation programs that do not invest actual cash into startups or VC funds. My view is that when you invest capital you are more accountable for what you are doing than if you just decide to attempt to partner with startups. Once there is real money on the line the quality of your due diligence and commitment goes up radically. Again, if you can't get your corporate to create a CVC then these programs may be your best option to access external innovation or use that as a stepping-stone to get support for a CVC program.

Patrick's InnoLeaps program is different. He's actually helping large corporates carve out some of their entrepreneurial ideas and teams and spin them out, dock them inside of his beehive of entrepreneurial buzz and scene and then spin them back into the corporate. His program adds big value, but it's different from most "open innovation programs" that I generally give the thumbs down. These other programs may have value for the internal staff and some startups, but I would not make time for them myself.

A large Japanese corporate recently asked me to ask my portfolio companies to fill out an online form and "apply" to their innovation program to fly to Tokyo and meet with their large corporate and explore partnerships with their corporate as part of their innovation program which does not have any capital to invest. I would never bother my startups with this and that entire program is delusional that they will ever make any progress on this path. I personally do not take time to entertain such strategy moves and I would go as far as protect my startups from dealing with low level managers at corporates that I am certain are helpless to get any partnership going with our portfolio. If Claudia Munce who used to report to Lou Gerstner and founded IBM Ventures only succeeded half the time to get a partnership with a BU when she was investing hundreds of millions of dollars then why should I take the risk that the open innovation middle manager has the mojo to get anything done with the corporate? As Cuba Gooding's character put so well to Tom Cruz's Jerry McGuire, "Show me the money!" I attended the launch Super Bowl party of Steinberg Ventures (http://steinbergventures.com), which is a VC fund focused on sports related startups founded by Leigh Steinberg, who is the character that the Jerry McGuire movie is based on.

CASE STUDY - CITRIX STARTUP ACCELERATOR - MICHAEL HARRIES, COFOUNDER AND CHIEF TECHNOLOGIST OF CITRIX STARTUP ACCELERATOR

I met Michael at the launch party for the Citrix Accelerator and sat down with him four and a half years later to discuss the program and how a corporate accelerator can be an option for large corporates to access innovation and achieve other goals outlined in Chapter 1.

Michael Harries cofounded the Citrix Accelerator program in the beginning of 2011. As a bit of context, Citrix is a 25-year-old company that was essentially a single product company in 2000 and developed ten years later into a company with four major lines of business. As the business became more complex the research group found it increasingly challenging to maintain the quality of innovation over multiple business areas such as cloud computing, mobile and virtualization. Part of the birth of the Citrix Accelerator program was to extend the applied research mandate to use startups to explore 1) what is emerging in the technology world related to their enterprise customers and the future of work and 2) how the market is responding to these technologies. The core mandate for Citrix Accelerator is NOT to invest in companies that plug into Citrix's businesses, but technologies that could potentially introduce discontinuities disruptive to Citrix's core business or the broader technology ecosystem in markets Citrix cares about – namely enterprise work technologies. Harries explains that the return on investment to Citrix in running the accelerator can be measured across many different areas of the business, starting with strategic insights. Measurable advantages also include market perception of Citrix as an innovative company, HR retention, recruitment, positive local community profile, positive contribution to the ecosystem, driving positive culture change inside of a large organization, a path for intrapreneurship, development of new skills and training of employees from top to bottom of the organization, new perspective and specific opportunities for build, partner or buy.

Most accelerators, like Y Combinator, TechStars and 500Startups, offer a specific amount of cash such as $18k, $100k or $150k on the high end; they have large cohorts, batches of 30 companies or even 100+. Citrix invests $250k into up to eight new companies per annum. Citrix doesn't usually operate the Seed program with batches, other than the Innovators' Program described below. These companies are not given a farewell with a demo day after 3 months, but are welcome to work out of the Citrix Accelerator facilities for up to 18 months. Startups typically move out once they secure a major funding round.

Citrix invests the $250k on founder friendly terms of an uncapped convertible note, but this then changes to the terms of any other convertible note the startup may raise on. For example, a startup might raise $250k from Citrix Accelerator and then raise an additional $1m from angels and micro-VCs with a specific cap. Once that happens the $250k from Citrix adopts the same cap and terms of the new note. I would call this founder friendly.

In 2014, Citrix Accelerator added a more conventional accelerator called the Innovators' Program with a 3-month program and a grant of $25k per company. In this case the startup has zero dilution to their cap table and Citrix does not become a shareholder. So far, Citrix has run programs in major cities where Citrix has offices, including their Santa Clara HQ in the heart of the South Bay of Silicon Valley, arguably the global epicenter of enterprise technology; Raleigh-Durham, a pillar of Research Triangle Park (RTP); Santa Barbara and Bangalore, India. These programs each have local groups of mentors and company advisors and also enable internal employees to spend three months in the same program as "intrapreneurs" in order to develop an idea into a viable business. The curriculum for this program is a formal mix of design thinking, customer development and leadership training. The goal for entrepreneurs and intrapreneurs is to develop and prove a business model.

In most cases, employees work on ideas that are directly additive to Citrix, so they remain on payroll, and through proving out the business, develop their skills and value to the company. Teams that have a viable idea after the innovators' program are funded to continue developing the business, with a very clear set of expectations and timelines. This enables internal corporate innovation to be insulated from the existing corporate environment and to be inspired and surrounded by outside entrepreneurs and local business leaders.

The Innovators Program is funded through a combination of Citrix research funding, and local partner sponsorships. Local partners include other corporates, local investors, and often municipal authorities.

The Seed program investments are made off the Citrix balance sheet, but initially expensed as research. There have been some exits, and valuations are at break even today, with the expectation that as companies develop, these investments will drive significant multiples, which should establish the long term viability of the Citrix Accelerator program.

I asked Harries what he felt would motivate a very hot startup to choose the Citrix Accelerator program over Y Combinator, 500Startups, TechStars or any other independent accelerator. He gave the following top reasons:

1. A community of fellow enterprise computing startups
2. Offices in Santa Clara, class A space
3. The halo effect that a major industry titan like Citrix gives to what the startup is working on
4. Very focused and experienced advisors largely from inside of Citrix but also outside
5. A process for customer development where a startup may have succeeded at developing a disruptive technology and business model, but now needs help accessing meaningful enterprise customers.

Citrix Startup Accelerator's focus on a specific range of enterprise oriented startups, covering infrastructure software and future of work, means that the community effect is huge. Our CEO sessions are very well regarded and the shared experiences are extremely valuable. Also, our input, at individual and board level, is highly focused around proving the business model for these types of organizations.

I found the "halo effect" to be the most compelling of Harries' top reasons and the true differentiator. Joining the Citrix Accelerator before or after any of the others is not mutually exclusive. Most accelerators without major corporate participation fail to provide a tech startup to a network of relationship managers that can access large prospective corporate customers at an early stage. Such access drives product and business strategy, feedback and ultimately, meaningful revenues. Often YC (Y Combinator) companies boast of having taken 60+ customers onboard during their three months in the program. If you dig deeper you may find that 58 of them are in the same YC batch or YC alumni. Now that is a powerful thing and a good reason to go to YC, but having Citrix introduce you to the Fortune 500 is also meaningful. Without any doubt, enterprise technology startups would be wise to consider Citrix as an option. Corporates considering using venture capital as a tool to achieve the objectives in Chapter 1 can learn from the Citrix example.

Citrix Startup Accelerator is an example of the transition of corporate research into 'open innovation,' where insights are sought into the combination of both invention and market response through working with startups. For any organization seeking to follow this direction, it's critical to be very clear about which strategic goals are being sought, and how it can align with corporate dynamics. Citrix seeks longer term, larger trends, so aims to invest in big picture startups, doing something new, where there is a significant IP position, and where the market is not yet proven, hence high risk. Others may seek very targeted innovation areas, extensions to the ecosystem, or new products for an existing channel. @citrixaccel, @citrix

Note from Andrew Romans: Since sitting down with Mike Harries, Citrix has decided to cancel this program, giving it a life span of five years and two months. I commend Mike on the important work he accomplished investing in and helping 31 companies and look forward to working with him wherever he goes. This is now another real-world example in this book that corporates need to make a long-term commitment to harvest the dividends and why many in the VC ecosystem are skeptical that corporates will stay in the game until they establish a consistent track record like Intel Capital.

CASE STUDY - SILICON CATALYST - RICK LAZANSKY - COFOUNDER & MANAGING PARTNER; BOARD DIRECTOR, SAND HILL ANGELS

I caught up with Rick Lazansky to learn about how he is partnering with corporates for an incubator solely focused on semiconductor related startups. He also knows more about semiconductors (semis) than anyone else I know. (Full disclosure, I have known Rick for many years and he is an active investor in Rubicon Venture Capital's funds.) Here are Rick's words on how he is partnering with corporates to put the silicon back in Silicon Valley:

I was VP of product development at Xpedion Design Systems, which was acquired by Agilent Technologies, where I stayed on for several years. I was also Chairman and founder at Denali Software and a string of four other companies that were either directly in semiconductors or servicing semis. I think I was attracted to the hard software problems that needed solving in the industry. I am also an active angel investor via Sand Hill Angels and an early investor in Andrew's VC funds at Rubicon.

In 2001 I got pulled back into Xpedion, focused on RFIC simulation tools. In the 2000's this was the only double-digit growth area in the industry. From 2001 to 2014 we achieved 150 releases - roughly one new release per month, keeping up with the pace of our customers' design activity. At the beginning, half of our customers were VC backed startups and the other half were big companies. By 2009 to 2010 we noticed that there were no more startups. It became clear that the VCs had turned off the tap and all the VC backed startups we were servicing either became acquired or died off.

I decided that with so much depending on the industry downstream, something needed to be done. It's no mystery to insider guys like us why this was. The cost to make a successful semiconductor company is high. In the Valley, from a venture capital perspective, semis are pretty much the definition of "capital intensive." Essentially a semiconductor startup can spend $200k per year per engineer on EDA companies paying for tools. You will then do shuttle runs that will cost a lot – ranging from $100k to a quarter-million or more per run - and you can expect to do up to a dozen runs. Test labs can cost half a million to a couple million to set up. There is a lot of uncertainty in angel and VC investing and founding companies, but one thing is certain. With semis it will cost a lot to get your technology working and best of class yield (meaning what percentage of produced products work well enough to be sold).

For example, if you were to write a $10m check to a startup doing an integrated circuit design, it is very likely that the lion's share would go to pay for tools and services. Most of your dollars end up going into a big company, not into the development of the intellectual capital of the startup. That has always been a very upsetting reality for me. Compare this to investing in an internet or software startup where nearly 100% of your dollars go into developing the startup's intellectual property (IP) and growing the company. The amount of money you need to invest into the Internet company compared to the semi company is 20% or less than required for the semi startup.

So there was a clear gap in the market. Innovation in semis has pretty much dried up at a time in human history where we need more innovation than ever before for the Internet of Things, Industrial Internet of Things, Internet of Everything and health care technologies. These new devices and sensors will need to function on a very different scale and require a ton of innovation that does not exist yet. So just when the VCs cut off the flow of capital into semis in search of more capital efficient startups, we happen to be at the dawn of a new age requiring more and faster innovation.

Another point of inspiration for me to start Silicon Catalyst was SEMATECH, which was a not-for-profit operating in the late 80's and 90's where Intel and a bunch of others joined to deal with some very costly issues to keep the industry going. I am pleased that we recruited Dan Armbrust, former President and CEO of SEMATECH to be the CEO of Silicon Catalyst. Dan also previously led IBMs 300mm semiconductor operations.

I also had a skeptical view that most corporate incubators are an attempt for the corporates to see what they'd like to acquire. So here's what we did. I first took the time to recruit the very best senior executives from the semiconductor industry to run and advise Silicon Catalyst. So just like other accelerators have their group of mentors, we have our mentors, but ours are grizzled grey haired titans in the semiconductor industry.

We took a view to create a unique incubator that could strip out the cost that makes semi solutions capital intensive and structure these start-ups so that they can put 100% of their investors' dollars to work growing their unique IP and so their businesses. We assembled a number of corporate partners that made hundreds of millions of dollars of in-kind tools, products and services available to our startups. Some of our current partners include Synopsys, TMSC, IMEC, Keysight Technologies, Advantest,

PDF Solutions, Open-Silicon and Autodesk. All of these companies are giving us goods and services for free, including other things startups need such as office space.

Our business model is to take a meaningful percentage of common equity in each startup. This is shared with the group of volunteer mentors that help support them. As with most accelerators our mentors often negotiate direct deals with the startups so that they get additional economics for their time and value. We bring everyone together.

We believe the chip business is the wrong business to be in. There is a new generation of entrepreneur out there that has learned from the internet and software guys; these hardware guys are finding ways to fail fast and iterate quickly. It's easy to build very profitable pure IP businesses, which is where the growth is. ARM is an example of a company that does not build chips - they license designs to bigger companies and sell IP. IP is a great business to be in.

On the other side of the spectrum it can be even better to be a solutions business. There are very few companies building chip solutions for IoT. Companies like Fitbit end up building hardware because they need something that does not exist but the revenue models become subscription models and other recurring revenue streams.

A big difference between a semi incubator and a software accelerator is to give the startup 24 months not 3 months. I think of Silicon Catalyst as more of a long-term incubator than a short-term accelerator that kicks everyone out after 3 months in search of new meat. We typically bring in new companies each quarter; one-third do not work out but we get to those failures quickly. With our network we think we are the closest thing to 100% deal flow coverage in the semiconductor and solutions industries. I often say to our large corporate partners - if all you get out of this is a few acqui-hires that could generate hundreds of millions of dollars for the big balance sheet companies and then it's all worth it right there.

We originally wanted to show the VCs that it was safe to come back in the water. Now I think we are addressing a huge gap in the market and invite large corporates to come and work with us to put the silicon back in the Silicon Valley (http://www.sicatalyst.com). @SandHillAngels

CASE STUDY - TECHSTARS CORPORATE ACCELERATORS - BRAD FELD - AUTHOR & MANAGING DIRECTOR, FOUNDRY GROUP

I asked Brad for his perspective on whether a corporate is more likely to achieve their goals establishing and operating their own accelerator, partnering with a group like Techstars that can run an accelerator for them, or simply investing in an independent "corporate-neutral" accelerator and being active as a mentor. As a cofounder of Techstars, Brad clearly came down on the side of partnering. In Brad's words:

It's one thing to say you will create a top performing accelerator, but it's another thing to pull it off and run a truly good one. One should think of this from the different perspectives of the startup, the corporate, the team running the accelerator, and the network of advisors and mentors around the accelerator. Going solo without a partner who knows how to create and run an accelerator will make the experience more insulated for all. On their own, most corporates might be willing to make a three-year commitment, but this type of endeavor requires a ten-year commitment. Priorities and management at large companies change regularly, which can cause the focus on the accelerator to vanish in one budget cycle. This lack of continuity may not damage anything for the corporate or its executives, but it will have a negative impact on the startups that go through these orphaned accelerator programs.

If the goal is to help the startup, the accelerator needs a broad network to draw on. Large companies with significant balance sheets can act on multiple options at the same time. They can create their own accelerator program, invest in an independent accelerator or accelerators and be active in all of those while making LP investments into VCs that are willing to take their money and create a team to operate their own CVC to make direct investments.

Disney is a strong example of this. Disney partners with Techstars to establish and run the "Disney Accelerator powered by Techstars." Each company participating in the program receives $20,000 in funding upon acceptance, and access to an additional $100,000 convertible debt note at their sole option. Thus, $120,000 in investment capital is available to each and every company immediately upon acceptance into Disney Accelerator. The Disney Accelerator office is located in greater Los Angeles, the heart of the entertainment industry, providing access to mentorship from more than 60 Disney executives as well as 70 entrepreneurs and investors from the business community.

Brad pointed to the story of Sphero and the BB-8 robot. Sphero, headquartered in Boulder, Colorado, had raised over $34m at the time that they joined the Disney Accelerator and accepted the relatively small $120k investment from the program. The relationship with Disney created a Star Wars focused product, which became transformational for the company. @bfeld, @foundrygroup, @techstars

CASE STUDY - TECHSTARS AND THE DISNEY TECHSTARS ACCELERATOR - DAVID COHEN - FOUNDER, CEO & MANAGING PARTNER, TECHSTARS

David Cohen wrote much of the chapter on accelerators for my first book and as a selfless supporter of the startup ecosystem was quick to contribute to this book. David's words:

Techstars is a global ecosystem for entrepreneurs to bring new technologies to market, powers accelerators for major global brands such as Disney, Nike, Barclays, Ford, Sprint, Metro, and more. Corporations can avoid the "signaling" issues that lead to adverse selection, by outsourcing innovation programs in partnership with Techstars instead of rolling their own. This partnering attracts the best entrepreneurs and follow on capital.

In one example, Techstars powers the Disney Accelerator (www.disneyaccelerator.com), based in LA and focused on digital media and entertainment. In the inaugural class of companies, Techstars recruited a digital play company called Sphero through their network. The company attended the Disney Accelerator, and post program attracted investment from Disney and others of an additional $45m.[3] This is a great outcome to be sure, but Disney and Sphero were both further impacted. One of the Sphero products is an amazing robotic ball, controlled remotely by a smartphone. Sphero inspired Disney CEO, Bob Iger (one of their lead mentors during the program), to create BB-8, the next "R2-D2" for the newest star wars movie "The Force Awakens." BB-8 nearly broke the internet when it was announced, and the buzz was incredible[4]. This is a great example of how both the corporation and the startup benefitted tremendously from a corporation "giving first" using the Techstars platform and getting back much more in long term value.

In another example, DoPay was a participant in the Barclays Accelerator, powered by Techstars. This London based program is focused on FinTech. DoPay had a solution to a problem that Barclays had been wrestling with for some time. How do you bank the unbanked around the world? Barclays took a chance on DoPay to help them create a payroll service in the cloud, and in the first few months had over one million new accounts created around the world, while solving a perplexing problem for their own customers in working with unbanked employees around the world[5].

What we've experienced at Techstars is that the spirit of "give first" does not necessarily come naturally to major corporations. They view their distribution and customer base as priceless. The smartest corporations are learning to give before they get in the context of entrepreneurship, knowing that it's not the competitor that they're aware of that they should fear. It's the one in the garage that will either be friend or foe in the future. Might as well make friends early, and benefit together. @DavidCohen, @DisneyAccel, @techstars

---

3 (http://techcrunch.com/2015/06/02/star-wars-bb-8-designer-sphero-raises-another-45m-from-mercato-disney-and-more/).

4 http://www.gosphero.com/blog/sphero-and-disney-team-up-on-star-wars-the-force-awakens/.

5 http://techcrunch.com/2015/04/30/dopay-seed/

SPONSORING INCUBATORS & ACCELERATORS - VICTOR PASCUCCI III, FOUNDER & FORMER HEAD OF USAA VENTURES & HEAD OF CORPORATE DEVELOPMENT

Plug and Play – As a corporate you pay a sponsorship fee for the relevant sector you like and you then provide input as to which companies enter the accelerator. Business partners can get engaged in the demo days. USAA is the financial services sponsor. @victorpascucci3

CONCLUSIONS ON ACCELERATORS AND INCUBATORS - ANDREW ROMANS

I personally think that the unit economics of most accelerators don't add up. Most of them raised enough capital to get them through two or three years of burn rate and unless they get very lucky the exits will not come in fast enough to make them break even or sustainable. Some will raise more capital for the same accelerators and others will open new accelerators in new cities or around new industry vertical topics to keep the lights on. Corporates thinking of accelerators should be aware of the fact that most accelerators have losing unit economics and note that this is the most likely unprofitable end of corporate venturing. Unlike entrepreneurs founding accelerators, corporates can afford to back a loss making business.

The days of accelerators not having a fund to invest into the startups are either coming to an end or those accelerators will suffer from adverse deal flow selection. If you are CEO of a startup and consider joining one accelerator that will invest $150k into your startup or provide you with enough cash to fly your team to Silicon Valley for three months or go to another accelerator that just provides mentors or office space, which one would you chose? All things being equal, the accelerator with a fund wins.

It appears that 500Startups invests $150k into the startups that go through its accelerator and then requires them to pay $25k back to 500Startups as revenue for the office space and accelerator experience. 500startups' McClure will argue that the in-kind services and products they get, like cloud web hosting services, etc., are worth $125k, so $25k is a bargain. I do not see other accelerators doing this. McClure, however, has the experience to know his unit economics and is probably positioned not to be forced to sell equity in his management company to survive. He also organizes a string of different events throughout the year and has a thriving events business that generates an additional line of revenue. I think he's brilliant to run an accelerator with profitable unit economics while many other lemmings are heading towards a cliff. Lastly, he has evolved to raise substantial VC funds in different parts of the world and has fully graduated from the limitations of the accelerator business model. He attends demo days of other accelerators and invests into the best startups he can find and does not limit his VC funds to only invest into startups that go through the 500Startups programs. It is truly genius that McClure is getting management fee and carry on his own revenue! I'm continually impressed and that's innovative. I tip my hat @davemcclure.

In some cases it may make sense for a corporate to establish its own accelerator program like Microsoft or Citrix. For others like Disney the best plan may be to partner with someone like TechStars to help run the Disney accelerator program. Others may find investing into an independent accelerator / fund like TechStars or YC provides strategic value. I personally think, for most corporates, money invested into an accelerator program or accelerator fund is risky with regard to generating a strategic return. It may not deliver the strategic value they seek. The simplest way to get access to the strategic goals is offer to populate multiple accelerators with employees of the corporate that can act as mentors. This way the only expense to the corporate is salaries of local employees who can roam the startups seeing all the cohorts and gain strategic knowledge while being supportive of the ecosystem. Better yet - make a few investments at demo day and get your hands dirty.

Four

CVC Investing in Other VC funds – Fund of Funds (FoF)

"Quickness is the essence of the war."

- SUN TZU

See the case study on Cisco to learn how Cisco invested in 47 VC funds in 4 years. See as well Telefónica, Fininvest, Telecom Italia and other case studies that illustrate the combination of FoF and direct CVC strategies as a best practice.

WHY FUND OF FUNDS (FOF) MAKE SENSE FOR CORPORATES, STARTUPS AND VCS - JOHN FRANKEL, PARTNER, FF VENTURE CAPITAL

John runs ff Venture Capital in New York. As an NYC and Silicon Valley VC, we see John often and have co-invested with him in the past. Here are John's words:

Corporates are about profit generation in the field of focus, and often march to a quarterly beat. Their time horizon is often less than the 5-7 years of illiquidity implicit in a venture capital fund and their objectives are often different. This lack of goal congruence can lead to disappointment over time. In addition, corporate decisions are made by a team that might not be there for the life of a fund, and so the decision rationale to become involved might not be consistent over time as the decision makers at the corporate change. So, why get involved at all?

Simply put, businesses have never been as challenged by technology as they are today. Society, however, has faced the challenge of disruption, namely in the Industrial Revolution. The Industrial Revolution brought about the formation of many businesses and industries and enabled the companies we have today. But the advent of chips in everything, mobile super-computers, and the ubiquitous connectedness that social networks bring - plus the accessibility and the sophistication of modern software languages - means that corporates do not have the same research and development advantage they used to have. The costs of starting a company and attacking a previously defensible part of their operations have dropped effectively to zero, so smart folks with an insight or two can rapidly start to attack their business, seemingly coming out of nowhere and with potentially limitless access to funding. The taxi companies with regulatory moats around their business are defenseless from a multi-billion funded Uber and Lyft.

In addition, large companies tend to have a political layer that simply is resistant to change and questioning. This makes them slow to make decisions that can defend themselves. Many companies are unable to transform themselves, in such a way to be willing to build low-margin alternatives of lesser quality that will over time overtake large parts of their existing high-margin business. Goldman Sachs, Apple and a few others may have, but examples are few and far between.

The other factor that gives this urgency is that growth is simply hard to come by in a world awash with artificially low interest rates and a greying population. In a zero-growth world, corporates need growth, and that growth is coming from startups. They are the new R&D labs for corporations. But what is the best way to tap into them? Simply put, by becoming a significant investor in the right early stage funds, corporates will be exposed to these disruptive ideas and companies far earlier than they would be otherwise. Not only that, but by investing in venture funds, it should not cost them money for the information, rather they should actually make money. Corporates and their CVC units can bring customers to startups and eventually acquire these portfolio companies - this goal alignment is key to why this can be a successful strategy. @john_frankel @ffvc

FUND OF FUNDS (FOF) IS THE FIRST STEP, DIRECT CVC INVESTING COMES NEXT – ANDREW ROMANS

My advice to corporates seeking to get into corporate venturing is to follow in the footsteps of Novell, Intel, SAP, Nokia, Cisco, Microsoft and many others and start by investing into other VC funds and then making direct investments. This has proven to work best. It helps you achieve your strategic and financial objectives and turbo charges your own direct investing program. If you make a list of your goals and objectives adapted from Chapter 1 of this book, then get the key folks in your C-suite to agree on this customized set of objectives, I assure you the quickest and most certain way to achieve these goals is Fund of Funds (FoF) investing, followed by a direct CVC investment strategy. This path also takes away much of the financial risk of losing time and capital by starting with direct investing without buying into the game.

There are a few realities that should be considered. Most startups want to raise money from Sequoia, Kleiner Perkins, Benchmark or other new hot name VC brands like Andreessen Horowitz. The big brands and the hot new emerging managers always get the best deal flow. The new guys always make better returns for their LPs, but it's hard to predict who the next hot VC newcomer will be. It's kind of like the music business. There are always a few bands and acts that have momentum and their next album will sell well, but there is always a new sound coming along.

The entrepreneurs' dream is not to raise funding from John Deere Ventures, Campbell Soup Ventures or other corporates. That is the simple truth. Don't let anyone lie to you suggesting otherwise. The innovation you seek does not instinctively want you.

Many young entrepreneurs probably should take funding from a CVC, but they don't, because they fear that this irreversible action will prevent them from doing business with or selling their business to the competitors of that one corporate. Most CVCs have a negative reputation and so the CVC has historically been somewhat the funding choice of last resort or only makes sense when the startup is truly in hyper-growth scaling mode of Series C, D or even later stage. The startup may be better off taking the CVC funding and benefit from a direct partnering relationship, but most young CEOs must make this mistake for themselves. If they see a financial independent VC with corporate LPs offering the same partnership the answer is an easy yes from the CEO and the corporate gets its Chapter 1 goals and objectives.

The CVC should have a mix of internal and external hires running the CVC. To begin with they should depend on the deal flow that comes directly from the VCs in which they are LPs. If they focus their time on those deals they will get into good deals that bring strategic value and are financially sound. This will put the CVC group on the right path of instantly achieving their Chapter 1 goals with minimal risk. They will then become hot by making hot investments. The hot investment pace is what makes any VC franchise relevant and builds their brand. Then the deal flow will find the CVC directly and the CVC will not need to rely so heavily on the other VCs they invested in. Again, there is nothing strategic or transformational about investing into a startup that goes bankrupt. Working closely with a group of financial VCs that have twenty years of experience is solid insurance.

I think corporates need to buy their way in. For sure this will collapse the time to achieving Chapter 1 goals. If you do this correctly you will invest into a few different funds and get geographical coverage. It might make sense to invest into a few funds in Silicon Valley, New York, London, Tel Aviv and China. Get some sector diversity as well. Maybe invest into something specific like a fintech or IoT fund and then put the rest on internet VCs. Many people disagree with me on this and I respect that, but I am all for not investing into specialist VC funds. Tomorrow's innovation is coming from somewhere that none of us predicted and you don't want to be pigeon-holed in a cleantech fund that might have been all the rage a few years ago and now you are missing the smartphone shared economy deals. Most of those specialist cleantech funds also lost money for their LPs.

The most successful entrepreneurs are the truly versatile ones. It's not what life throws you, but how you deal with it. The best entrepreneurs faced major challenges and they traversed from risky to rich by being versatile and flexible. I believe the same is true for VC funds. I want maximal ability to be flexible and say yes if I want to. I don't want any restrictions on our ability to follow our strategy investing across industries that software is about to eat.

If you are a large corporate you have your core business and peripheral business to consider, but you also have many big company issues that are not related to your core customers such as dealing with your employees and other expenditures. Do not make the mistake of only investing into VC funds you think are going after your limited shopping list of topics to invest in. The big deal is the internet, smart phones, big data, IoT, new business models, who owns what and how it will be paid for in the future. It's all changing and it seems to be changing faster. The one thing we know is no one knows what's going to happen. Throw a net that keeps you in the big picture know. FoF integrated into your overall CVC strategy enables you to get away with this.

When you make a FoF investment make sure that the GPs (General Partners) at those funds are willing to talk to you about specific investments and position your direct CVC investing practice to invest into the future rounds of their portfolio companies. Sometimes you will get access to co-invest alongside the financial VC, but you will probably be too slow and the best you can do is access the next round or you might force a strategic financing with just you after the financial round closes.

Now just as the entrepreneurs would prefer to take funding from a financial VC like Sequoia and not tie themselves to a strategic that opens one door and shuts ten other doors; most financial VCs do not want to take LP dollars from a corporate. Brad Feld says in this book that he would only accept funding from a corporate if they agreed to commit to his future funds so long as Foundry Group met a minimal fund performance. There is a reason financial VCs do not want to take LP dollars from corporates. They are famous for not re-upping and investing into future funds. Just like their own CVC groups had an average life span of 2.5 years and that appears to be trending at 5 years today; they don't invest in more than one or two VC funds for the financial VC. When you are a financial VC you want to raise a new VC fund every three years. Ideally you want all of your existing LPs to re-up and have your fund be oversubscribed. You want to close your fund quickly. NEA seems to open a new fund on a Monday and close billions by Friday. This does not happen with corporate LPs. Change of a CEO, economic downturn, or gridlock – take your pick. These are not reliable LPs to commit loyally to all future funds. In an ideal world the financial VC would get a legally binding commitment from a corporate to invest in the next three funds over a ten year period contingent upon minimal performance of the financial VC and minimal financial performance of the corporate.

At Rubicon we believe in all of this Holy Grail stuff that the corporate can be leveraged to deliver value to the startup. Delivering value to the startup is what it's all about for us; so writing this book and bringing on corporate LPs makes sense to us at Rubicon as we are disrupting the VC model ourselves.

CVCS SPINNING OFF TO GP-LP, BECOMING INDEPENDENT AND REBRANDING – ANDREW ROMANS

"Look! It's moving. It's alive." Dr. Henry Frankenstein – 1931 film

I remember Joerg Sievert walking into my office on Trafalgar Square in London two days before I relocated to Silicon Valley with my family. He was walking tall that day and proudly announced that SAP Ventures, which until that moment had been investing off the balance sheet, had transformed to a GP-LP structure and closed a $300m+ VC fund with SAP as the sole LP. The General Partners would get a 2% annual management fee and 20% carry, which is 20% of the fund-wide profit from their investments. Joerg a few years later left SAP Ventures and joined the family office of one of the founders of SAP in Switzerland.

I think the SAP Ventures story is interesting. It started off like most CVCs investing off the balance sheet and paying the team of investment professionals a base salary and bonus possibly more tied to the performance of the multi-billion dollar corporate than the performance of their investments. It is no mystery that many CVC investment professionals that co-invest with independent VCs into the same deals, do much of the same work, also think they should be compensated with a 2&20 scheme like us. Another motivation to spin out with an independent structure is to assure the longevity of the program. When you are investing off the balance sheet, the investment professionals worry that the program could be cancelled, reduced or paused at any moment. A new CEO, an economic downturn, the next reorg, McKinsey poking around and recommending the corporate "get back to its knitting" can all spell the end of the CVC. This can happen at a moment's notice. Another motivation to spin off can be to gain more autonomy and free the investment professionals from the investment committee or head of a business unit to get a deal done. Big corporates are slow to act. Working at a CVC can be an exercise in frustration chasing the CFO of a $20bn revenue company to review and sign off on a $1m or $5m investment that is closing this week! Speed is important when you are in the fast lanes of Silicon Valley.

As soon as a CVC group spins off to a GP-LP structure the newly minted GPs start attending GP-LP conferences, establishing relationships with institutional investors, selling their story as an independent VC fund, and trying to diversify their LP base. One driver to diversify the LP base is that the parent corporate may suggest the fund be operated as an evergreen vehicle and stop the flow of capital into future funds making CVC a zero cost R&D program. Being dependent on one LP may get you one fund only. If the newly minted GPs want to raise a new fund every three years, they better diversify and try to get their birth LP down to 50%, 33%, 20% or even 10% as quickly as possible. If they want to be viewed as an independent VC in the market they would be wise to get any one single corporate down to 30% or 20% of the future funds. This is important, because many startups may worry that if they take funding from SAP Ventures that will inhibit their ability to sell their company to competing Oracle. This may or may not be true, but perception is functional reality and entrepreneurs worry that if they take money from SAP Ventures, even if SAP is just a big LP and even a minority LP it worries them and why take the risk when other independent VCs are knocking on your door.

I have been on VC panels with SAP Ventures execs many times and I think every single time the SAP Ventures person managed to make the statement early on "We are totally independent from SAP and in fact we have sold more of our portfolio companies to Oracle than to SAP." Clearly they have a chip on their shoulder if they keep saying this every time. Eventually SAP Ventures changed its name to Sapphire Ventures to further distance themselves from SAP. I know a bunch of folks at Sapphire Ventures going back years where I knew them when they worked at independent VCs before joining Sapphire, but despite these relationships they declined to be interviewed for my book, stating that they are not a corporate VC and do not want to be seen as one in the marketplace. So there you go – the evolution of a classic CVC to a totally independent financial VC. I know others that made the same journey and they also declined to be in this book as they do not want to be misunderstood to be a CVC when they are now independent financial VCs that went through great efforts to break free and rebrand.

The pattern I've seen is to start investing off the balance sheet, leverage the corporate to generate top performing IRRs, then break off with the corporate as the sole LP, then diversify the LP base, then change your name to distance from the stigma of CVC and lastly move your office out of the building of the corporate.

Sapphire Ventures, last I looked was still in the SAP building on Hillview Avenue in Palo Alto and also in the SAP building on King William Street in London. Maybe they should move into new offices in San Francisco and Mayfair and make the final step.

Now it's easy to understand the logic of anyone at a CVC to be motivated to make this transition and follow in Sapphire Ventures' footsteps, but let's consider this from the perspective of the corporate. Remember the objectives the corporate outlined in Chapter 1. What were the primary and secondary goals of the corporate to get into corporate venturing? When your CVC group spins off like Sapphire I am not sure how much the corporate is achieving its goals. It is possible that they are achieving their goals more effectively than they were when the group was tucked into their organization, but this should be clarified and locked down.

My take away here is that if the CVC group spins off like Sapphire and the corporate wants to maximize its strategic gains outlined in Chapter 1 they should ensure that they will have frequent communication with this new independent VC now and into the future so that strategic goals are achieved.

The logic for the investment professionals to go independent is very clear. The logic for the corporate to support this looks more like the Fund of Funds chapter of this book. Funny enough Sapphire's strategy is a mix of Fund of Funds and direct investing. Sapphire invests directly into other VC funds and uses that position to access deal flow from the portfolios of the VCs they invest in to generate solid deal flow for later stage direct investments – makes a lot of sense to me and Sapphire has become a strong VC franchise.

I bumped into an old friend of mine recently at a networking event in the Valley and he told me that he had just joined the newly formed CVC group of a large corporate. This old friend of mine is an entrepreneur that has wanted to be a VC his whole life and even tried and failed to raise an independent fund. Even before starting his new job as a CVC he laid out his plans to me to spin this nascent CVC group out following the Sapphire path as quickly as possible. He even had a new name in mind...and he hadn't even showed up for his first day at work yet. The point here is to keep in mind that the team you put in charge of your new CVC may be a mutiny waiting to happen.

All corporates that authorize these CVC groups should recognize they've possibly created a monster and it's alive! I think some thought should even go into employment contracts when appointing the investment professionals for a CVC. For example, the corporate might deserve to own part of the GP if it spins off. They might give some legal thought to what the corporate wants if the CVC breaks away or the team breaks away as a group.

VCs and placement agents (bankers that help VCs raise funds) sometimes send me their VC pitch decks to solicit investment into their VC funds or introduce them to prospective LP investors. I recently saw a deck for a fund that was the entire team of a big CVC, but distributed across

Asia. So sometimes the team shops a new fund without even breaking away and tries just to walk off with the team once a few anchor LPs are secured.

One other comment I will make on this topic is that most CVCs beat their chest showing the alchemist performance of their investments and seem to expect that this track record will transfer and follow them when they leave the CVC and become a GP at an independent fund or start one of their own. Unless they find a way to remain connected to that corporate that can become a first big reference customer or leverage their sales force to work with the startup, their stellar performance may not transfer. CVC is a very different skill set and most classic VCs are not set up to make the relationship with the corporate work. Moving a CVC executive into an existing independent VC, bringing the corporate LP making a FoF LP investment into the fund, might help in transferring performance.

CASE STUDY - NOVELL TO PELION VENTURES - BLAKE MODERSITZKI - MANAGING DIRECTOR, PELION VENTURES; COFOUNDER & MANAGING DIRECTOR, NOVELL VENTURES

Another interesting transformation story comes from my friend Blake Modersitzki, cofounder of Pelion Ventures. Blake started off as the international product marketing manager for WordPerfect. This was an old school company that competed with Microsoft Word as a word processor. They merged with Novell, which became the king of the mountain, making a ton of money dominating the computer networking market for a time. Novell literally is king of the mountain with incredible mountain views based in beautiful Utah. Blake became a director in their corporate development group and, out of that group, helped form Novell Ventures. The capital was from Novell's balance sheet and had a double bottom line focus: make money for Novell's shareholders by investing into great companies and only invest into companies that are part of the broader networking software infrastructure ecosystem. They started with a FoF strategy and Blake invested into some of the best independent VCs on Sand Hill Road. They then came to the conclusion they could make direct investments themselves and coordinate this activity with corporate development.

In 2001, when Eric Schmidt left Novell to become CEO of Google, the new management team at Novell decided to focus on their core business. Novell's corporate venture activity became less of a focus. Through an introduction by one of the cofounders of Accel Partners (via the FoF program at Novell, they were an LP in three of Accel's funds), Blake met the team from Utah Ventures, a small regionally focused venture fund in Utah. Over the course of several conversations the team from Utah Ventures and the team from Novell's venture activity concluded that teaming up was in both of their best interests. The idea was to carry forward the strategy and focus from Novell's Venture activity on the direct side. Blake noticed that the fund was not attracting the best deal flow from California and around the country so they changed the name to UV Partners. Even with the new name there seemed to be some association to a regional strategy. So another name change happened with the new name being Pelion Ventures, which I view as a strong, lasting VC franchise. The evidence is a 20-year history of successful venture investing. Novell's venture actives were from 1996 to 2002. The current incarnation of Pelion Venture Partners dates back to May 2002. They successfully closed their sixth fund at $240m which is well above both their target and hard cap. Pelion's investment strategy and sector focus can be traced back to what they did at Novell. @blakemod

Five

Advice & Best Practices for Corporate Venturing Related to CVCs, Entrepreneurs & Financial VCs

"Success consists of going from failure to failure without loss of enthusiasm."

- WINSTON CHURCHILL

TIM DRAPER'S THOUGHTS ON CVC – COFOUNDER OF DFJ, DRAPER ASSOCIATES AND DRAPER UNIVERSITY

Tim Draper is one of my heroes and has as much experience and perspective on this topic as anyone alive. Here are his key points:

1. CVCs are best when they are in it for the long haul. Intel Capital has been terrific this way. They have been the best at diving into the venture capital business and sticking with it. Many CVCs come into the business at the top of the market and leave at the bottom. This is clearly not good for the corporates, but it is also damaging to the companies when they withdraw support when it is most needed.

2. CVCs can be amazing partners for startups when they help introduce the startup to the appropriate people in their company who can test their products. When corporates come in as investors,

entrepreneurs love it when they beta test their products and operate as their early customers.

3. When an entrepreneur takes money from a CVC, he or she should beware and understand that the CVC's first loyalty is to their corporation. This makes perfect sense, but can be very frustrating when a CVC has a board seat on the startup board and seems to be acting in the best interest of their corporation and not necessarily in the best interest of the startup.

4. It is a good idea for an entrepreneur who has taken money from a CVC and given the CVC a board seat to have a separate advisory board that does not include the corporate. Often the interests of the corporation and the interests of the startup diverge.

5. Entrepreneurs are often worried that a corporate only invested in their start up because they want to kill them or starve them until they can buy them cheap. This is almost never the case. The CVC representative is almost always cheering for the success of the business, even if the CEO might see them as a competitor, or just concerned whether they are friend or foe.

Follow Tim on Facebook, LinkedIn and Twitter @TimDraper

BRAD FELD'S THOUGHTS ON CVC - AUTHOR & MANAGING DIRECTOR, FOUNDRY GROUP; COFOUNDER, TECHSTARS

I caught up with Brad Feld, cofounder and Managing Director at Foundry Group in Boulder, Colorado, on the topic of CVCs, classic mistakes they make, and the difference between independent and corporate accelerators. For any of my readers that do not follow Brad Feld, he is possibly the leading author of books related to venture capital and entrepreneurship. I highly recommend all of his books; Venture Deals is the most widely read. In Brad's words:

It was in the late 1980's when I went to business school and corporate venture capital was all the rage way back then. What I have witnessed over many years is that companies fail to be consistent in their involvement with venture capital and ultimately suffer from this inconsistency.

Today it seems that large companies are again remembering the importance of innovation. In general, these companies are good at incremental improvement of their products but struggle with radical innovation, especially when it disrupts their existing business.

Companies are wise to use venture capital to counter balance their natural struggles with radical innovation. One approach is to participate in accelerator programs, which tend to be most effective when done in partnership with organizations like Techstars who are experts at creating and running accelerators. Direct investments in companies and LP investments in VC firms are other options large companies can use to engage with startups, as well as a classical corporate development program that will often include acquisitions of smaller companies.

It is useful to look at the example of Microsoft and their investing activity over time. Over 20 years of VC investing, I have witnessed Microsoft go from actively investing in other companies, to establishing a policy of not investing in other companies, and then returning to a program investing in other companies, then stopping for another period of years, only to start again. This inconsistency, especially over a long period of time, undermines and minimizes the potential outcome, as the large company is constantly adjusting its strategy, rather than focusing on a long-term approach around startups and innovation.

Many companies get it wrong by not being consistent and committed to corporate venturing for the long term. They should take a long-term view and put in place a structure that can survive a change in the CEO and CFO.

As an independent and financially driven VC at Foundry Group, I have lots of experience in co-investing with corporate VCs. My experience is mixed. Sometimes the CVCs are awesome and sometimes they are horrible. Oddly enough, in my experience sometimes a company could be horrible in one investment and awesome in a different one. In these cases, a different person from the corporation was involved in each deal, but representing the same CVC. If the CVC executive has less power inside of his organization, in challenging situations (which happen continuously through the life of all startups), he will tend to behave irrationally and self-interested, rather than in a clear way that has the interest of the startup in mind. He might be worried about losing his job and, through his behavior and decision-making, destroy value at the startup. In other cases, a CVC might simply be passive or the executive involved might fail to get anything synergistic done with the corporate. In these cases, the only value of the CVC is the cash they invested.

While doing nothing is fine, despite the promises they made to leverage the big company, responsiveness on the part of the CVC is still important. I've been in many situations where a CVC promised an answer on a request by the following Wednesday but failed to mention which year!

Some CVCs or individual execs at those corporate venturing groups develop a reputation for being bad operators. As a result, it is important not to give a corporate investor a special deal over the other VCs. In some cases the CVC is quite independent of corp dev and other times it is the same group doing both corp dev and CVC or the two separate groups report to the same person. Especially try to avoid giving up Right of First Offer (ROFO), Right of First Refusal (ROFR) and negative blocking rights.

An example of bad CVC behavior occurs when a startup gets into financial distress and the board is trying to decide to bridge the company to another financing. In this case, if the CVC has a board seat, they get caught in the track of not paying attention to their fiduciary duty to the company as a board member. In the worse examples, they stall while the financial distress increases, with the underhanded goal of acquiring the company for a relatively small amount when it ends up against the wall with a very short list of options. This is something I have seen many times and is most likely one of these situations that Fred Wilson at Union Square Ventures was reacting to in a well-known blog post (https://goo.gl/Cq3guc) when he was quoted saying he would never, never, never, never co-invest with a Corporate VC ever again.

There are CVCs that manage to maintain a level of independence from their corporate to insulate from this sort of behavior. Google Ventures (now called simply GV) is a strong example of this. Google is more of a single LP in GV, which is positioned as an independent VC fund, committed to a long term 20 year+ time horizon, and in the case of a conflict of interest theoretically adhering to a Chinese Wall policy to prevent the above from happening. At the same time the investment professionals at GV have deep linkages into Google to unlock synergies for the portfolio companies.

Regarding corporates making LP investments, at Foundry Group, we are unlikely to accept an LP investment from a corporate unless they were able to demonstrate a long-term commitment to investing in our funds. We tend to raise a new fund every three years. If we do what we say we would do and we perform, we expect renewed commitments to invest in our future VC funds. It's hard for us to truly believe a corporate will continue to support our future funds. Often a senior executive is pulled into a VC's orbit and simply wants to reinforce his position in that orbit. This lack of consistency makes it hard for corporates to be dependable LPs.

To be sustainable, the partners in a CVC need appropriate compensation that is similar to that of a partner in a VC firm, which is often hard for companies to get their minds around. If the company doesn't provide the appropriate compensation, the best CVC partners will be recruited by VC funds, and the CVC will see significant personnel turnover. This can create an adverse selection effect, where the CVC execs who stay long term at the CVC are the ones who most likely are the underperformers. Ideally the company should reward strong experience, not only in the role of investing, but also in the context of knowing how to work with the rest of the large corporation and maintain a team of individuals who establish a long history working together over many years. Many corporate VCs seem to be achieving the exact opposite. @bfeld, @ foundrygroup

THE DISAPPOINTMENT OF CORPORATE VC - TOM FOGARTY, INVENTOR OF THE BALLOON CATHETER AND 165 MEDICAL PATENTS; FOUNDER OF THE FOGARTY INSTITUTE FOR INNOVATION; PROLIFIC INVESTOR

I had a chance to sit down with another one of my heroes - the legendary Tom Fogarty at The Fogarty Institute for Innovation in Silicon Valley. I was lucky enough to meet Dr. Fogarty as he is a major investor in Biomedix, a great medtech startup where my brother is CEO (no bias there ;-). Dr. Fogarty has been a surgeon, Stanford University professor and inventor of the transformational balloon embolectomy catheter and over 65 other very important medical inventions. He later became a prolific investor. His important work has saved millions of lives and generated billions and billions of dollars for his portfolio of startups. Dr. Fogarty recognized that VCs were not funding important early stage healthcare related startups and he created The Fogarty Institute to address this gap, partnering with El Camino Hospital and numerous other corporates in the healthcare ecosystem. Healthcare corporates should take note and get in touch with this unique institute packed with tomorrow's transformational healthcare startups. Here are some lessons from my interview in Dr. Fogarty's words:

Corporate VC is not the benefit I thought it was going to be. Corporates are just like VCs, in that they act like they know how to do everything. Most big companies don't want to make investments in spaces where they're already represented because it's an admission of failure for their internal R&D groups. Medtech entrepreneurs shouldn't ask companies for what they want, but tell them what they need.

That said one should not paint all VCs or CVCs with the same brush. It comes down to the individual you are working with. I've seen large corporations buy our companies and then later try and sell them back to us. Whenever they acquire, you need to treat them like a partner, at least for the first year.

Within the field of medicine some of the worst VCs are the physicians that are disappointed in their career choice of being a Medical Doctor. If you want to stay out of trouble in medicine you should do what you were taught to do. It's necessary because if people do not stick to the accepted procedures that's bad for safety. It takes a combination of being bold and a little crazy to venture out and do something new or different. You need to think differently. Industry and corporates need to work with physicians and not fight with them. One needs to recognize the difference between iterative and big changes in medicine. If you have a new technology that is saving 10 out of 10 people, how many more need to die before introducing this as the way you teach physicians to address a topic. It's a reality that technology is changing faster than the regulatory process. The regulators are getting better, but sometimes you can get more done off shore before you get the first letter back from the FDA. With so much change, reduction of the cost of launching startups and new things like miniaturization truly working, I would advise corporates to play a bigger role in the early stage venture ecosystem.

You're not going to know what's going on from just looking through the window from the outside. You've got to get closer than just looking. That will come from investing. @FogartyInst

CORPORATES MUST ADJUST TO LEVEL OF STARTUP SPEED - ANONYMOUS, MANAGING DIRECTOR, LARGE JAPANESE CVC ACTIVE IN JAPAN AND SILICON VALLEY

One early stage startup was introduced from a top Sand Hill Road VC through a closed loop. At the first meeting, the impression was good because the founders had a multiple track record of success and clear vision. Then one year after the first meeting, we started a conversation on how to collaborate. From the vantage point of the big corporate the startup still looked too early to work with. Our CVC team worked hard to convince the business unit and managed to set a couple of meetings to start supplying the sample product for trials. While continuing to talk about how to progress our collaboration, we heard a lot of good stories about that start up from other corporates. Our CVC team tried to accelerate the trial. Then the startup was acquired and so the story has gone. The lesson here is to find a project champion at the big corporate in the early stage of a project, difficult but important to achieve. Imagination of venture capitalists is hard to sustain among execution oriented corporate executives who seek short-term results.

ANONYMOUS, FINANCIAL VC ACTIVE IN THE SILICON VALLEY

The key to successful CVC investing is having the right team, the right long-term commitment from the absolute top of the corporate executive team (CEO), and an objective investment strategy focused on fundamentals of venture capital success metrics. These require recruiting staff from outside the corporate and giving them enough leeway to invest and build long-term relationships with the VC and entrepreneur community.

CVC investing requires good political maneuvering within the enterprise to build strategic ties, "sell" the investment to a bureaucratic team, and walk the walk by building a reputation in the venture community, and helping the CEO entrepreneur manage to success.

TOBY LEWIS' THOUGHTS ON CVC - EDITOR OF GLOBAL CORPORATE VENTURING

I caught up with Toby Lewis of Global Corporate Venturing, a great resource for the CVC community with publications and events and a unique source of data I don't see in other places. http://www.globalcorporateventuring.com/. Here are some of his key points:

Fifty percent of the Fortune 50 has active CVCs and 30% of the Fortune 500. Many corporates are thinking, if the other guys are doing CVC then maybe so should we. Here are a few considerations for those pondering forming a new CVC group.

The CVC initiative is often a personal project of the CEO, founder or one senior person pushes it and then quite often, shortly after launching, everyone moves on and the program ends. The average lifespan of a CVC is less than five years. A CVC probably needs to get through three CEOs to see if the CVC program will truly survive.

The number of patents that are filed from startups has grown from only 5% of all patents a few years ago to now 30% of all patents. If corporates wish to capture this shift in innovation they need a strategy. In the past the top graduates of the elite universities wanted to join the biggest name large corporates, banks and consulting companies, but this has changed. It has changed in the US, China and Europe and is likely to begin to change in Japan. If you are hiring in the US, Europe or China and want to access the full talent pool, having a robust CVC and corporate development program is one of the best ways in.

One-person CVC teams fail just like one-person startups fail. Seventy-five percent of CVCs have five people or less on the team. They should look at the financial VCs when considering how to construct and staff their teams.

The biggest mistake is failure to build a portfolio that's relevant.

Compensation is the other huge problem for CVCs. Fewer than 10% of CVCs offer a 2&20 compensation plan. Conversely, if you go 2&20 you will end up with a financial VC and there may be no point to that for the corporate. The correct answer is some balance of strategic corporate and financial incentives. Those CVCs have the best chance of being successful. The average salary for a CVC exec is $300k. Most financial VCs make a base of $1m+ and the variance on what they get from carry is huge. Without a doubt the CVC needs a stable team to enable the CVC to achieve its goals. Poor compensation assures the goals will not be met.

Making Fund of Funds (FoF) investments is the quickest way to get the results you want. 30% of all CVCs make FoF investments.

The easiest way to double check what you are doing is to ask what is your motivation to get into CVC. The CEO should ask this of the exec that is gunning to start the program.

In my view, if you are a big corporate and you do not have a CVC, well, that's a huge mistake. @TobyLewis2

FRED WILSON'S FAMOUS QUOTE ON WHY CVCS SUCK – FRED WILSON, FOUNDER & MANAGING PARTNER AT UNION SQUARE VENTURES AND FLATIRON PARTNERS

Fred gave me the OK to include his previous comments on CVC. You can view a link to this famous interview here: scroll down at https://goo.gl/Cq3guc. You can find his direct comments on his personal blog – www.avc.com and search for "corporate VCs" as well as Twitter @AVC and @FredWilson.

"I do think that venture investing is not the best use of a corporation's capital and that it is inevitable that it will produce sub-par returns at best and significant losses at worst." On Pando Monthly when asked about the lessons he's learned as a VC, Wilson was quick to reply that investing with corporate VCs was something that he "never, ever, ever, ever gonna do again – never, ever, ever – never."

Asked why he felt so strongly, he replied, "They Suck! They are not interested in the company's success or the entrepreneur's success.

Corporations exist to maximize their interests. They can never be menschy or magnanimous. It's not in their DNA, and so they suck as investors."

"I just think corporations are very bad partners. They should not invest in your company. They should buy your company. That's how you should think of a corporation. They are your exit. They're not your financial partner. Entrepreneur says I can get a better valuation with a corporate." Fred continued, "They [corporates] should buy."

Andrew Romans weighing in here again: Fred later wrote in his blog differentiating between passive corporate VC arms – like GV (Google Ventures), Intel Ventures, SAP Ventures, and Comcast Ventures – and active strategic investments, calling the former a good source of capital and the latter at odds with the objectives of the entrepreneur and company.

At the risk of bringing up an emotional point, I felt compelled to include this in the book to let corporates know that there is a widely held view of CVC tied to a steady flow of negative bad operator real-world experiences. Fred is an important influencer in the global tech ecosystem and people care what he says and writes. Fred's video clip on this matter is famous and the point I want to make is that CVC is a big opportunity for the corporate, the startup and the financial VC, but it needs to be structured in a way to be in Fred Wilson's good books and not the camp he will not work with. He's not alone in voicing this view.

Legendary VC Ted Dintersmith of CRV once said to me, about taking capital from strategics, "Be careful. You'll have sold your company. You just won't know it." - Micah Rosenbloom, Founder Collective

ADVICE ON HOW TO STRUCTURE YOUR CVC DEAL SO YOU CAN OPTIMIZE FOR YOUR EXIT - GAURAV BHASIN, MANAGING DIRECTOR, TECHNOLOGY INVESTMENT BANKING, PAGEMILL PARTNERS, A DIVISION OF DUFF AND PHELPS SECURITIES, LLC

While our firm generally does not do early stage VC raises (we primarily focus on technology M&A, with any capital raising activities focused on growth equity and late stage financing), we have at times provided advisory services on capital raises to companies and former clients with whom we have had longstanding relationships. One of these companies provided critical technologies for smartphones and was looking to raise capital from three corporate investors and a larger, traditional VC firm. Aside from capital, the corporate investors provided access to end-customers as well as manufacturing expertise and relationships (process knowledge for making the components along with access to assembly lines in Asia). They also provided strong future integration opportunities for the company's products, something that the traditional VC did not offer.

During the negotiations, one of the corporate investors requested a 30 day Right Of First Refusal ("ROFR"). While ROFRs are less commonly requested by Silicon Valley corporate investors, they are more frequently requested by corporate investors based outside of Silicon Valley. Given our previous experience with ROFRs (including how challenging they can make an M&A process), we advised the company not to accept the ROFR; but instead to propose a Right Of First Notification ("ROFN") which would only require notifying the corporate investor in the event the company received an inbound offer or decided to commence a sale process; this is something we would do normally since the corporate investor was also a potential buyer. After multiple rounds of negotiations, the corporate investor dropped its request for a ROFR and accepted the ROFN.

After growing for several more years, the company decided it was the right time to pursue M&A and formally engaged us as its financial advisor. Our previous efforts in helping the company think through the implications of a ROFR vs a ROFN and ultimately negotiating for a ROFN paid off, as almost every prospect that we contacted, while impressed by the support of the corporate investors, inquired if the corporate investors had any special provisions such as a ROFR or special license agreement in place. Several of these prospects stated that they do not spend time reviewing opportunities where the target company has a ROFR in place for fear of being used a stalking horse. Because there was no ROFR in place (only a ROFN), we were able to showcase the company to a larger number of interested prospects, which maximized competition and ultimately resulted in the company being sold to a strategic prospect that was not a current corporate investor.

When seeking corporate venture capital it is important to keep in mind that term sheet provisions matter. While corporate investors can provide a wide array of benefits beyond just access to capital, they can also insert provisions that limit a company's independence and complicate (and potentially disrupt) a sale process. In addition to the aforementioned example of a ROFR vs a ROFN, another common issue to watch out for involves restrictive provisions or limitations placed on the company by the corporate investor. For example, the company should ensure that the IP developed by the company fully belongs to the company and is not licensed to the corporate investor under restrictive provisions, or that products jointly developed by the company and potential corporate investor can be sold independently, or that the company has the ability to sell to or partner with more than one competitor (on a commercial basis).

CONSIDERING RIGHT OF FIRST NEGOTIATION AND RIGHT OF FIRST NOTICE WHEN NEGOTIATING CVC FUNDING - CURTIS MO - PARTNER, DLA PIPER

Curtis Mo is partner at DLA's corporate securities group in Silicon Valley. He has represented over 1,000 startups, public companies, VC and PE funds, investment banks and other clients and was kind enough to catch up with me on the topic of CVC.

If the main motivation of a CVC to make a minority VC investment into a startup is to position the corporate to acquire the company (one of the original motivations for CVC activity in the early days of CVC investing in Silicon Valley), this can create the dynamic of a 3-D chessboard. Often, at the time of making the first investment the corporate would like to negotiate a Right of First Refusal (ROFR) to acquire the startup and get this into the corporate securities documents. The problem this presents to the founders and independent financial VCs is that it may cap out their upside. It may be better to go for a Right of First Negotiation. Although less restrictive this can also put a chill on the process to sell the business. A Right of First Notice may be best, but it is important to precisely define what the Right of First Notice truly allows for. If the startup gets a blow-out bid with a no-talk clause that prevents the startup from shopping the opportunity to sell the company, the Right of First Notice may upset that transaction. This creates the 3-D chessboard dynamic and the company may need to establish an independent committee to contain conflicts of interest and the flow of information. The corporate and outside buying corporate may both be concerned about the flow of information related to their products, technology roadmap strategies and so on. Regardless of how these issues are addressed, a buyer for the startup may view the incumbent CVC investor as a wolf in the hen house.

BEST PRACTICES FOR FORMING NEW CVCS - ARMANDO CASTRO, JR. - PARTNER, PILLSBURY WINTHROP SHAW PITTMAN LLP

Over the years I have worked with a number of CVCs including: Pfizer, Hoya, Cisco, Samsung, Intel, Broadcom, Qualcomm, Bosch, Siemens, Honda, Takeda, NVidia, Imagination and others. As to best practices on establishing CVCs, there is a wide range of structure used in establishing a CVC and best practice choices to make. Corporates will benefit from making clear decisions around some of these topics:

- Will the fund be formed as a separate fund or merely be a business unit that reports to Corporate Finance or Treasury?
- Will the fund seek to generate capital gains or will the focus be to acquire access to strategic technology for the "Parent"?
- Who will the fund use to identify and make investment decisions?
- Do all investments also have to have a business unit sponsor or champion to promote the deal at the business level, or can the fund make independent investment decisions?
- Will the fund be allowed to be the lead or sole investor in a financing round?
- Will the fund be allowed to be the first outside money into a new venture?
- How will the fund employees be compensated? Will they be eligible to get a carried interest?

During the 1990s and early 2000s, Silicon Valley enjoyed a boom in the networking and communications space. One of the funds that drove this growth was not a traditional venture capital fund. It was the venture investment arm of Cisco Systems. During this time span Cisco was not only an active investor, it was also one of the top acquiring companies in the networking space. Their efforts eventually led them to become the number one valued technology company in the world during parts of 2000 and 2001. Much of the growth and influence that Cisco enjoyed was generated through the strategic use of their corporate venture investment arm. Cisco used their corporate venture arm to stay informed on the latest technology developments in the space as well as to identify top talent that could be considered for other business units and to identify likely acquisition targets.

In the early 2000s, Samsung established its venture investment arm in Santa Clara, California. Their goal in large part was to match the success that Cisco had enjoyed through their investment arm in order to extend their influence in the Silicon Valley technology community and beyond. This goal led to the creation of one of the most active CVCs in Silicon Valley today.

CVC AND CLIENT DEAL STRUCTURE DELIVERY - MATTHEW MYERS - SENIOR EXECUTIVE, BNP PARIBAS BANKING GROUP, RESPONSIBLE FOR INTERNATIONAL CVC TRANSACTIONS

Investing in businesses that are only related to a corporation's core business is a flawed investment approach. It is critical that a Corporate Venture Capital (CVC) firm invest in focus areas that fall outside of its traditional purview. Too many of the CVC corporations in Silicon Valley, New York and overseas invest in technologies that only have the potential to supplement their existing operations and business lines. This is an extremely myopic vision. It overlooks startups, brands and investment opportunities that have the potential to shape the internal efficiency of the CVC institution's parent organization.

For example, Citi Ventures focuses on investing "in startups solving critical challenges in areas that are relevant to Citi Group, Inc.'s businesses." By directly framing the objectives of the program to create investments that only mirror the parent corporation Citi Ventures has lost out on significant startups and technologies.

A startup that builds software or technology to constantly streamline their HR systems or re-define their corporate culture would be far more valuable for Citi Ventures to integrate into their portfolio of acquired companies. Why? An organizational culture shift will prevent the company from investing in technologies, that although related to their core mission (internet banking), are not exceptionally profitable over the long run. Adding support for more and more technologies within the corporation makes it more top-heavy. An unwieldy corporation is not wanted by anyone: not by shareholders, institutional investors, employees, clients or customers.

Why not shift the focus of their program to include businesses that are not relevant to their core operations? GV (Google Ventures) investment in Uber is a good example of this. But this investment for GV, and Alphabet Inc. is not radical enough. A CVC subsidiary needs to invest in companies that have the potential to upheave their own corporate culture and make their internal operations more efficient. This is not accomplished by investing only in early-stage or late-stage companies that support core businesses. Why aren't Google's acquisitions creating new products that rival Search or AdWords?

Google launches a large number of products that mirror their competitors (Google+ for Facebook, Google Collections for Pinterest, etc.). Why is Google replicating their rivals instead of constantly building and re-building their internal corporate culture and teams to support new groundbreaking advances? Alphabet Inc., Google and GV must do this. GV can invest in technologies and startups that will disrupt Google itself. This is the type of strategy that will produce the next groundbreaking product within Google and revitalize the company.

Going to a CVC company's sponsored demo day after these startups emerge from their 3-month accelerator or incubator program is painfully boring. The companies often use canned language in their presentations. The technologies aren't groundbreaking. Once the 3-month program and initial investment is made, the startup and CVC firm go their separate ways. The same is true with stand-alone investments by a CVC firm in a more established company that imposes legal and financial terms that don't support the acquired company. It doesn't have to be this way.

Startups and early stage companies that have invested an extraordinary amount of time and resources in their ventures need to have the same corresponding level of institutional commitment. This translates into real investments ($1m or more) and support (greater than one year). It also translates into the CVC enterprises taking stakes in companies that fall outside of the scope of their traditional businesses. Anything less than this is superficial. It's a cursory investment. There is no substance to many of these partnerships because the corporation and their leadership aren't really taking meaningful stock in the companies (financially or otherwise). That's why a lot of these cookie cutter CVC firm purchases are shuttered, fail or result in acqui-hires. The parent company's leadership didn't take any calculated risks. They need to. For every deal they make. This will disrupt the overall CVC investment culture, produce groundbreaking companies and change the CVC firms' parent companies internally." @ InfraUpgrade @iuienterprise @iuimobile

ROMANS' THOUGHTS ON SECTOR FOCUS OR BROAD FOCUS

I was partly motivated in include Matthew's contribution because it brings into focus the issue of what sectors a CVC should invest in. Many CVCs require the support of the head of a business unit before they can complete an investment. This in theory makes sure that the CVC is making investments that are strategic to the corporation and not purely financial. Other CVCs adhere to strict shopping lists and invest in topics and industries directly related to their core and peripheral businesses. Obviously a CVC should cover those topics, however, my research in speaking with over 100 CVCs for this book has led me to conclude that a CVC should have a broad sector focus. I believe it is a mistake to focus exclusively on investing in topics related to the core and peripheral businesses. If the CVC invests with too limited a mandate they are unlikely to achieve the main goals outlined in Chapter 1. They are likely to miss the disruption that will shake up their industry or spot opportunities to access innovation and diversify their products and services, lower costs and make their employees happier and more competitive. Your CVC activities should not be limited to the products and services you sell, but also those that you consume. Your business is in fact much broader than what's for sale on your web site.

At the beginning of the process of writing this book I looked at GV and scratched my head wondering if they were skiing too far from the piste. Now I think they are doing the smartest thing. I do not expect most Fortune 500 CEOs to become enlightened from reading my position on this issue, but I urge them to open their minds to the logic that they are motivated to find something different and not more of the same. Following the hottest deals in the Valley and other important tech corridors and co-investing with the best financial VCs will lead the corporation to the most interesting innovation wherever it is, doing whatever it is...disrupting. I am in favor of declaring some core focus and then taking meetings looking at deals outside of this area of focus 25% to 50% of the time depending on how comfortable you can get with loosening your industry focus. If you are a big company with many employees, I am sure your skilled CVC execs will find ways to add value to those unlikely startups with a balance of "gives and gets." Your shareholders will not complain when they see you increasing earnings per share after a few years of success.

HOW CAN CVC ADD VALUE TO JAPANESE CORPORATIONS? - IAN MYERS - CORPORATE ADVISORY, SUMITOMO MITSUI BANKING CORPORATION; STANFORD UNIVERSITY MASTERS GRADUATE; AUTHOR, "CORPORATE VENTURE CAPITAL AND SILICON VALLEY:

CREATING INNOVATION FOR JAPANESE FIRMS" (JUNE 2015); FORMER INTERN, WORLD INNOVATION LABS – WIL

Ian Myers shared his findings from completing a master's degree at Stanford University focused on CVC specifically related to Japan and other Asian markets, while acting as an intern for World Innovation Lab – WiL – a Silicon Valley VC fund with multiple Japanese corporate LP investors who introduced me to Ian.

How Can CVC Add Value to Japanese Corporations?
Here, the benefits of CVC are broken down into two parts. The first lays out generalized benefits that can be achieved across industries as a natural outcome of CVC activity (including Japanese firms)[6]. Then we examine how CVC can have certain specific benefits to Japanese Corporations because of their relatively intensive R&D activities. These general benefits are:

- Agility – The insights gained from CVC activity allow companies to respond to rapidly transforming markets, by owning or utilizing emerging technologies
- Protection from threats – Companies who rely heavily on internal R&D are narrowly focused on incremental improvements of existing technologies and are not well positioned to identify potential competitors. The due diligence that CVC operations provide can help corporations protect from emerging threats
- Developing complimentary technologies – CVC operations allow companies to invest in and assist startups that are developing technologies, which rely on the parent company's existing technology. This is a relatively less labor intensive way to speed up the adoption of said technology, while offering more features to users

---

6 Lerner, Josh. "Corporate Venturing." *Harvard Business Review* (n.d.): n. pag. *Harvard Business Review.* 01 Oct. 2013. Web.

Alongside these general benefits, Japanese firms are able to realize high returns from CVC because of their heavy reliance on R&D. Young Gak and Ito, in their comparative study of Japanese/Korean R&D investment and productivity found that Japanese companies have high levels of spending on R&D, but low levels of returns from those expenditures.[7] Yet, it is precisely because of their high levels of R&D spending that Japanese companies have an advantage when engaging in CVC. Research shows that companies with strong internal R&D programs have a relatively high absorptive capacity, which serves as a strong foundation when exploring new opportunities through CVC.[8] These findings extend beyond just CVC and R&D—companies with multiple means of investing in technological innovation (R&D, M&A, intrapreneurship) can benefit the most from CVC as a means of acquiring knowledge that is complimentary to their existing operations[9].

This knowledge acquisition does not occur only after the investment is made. Japanese companies can expect results from even the initial activities of a CVC operation. Dushinksy and Lenox found that this knowledge could be acquired at three stages of the investment process. First, before committing any capital, companies can gain some preliminary knowledge through due diligence. Second, after the investment, the corporation can gain information through board seats or by acting as liaisons between the portfolio company and the parent company. Lastly, even when a venture fails, companies are given insights into potential technological pitfalls

---

7   YounGak, Kim, and Keiko Ito. *R&D Investment and Productivity: A Comparative Study of Japanese and Korean Firms* (2013): n. pag. *RIETI*. Research Institute of Economy Trade and Industry, May 2013. Web.

8   Sahaym, Arvin, H. Kevin Steensma, and Jeffrey Q. Barden. "The Influence of R&D Investment on the Use of Corporate Venture Capital: An Industry-level Analysis." *Journal of Business Venturing* 25.4 (2010): 376-88. Web.

9   Vrande, Vareska Van De, W. Vanhaverbeke, and G. Duysters. "Additivity and Complementarity in External Technology Sourcing: The Added Value of Corporate Venture Capital Investments." *IEEE Transactions on Engineering Management IEEE Trans. Eng. Manage.* 58.3 (2011): 483-96. Web.

or unattractive markets, which can be used to evaluate the relevance of existing internal R&D.[10]

While domestic sales are still strong, many Japanese technology companies are seeing the products that were once a hallmark of their ingenuity and quality, such as televisions, phones, radios, household appliances, rapidly losing market share around the world—displaced by disruptive technologies, innovative business models, and commoditization by low end products.[11] In February of 2014, Sony announced that it was shutting down its PC business. One month later Panasonic put an end to its plasma TV division.[12] Hitachi, Sharp, Toshiba, and Sony, have all either drastically reduced their production of televisions, or eliminated/spun off those divisions entirely. This turning away from what used to be core businesses is necessary if Japanese companies wish to cut costs, become more productive and confront current market realities.

Many Japanese companies have recently seen a surge in profits, giving rise to the question of why CVC is necessary if a company is already finding success with its existing core businesses. The answer: it is precisely for that reason that this contribution to Andrew's book draws attention to the possibilities for conducting CVC. Research shows that resource rich companies who are in highly dynamic industries are less likely to commit to venture investing because they seek to utilize resources on less risky, more successful business opportunities[13]. This is paradoxical given that they must continuously create and spread knowledge in order to remain

---

10 Dushnitsky, Gary, and Michael J. Lenox. "When Does Corporate Venture Capital Investment Create Firm Value?" *Journal of Business Venturing* 21.6 (2006): 753-72. Web.

11 "Eclipsed by Apple." *The Economist*. The Economist Newspaper, 12 July 2014. Web.

12 Eha, Brian Patrick. "Sony Now Predicts a $1.1 Billion Loss, Shuts Down PC Business." *Entrepreneur*. Entrepreneur Magazine, 06 Feb. 2014. Web.
"Panasonic to Shut down Plasma TV Production by March 2014: Report." *NDTV Gadgets*. N.p., 9 Oct. 2013. Web.

13 Basu, Sandip, Corey Phelps, and Suresh Kotha. "Towards Understanding Who Makes Corporate Venture Capital Investments and Why." *Journal of Business Venturing* 26.2 (2011): 153-71. Web.

competitive and respond to rapidly changing markets.[14] This need has created an imperative for companies to expand beyond traditional operations and locations in order to offer better products to new consumers. As their traditional R&D operations fail to produce innovative or disruptive technologies, these companies are beginning to use CVC funds as a means of responding to industry challenges through seeking to identify opportunities in emerging or complementary markets and co-opting related knowledge. [15] By engaging in corporate venturing, Japanese companies will be able to add to, or reorganize their internal knowledge networks, thereby increasing their ability to remain globally competitive.[16]

Where Should Japanese CVC Focus Their Operations?[17]

Having shown that Japanese technology corporations will be able to increase their ability to innovate through corporate venture capital, we turn our attention to the question of which region will be the most beneficial for Japanese companies to open CVC operations. We find Silicon Valley to be this region for the following reasons:

- In 2014, California was home to half of all VC deals in the U.S. Within California, the top 6 cities for CVC deal activity are all in the greater Bay Area. [18]

---

14 Eisenhardt, K. M. "Making Fast Strategic Decisions In High Velocity Environments." *Academy of Management Journal* 32.3 (1989): 543-76. Web. and D'Aveni, Richard A. Robert E. Gunther. *Hypercompetition: Managing the Dynamics of Strategic Maneuvering.* New York: Free, 1994. Print.

15 CVC activity in Japan has been steadily increasing, with year over year funding growth of 56.95%. – CB Insights Database

16 Williams, Christopher, and Soo Hee Lee. "Exploring the Internal and External Venturing of Large R&D-intensive Firms." *R&D Management* 39.3 (2009): 231-46. Web.

17 This is not limited to Japanese companies without CVC operations, even if companies have existing operations in Japan, they can benefit from expanding into the Silicon Valley region

18 *2014 Corporate Venture Annual Report.* Rep. CB Insights, Feb. 2015. Web.

- Existing Japanese CVC operations invest mainly in internet and mobile technologies - the highest concentration of such venture deals is in Silicon Valley
- Many Japanese companies already have a presence here through R&D centers and they are beginning to utilize Silicon Valley as a means to increase open innovation activities. Knowledge acquired through CVC can complement those existing R&D operations
- Exit trends in Silicon Valley continue toward M&A and away from IPOs; many Japanese companies have the cash to attract new startups who are looking for an exit strategy
- Japanese companies have large networks with many resources, especially for hardware startups looking for manufacturing partners, giving Japanese CVC a competitive advantage in terms of value added

CVC are much less likely to take initiative as lead investors, especially in the early stages of a startups growth[19], meaning that they must join financial VC led investment rounds as co-investors. This is largely because CVC investment managers do not have the experience required for growing new businesses and because founders are often wary of giving corporations too much control, fearing that their technology will be co-opted before their venture has a chance to grow.[20] This is supported by Hasegawa, who found that the CVC managers of Japanese electronics companies in America were often not comfortable as lead investors.[21] Thus, Japanese companies should seek to place their CVC operations in the area with the greatest number of financial VC deals - the more

19 This is especially relevant to existing Japanese CVC operations, for which Seed/Series A investments represented 78% of total deal activity in 2013-214 – CB Insights Database

20 Masulis, Ronald W., and Rajarishi Nahata. "Financial Contracting with Strategic Investors: Evidence from Corporate Venture Capital Backed IPOs." *Journal of Financial Intermediation* 18.4 (2009): 599-631. Web.

21 Hasegawa, Katsuya. "Evolution of the Corporate Venture Capital Operations of Japanese Electronics Companies." *First International Technology Management Conference* (2011): n. pag. Web.

independent venture activity, the greater opportunity for CVC to enter an investment round as co-investors. In 2015, California had nearly three times as many venture deals (2974) compared to the second ranked state, New York (1040).

Top 5 States for Venture Deals in 2015[22]

State	Deals	Deal Amount
California	2974	$44.4bn
New York	1040	$8.96bn
Massachusetts	676	$7.85bn
Texas	512	$2.43bn
Washington	383	$2.23bn

Within California, eight of the ten top cities by deal volume were in Silicon Valley as were the largest deals.

Top 10 Cities for Venture Deals in 2015 - California[23]

City	Deals	Deal Amount
San Francisco	1279	$24.6bn
Palo Alto	242	$3.66bn
Los Angeles	239	$1.97bn
San Diego	199	$1.76bn
Mountain View	165	$2.26bn
San Jose	109	$1.09bn
Redwood City	105	$1.61bn
San Mateo	86	$1.43bn
Sunnyvale	84	$693mm
Santa Clara	72	$691mm

Comment by Andrew Romans: If you add up all the deals for all the startups in other cities and towns in the San Francisco Bay Area you will find Silicon Valley simply has the most deals. This list is missing many other towns in the Bay Area with good startups.

---

22 *Pitchbook*, Web.

23 *Ibid.*

Investing in Silicon Valley, because of the high density of venture activity, will give Japanese CVC operations access to a larger spectrum of knowledge and technologies than anywhere else in the country.

Evaluating the strategic success of CVC operations has proven difficult—without concrete metrics, most CVC companies are judged based on their financial performance.[24] This is one of the biggest reasons that CVC operations have a reputation for short and sporadic lifespans. As markets turn down, investors see a lower ROI and executive management closes the operation.[25] Research suggests that investing in activities that are related to a company's core business will increase the financial ROI.[26] Existing Japanese CVC operations have displayed a preference for investing in the internet and mobile sectors—with 58% and 31% of investments made in the last two years going to internet and mobile respectively. In 2014, three out of five of the top cities for internet venture deals in were in Silicon Valley. The same is true for mobile venture deals, also made with three of the top five cities located in Silicon Valley. By investing in areas relating to their core businesses, Japanese technology companies can increase their financial returns, thereby creating greater incentive for executive management to support the continued existence of a CVC operation, a crucial component to success.[27] Moreover, they will have a greater chance of finding startups that align with their strategic goals and be better positioned to offer them advantageous resources for growth.

CVC can move faster than traditional R&D in order to gather information regarding emerging threats, disruptive technologies, and startups,

---

24 Hasegawa, Katsuya. "Evolution of the Corporate Venture Capital Operations of Japanese Electronics Companies." *First International Technology Management Conference* (2011): n. pag. Web.

25 Lerner, Josh. "Corporate Venturing." *Harvard Business Review* (n.d.): n. pag. *Harvard Business Review*. 01 Oct. 2013. Web.

26 Gompers, Paul, and Josh Lerner. "The Determinants of Corporate Venture Capital Success: Organizational Structure, Incentives, Complementarities." *Concentrated Corporate Ownership*. By Randall K. Morck. Chicago: U of Chicago, 2000. 17-54. Print.

27 Chesbrough, Henry. "Making Sense of Corporate Venture Capital." *Harvard Business Review*. Harvard Business Review, 01 Mar. 2002. Web.

which could complement the existing operations of a parent company[28] and they can also increase the effectiveness of existing R&D[29]. Japanese technology companies who have existing R&D centers or development offices in Silicon Valley will benefit from using knowledge gained through CVC operations to strengthen existing initiatives. Several of these companies have already either opened a CVC branch, or invested in financial VCs (Fund of Funds) and have begun working with Silicon Valley partners.

Some examples of this are DOCOMO, Toyota and Nissan. NTT DOCOMO, after twelve years in the area consisting of purely research activities, decided to open DOCOMO Innovations, as a means of pursuing innovation through collaboration with Silicon Valley companies. Nissan, hoping to accelerate research into autonomous cars, moved their research center from Japan to Sunnyvale. They have since begun to work with NASA, as well as Stanford and UC Berkeley/Davis research labs, as well as several local companies. Similarly, Toyota opened a research outpost in Mountain View in 2012 in order to work with Silicon Valley companies on data and entertainment systems. In November of 2015, Toyota announced plans to open a five year, one billion dollar research center for artificial intelligence in Silicon Valley in collaboration with Stanford and UC Berkeley. [30]

Executives from all three companies cited a desire to be at the center of innovation in their chosen field as a primary factor in the decision to open branches in Silicon Valley.[31] These instances show an increasing willingness among Japanese technology companies to collaborate with

---

28 *Ibid.*

29 Vrande, Vareska Van De, W. Vanhaverbeke, and G. Duysters. "Additivity and Complementarity in External Technology Sourcing: The Added Value of Corporate Venture Capital Investments." *IEEE Transactions on Engineering Management IEEE Trans. Eng. Manage.* 58.3 (2011): 483-96. Web.

30 Markoff, John. "Toyota Invests $1 Billion in Artificial Intelligence in U.S." *The New York Times.* The New York Times, 05 Nov. 2015. Web.

31 Ohnsman, Alan. "Nissan Opens Silicon Valley Center for Self-Driving Car Research." *Bloomberg.com.* Bloomberg, 18 Feb. 2013. Web.

Inagawa, Tak. "CEO Message." *DOCOMO Innovations.* NTT DOCOMO, n.d. Web.

Silicon Valley institutions in order to utilize external knowledge for their continuing R&D.

WHERE TO LOCATE THE CVC OFFICE WITHIN SILICON VALLEY – ANDREW ROMANS

I wrote a recent blog post after a Chinese corporate asked me where to locate their CVC within the Bay Area. In sum, I recommend putting an office in either Palo Alto or San Francisco. Sand Hill Road in Menlo Park is also fine, but I think it is a mistake to locate too far south in San Jose or Santa Clara. The deals and the events are all over the Silicon Valley from San Francisco to San Jose. It's good to be somewhere central so folks are willing to tolerate the traffic to come to you and so you can go to them without too much loss of time in the car. More detail on this important topic here:

http://rubicon.vc/understanding-the-changing-geography-of-silicon-valley-and-san-francisco/ (shortened URL for the same blog post: http://goo.gl/a817BX or find it here: http://rubicon.vc/blog/)

INTEL CAPITAL'S SALE OF $1BN OF PORTFOLIO ASSETS – ANDREW ROMANS

Intel Capital recently announced they were working with UBS to sell up to $1bn of their Intel Capital portfolio that is not directly strategic to their business. I think this is brilliant. Their portfolio is broad and mature enough that they can probably take a huge profit essentially selling shares of startups they invested in that have gone up in valuation and turn unrealized gain into realized gain. They can then redeploy those dollars back into Intel Capital's next $1bn of venture investments, seeking more strategic return than what they were seeing from good investments that have evolved to have no direct strategic link to Intel's business. They are essentially selling on the secondary market while most CVCs just wait for the definitive liquidity event for each portfolio company via IPO or M&A. This is the first time I have seen a CVC make open minded investments and prune the portfolio later to keep it more strategic, so their time and resources correlate more closely with their actual business units. When the news broke, the press misunderstood what was happening and got the story wrong, publishing headlines that "Intel Capital is abandoning venture capital." I received 30+ emails from friends making sure I heard the news. The press was wrong. Intel is uber-intelligent and this is a brilliant move. Hopefully the secondary buyers will add more renewed value to the portfolio assets they acquire. If any VC does not want to soldier on for their portfolio company they should step aside and get out of the way. *Note from Andrew Romans: like many things in this book, as soon as I write it down everything changes. Intel Capital has since announced they will not divest of any of its current portfolio. Good to keep one's eyes open on these never ending changes!*

US AND OTHER GOVERNMENT VC FUNDS – ANDREW ROMANS

When I was raising VC funding for my first startup as a founder in Washington DC in the late-1990's, it did not take long before we were introduced to In-Q-Tel. I have since gotten to know them better. Here's my understanding of what happened there.

Someone at the CIA started to ask - who works here that understands the internet? They came to the conclusion that they did not have anyone that understood the internet. I heard they even became very confused about who owns or operates the internet. Then someone said something along the lines that "Those VCs in Silicon Valley are the guys who understand the internet. Let's talk to them."

Then someone made the point that the CIA has limitless access to funds (tax payer money). Why don't we make our own VC fund and so In-Q-Tel was born. This was the CIA fund that then evolved to taking capital on from other parts of the US government and now has more "customers," to use their term, rather than LPs. From my perspective they have endless access to due diligence as they can ask anyone in the US government for help. Pretty cool. I think every government should create a VC fund. It's a no brainer.

I would go further and say that all governments should cancel their incubator programs that are failures and they should invest in VC funds that invest in startups that employ their nationals as founders and not require these companies be based in their home countries. Two good national funds that have helped address the lack of angel and seed investors are High-Tech Gründerfonds in Germany and Industrifonden in Sweden.

One European sovereign wealth fund approached me and offered to invest into Rubicon Venture Capital as long as we invested 2x their commitment level into startups that employ at least one founder from their country. They did not specify that the startup needed to be domiciled in their home country or have any strings attached, but simply employ one founder from their country on the founding team. I think this is very smart for the home country.

Let me pick an example. The government of Sweden should invest in VCs that are willing to invest in startups based in New York or Silicon Valley that have at least one Swedish founder. They should not restrict Swedish founders to focus on the Swedish home market. That's insanely limited. MySQL moved its HQ from Scandinavia to Palo Alto and was sold for $1bn less than a year later. The founders returned to Scandinavia with suitcases filled with over $300m in cash. They invested much of that into Scandinavian startups offering those startups not just cash but networks and experience. As much as the existing Scandinavian VCs are good people, now Scandinavia has a VC fund led by real founders that know the Silicon Valley. I call this a very positive development for the local Swedish economy. This fund even recently expanded to London, hiring my old friend Richard Muirehead, and are becoming a major financial VC player. Their new VC fund Open Ocean is probably one of the best VC funds in Scandinavia.

The politicians should actually support their entrepreneurs becoming ex-pats. I discussed the MySQL move to California and one billion dollar exit with a member of parliament from Sweden in Gothenburg. He still doesn't get it. He continued to say – what a pity that jobs left Swedish shores.

This is the model Israel has known from birth, but other countries have been slow to figure this out. I urge governments to abandon their weak startup programs and simply invest into VC funds at home and abroad that fund their nationals. I also advocate tax incentive programs that give their nationals tax breaks if they privately invest directly into startups or VC funds that back startups. The UK, France, and Israel have great programs for this worth copying. Local states in the US should follow suit. Just when you think your startup is a success you find out that you have not yet scratched the surface. That's what I think about venture capital in the US and around the world. We have not even started yet. It will take a few more generations for VC to hit a steady state in the US and most of the rest of the world will continue to grow their venture ecosystems and slowly progress to the amount of venture density in the US (VC dollars invested per capita).

RUBICON LIMITED PARTNER – IN – RESIDENCE PROGRAM (LP-IR) – ANDREW ROMANS

Most corporate venturing programs fail to achieve their potential and realize their list of stated goals, because there is no effective infrastructure to enable the flow of information and good communication among the startups, venture capital community and appropriate executives at the corporate and relevant business units.

A second problem is that many startups and their independent VCs do not want to encumber themselves by publicly aligning themselves with a single corporate and alienating the competitors of that one corporate. Additional problems exist such as the ability to close an investment transaction fast enough, as well as a myriad of other reasons why the cards are stacked against the CVC. A Fund of Funds (FoF) program can address some of this, but if the corporate does not get access to information and interaction with the startups and VCs, the FoF program can become pointless. It is also a challenge for the CVC investment professionals or financial VC with a corporate LP to reach out to business unit execs that can help evaluate working with a startup.

Many business unit execs resist working with the startup for a variety of reasons. Even if the startup has better tech and lower price points, "one never gets fired for going with Big Blue" and these BU managers rarely have financial upside in these startup partnerships. Even after the CVC manages to get a commitment from a business unit to work with their portfolio startups, these partnerships fail to materialize most of the time. So the entire process becomes one of frustration for the startup, the other financial VCs in the syndicate, the CVC professionals and the corporate itself gains nothing.

The Rubicon Limited Partner – in Residence (LP-IR) program addresses these issues by putting in place lasting and renewed human infrastructure we believe can address elements of the broken chain from cradle to grave. This program is partly inspired by the rotation model widely practiced by Japanese corporates, but altered to address failing points in these programs that we studied. As Masatoshi Ueno from Asahi Glass Corporation (AGS) put it, "There are too many pitchers and not enough catchers." His American baseball metaphor suggests that a CVC group in the Silicon Valley may throw ideas over the Pacific Ocean to the HQ in Japan, but there is no one at the HQ to receive or "catch" the idea. This can happen at the time the CVC is encountering interesting ideas, but not investing. It can happen when the CVC needs help conducting due diligence on a startup, including the formidable domain expertise from the corporate. This can happen post investment when the CVC is trying to create partnerships, information flow and make the CVC magic happen post-investment. From a FoF perspective we avoid these failures as we involve LP-IRs through each stage.

Rubicon's program includes an office inside of the Rubicon office for the LP-IRs, who are encouraged to spend 6 months in our Silicon Valley office and 6 months in our New York City office, or any mix of the 12 months between the two offices. LP-IRs may also spend the entire 12 months in one office and visit the other office at will. After 12 months Rubicon will return the executive to the HQ and take a new LP-IR. This is important as it will create a population of LP-IR alumni at the corporate HQ that Rubicon execs and future LP-IRs can contact, increasing the chances of strategic value transfer among Rubicon, its portfolio companies and the corporates. One of the criticisms I heard from Japanese CVCs was that their rotation programs lasted too long. Just when the rotating visiting exec was developing a local network that could add value they return home; and if they stay too long they are out of touch with what is happening at the HQ – so, no value there. Twelve months also puts in place a clear strategy to generate a lasting population of alumni, which is very important to manufacture "catchers" and remove resistance to innovation. I think of our LP-IR alumni as "double agents" that go back to the corporate, but I can call directly and know I have a friend to work with.

Current LP-IRs, as well as alumni of the program that return to the corporate, educate a generation of execs at the corporate on a continuous basis. This results in staffing the corporate's direct investing program at their own CVC and adopting best of breed CVC practices. More importantly this program provides real-time information exchange between the startup innovation and the corporate. It naturally creates a fiber optic line between the corporate BUs and the startup partnership opportunities.

All direct CVC programs suffer from missing out on deal flow and the ability to successfully close investment into startups that do not want to align themselves with a single corporate while still developing their business. Let me make this point a bit more bluntly. If one automotive VC wanted to invest in a connected car startup, that startup might choose NOT to take money from this CVC, because they think it would inhibit their ability to sell their product or service to the other automotive competitors. Let's also not forget that some VCs are hotter than others. It is rare that a CVC is so hot and attractive that they are truly the first choice investor for the startup founders. The independent VCs most commonly gain this status.

The Rubicon LP-IR program seeks to address this, by providing the corporate with access to deal flow they can otherwise not access on their own, but via the LP-IR program the corporate has their own team on the ground at Rubicon and alumni of the program to reach out to back at the corporate enabling the corporates to achieve their Chapter 1 goals in a timely manner when and where innovation occurs. Rubicon also manages confidentiality making sure startup CEOs agree to have any LP-IR present during pitch meetings. These CEOs can easily request a specific LP-IR not attend or access their confidential information. The startup CEO is in charge here.

Rubicon charges a fee per Limited Partner-in-Residence (per person) per annum to the Limited Partner to cover the costs of the program. In some cases, the same LP may choose to place one to four executives in the LP-IR program at the same time. The expense of the LP-IR program does not draw from management fees from the fund, but purely on those LPs that wish to participate. I view this as important as I have seen some funds structured to be multi-CVCs and the financial investor begins to lose when a meaningful portion of the management fee goes to babysitting corporate LPs. This model forces the corporate LPs to pay for what they eat and the financial LPs ride the wave all the way to the bank.

The LP-IR program also provides an educational curriculum teaching these executives how venture capital works, how to be a VC and how Rubicon specifically works closely with its strategic LP investors. Key drivers for a corporate to participate in the LP-IR program include all the motivations outlined in Chapter 1.

Rubicon's strategy to take LP commitments from corporates and facilitate partnerships is a clear win for corporates who often fail to achieve strategic objectives from their own CVC programs or LP investments into classic VCs who fail to provide transparency or infrastructure to enable communication and success. The startups are clear winners gaining access to large blue chip corporates as customers or partners to put their products and services into large sales forces without compromising neutrality or becoming legally encumbered, suffering from slow decision making and inability to deliver partnerships. In many cases startups can expect to collapse the sales cycle with multiple corporates and get direct access to the CFO, CTO, head of strategy, or routed to the correct business unit head at corporates via Rubicon. Even if Rubicon does not invest, it is worth it for a startup to try to pitch Rubicon in hopes of this business development opportunity. Investors in Rubicon's funds purely seeking a financial return will win as a result of superior deal flow and rapid growth in value for the startups. These relationships result in a faster path to IPO and in many cases M&A exits to the strategic LPs that "try before they buy" partnering and investing in startups before outright acquisition.

If you want to learn more about our LP-IR program please contact us at info@rubicon.vc.

Six

War Stories from CEOs, Founders and VCs – The Good, the Bad & the Ugly

"If you're going through hell, keep going."

WINSTON CHURCHILL

I t is important to share some negative perceptions entrepreneurs have of CVCs. You should know the bad news as well as the hoped for best practices. Many of the CVCs in this book have adjusted their practices to correct these issues, but these are real legacy perceptions of how CVCs operated in the 90's and 2000's and some of this persists today. Again, do not be offended reading this. The good CVCs are nothing like this but there is a generalization that CVCs are slow, can't lead and only invest in later stage. For many none of this is accurate, but if you were to poll hundreds of VC-backed CEOs you might hear some of this negative perception.

I want to share my own experience of what it was like meeting CVCs when I was an entrepreneur raising VC funding in the mid-1990s and early 2000's and again later when I was at Georgetown Venture Partners, The Founders Club and Rubicon. Literally on hundreds of deals, not least of which my own, I had a lot of interaction with CVCs. Usually there was a certain level of A/B testing where I pitched the same deal to 4 VCs in the same day and 20 in the same month and I could not help but notice the difference between the CVCs and the financial VCs. The first time an entrepreneur normally meets a CVC they can immediately feel the difference compared to the financial VCs. This is changing for sure, but I feel compelled to give this full picture to my readers.

What you can feel immediately is that the CVC guys feel like government workers compared to the financial VCs. You can tell financial VCs are trying very hard to make money. They have killer instinct. They are trying to move quickly if they want to get into a deal. Once in they are almost ready to strangle someone (for better or worse) to get to a good exit. In my experience with CVCs they often don't want to invest until the company has product market fit and throwing off nice revenue. So to some extent "where were you when I needed you?" is the feeling entrepreneurs have towards CVCs.

Even then they often can't lead. They can only join the B round and add some extra dollars and hope to leverage the corporate to add value to the business of the startup. The CVC team promises how they can add value making the corporate a customer or distribution partner for the startup and then in the end the CVC team does not have the clout to get anything done with the corporate. It becomes the same as a failed empty campaign promise from a politician who is not capable of making Washington DC do what she wants.

CVCs are also known for being slow to make an investment decision, get it approved and release cash. Often CVCs have internal processes that require the signature of the head of a business unit or executive committee. So not only do you need to "make the sale" to the VC unit of the CVC, but you need to get a business unit (BU) to put their reputation on the line saying they will do business with you. That's a double sale. Why not just keep it to a single sale with a financial VC?

Some CVCs are so huge as companies that they are worried about anti-trust monopoly issues and have commercial contract legal groups that are slow to sign your docs. Even when everything is signed off do not be surprised if it takes one to two months to get the payments group of the corporate to actually get a wire transfer off to you. This is the polar opposite of what you want in a VC. If the CVC needs the signature of both the CFO and the CEO who are frying bigger fish it makes perfect sense that these deals get held up when it's time to wire the cash.

After you close your deal with the CVC they do not "feel" like they are motivated to see your startup become a huge success. The other VCs are working on your startup to get their fund into carry or if they are already into carry they are planning on banking 20% of the profit directly into their pockets. When you are working with VCs this makes some of your VCs actually feel like cofounders. Most CVCs get a bonus that is related to the performance of the corporate and completely unrelated to the performance of your startup. Founders and financial VCs notice this.

In ancient times CVCs would always make the point to the pitching startup that if they end up owning 20% or more of the startup that they need to consolidate financials with the parent company, typically a publicly traded company, and that they don't want to do that. They position this as a positive to the entrepreneur stating that they are not greedy vulture capitalists that want to take as much ownership of your startup as possible but in fact work hard to avoid ever taking more than 19.99% ownership of the company for these GAAP reasons. I used to view this as a negative, thinking the CVC might not be able to support you with another check when things get tough even if they wanted to.

The other stereotype about CVCs is that they will really only invest when you are at the Series B or C stage and may be so slow that they will miss the round and end up joining the next one. Lastly, it is quite commonly viewed that shortly after the CVC makes the investment the individual or individuals at the CVC will change jobs looking for classic 2&20 VC compensation or get re-org'd into another group, or just go to another corporate or even jump to the entrepreneur side of the table and not stick around. So your champion at that big corporate may disappear on you. Many corporate venturing programs are discontinued after 2 or 3 years; so even if your team does not disappear, the entire program may go away and you will be an orphaned investment with dead weight in your cap table. Many of the folks that contributed to this book moved on and changed the company they work at from the time of my interview to the time of this book being published.

I advise entrepreneurs, when trying to decide from which VC to take money, to consider three elements in the decision making equation: 1) chemistry with the lead partner at the VC fund, 2) the reputation of the VC firm, and 3) the economics and terms of the deal (valuation, etc.) If the chemistry of the partner is at risk of changing on you then that's a concern. One investment thesis for direct secondary funds is to buy out a corporate investor that has orphaned a startup and replace them with an active investor that can add value.

Some CVCs are known for negotiating special deals seeking a better deal than other VCs such as performance warrants where they get more equity if they manage to land their corporate as a customer. Some of the CVCs in this book mentioned that they never do this as it is obviously viewed negatively.

Finally, many entrepreneurs and financial VCs are suspicious of taking a corporate into the cap table for fear of conflicts of interest. They fear that the corporate venturing arm is really just an extension of the corp dev / M&A group that may want to see the company run out of cash and then buy it on the cheap compared to maximizing the return on its investment, using this great outcome as the cornerstone for raising its next fund.

I held many of these views in my early days. I have gained more experience and, even in the process of writing this book, I have come to understand that while there is some truth to these commonly held views, they are certainly most often not the case. Times are a changing. That said, if you recently joined a CVC and think a big corporate name and war chest of cash will get you into the best deals, think again. You will need to earn your reputation just like the rest of us and in fact you have some things going against you already that you may need to dispel.

NEVER TURN DOWN A SMART STRATEGIC INVESTOR - KENNY HAWK - FORMER CEO, UBIDYNE; CURRENT CEO, MOJIO; SERIAL ENTREPRENEUR WITH IPO & M&A EXITS

Kenny Hawk is an old friend of mine that I met in Berlin when he was CEO of Ubidyne about ten years ago where he argued for giving the CVC the performance warrants they asked for, but failed to get his financial VCs on board. As fate would have it, T-Venture is an investor in his current startup. Here are Kenny's words:

Ubidyne, after raising a large successful series B during one of the most difficult fundraising environments in the last decade, had a 5 million euro term sheet from a key strategic investor - T-Venture, the CVC of Deutsche Telekom. The management team worked hard to secure the term sheet and saw great value in having one of the world's leading mobile operators as a strategic investor. T-Venture was flexible on their bite size and the makeup of the syndicate and had offered its CTO as a strategic advisor. Our existing venture investors were split on whether or not to accept their term sheet (which included performance warrants tied to their specific contribution to the company). While none of our investors had ever worked in a startup, some of them were frightened that an investment by T-Venture would damage our important relationship with Vodafone. The management team did extensive diligence speaking with each of the last 10 investments by T-Venture, and we found that each of them actually accelerated their traction with other operators. They also confirmed that the promised value add by T-Mobile was delivered above and beyond what they had expected. The best sample reference came from the founders of Flarion, who stated the company would never have made it if not for the early investment and support from T-Venture. Flarion was later acquired by Qualcomm for over $650 million and delivered a spectacular return for their investors.

The T-Venture issue began to polarize our management team and a subset of our investors. In the end those investors were able to block the deal. In a final meeting in Bonn, our investor actually told the executive management of T-Venture he saw "absolutely no strategic value" and that T-Venture should pay exactly the same price as the rest of the investors, (i.e., no performance warrants). Less than 18 months later, these same investors had to do an internal 6 million euro round at less than one-tenth the valuation that T-Venture had offered. The net effects of this strategic mistake wiped out the value of all founder and employee stock options, slowed the company while competitors including Huawei sped up, and gave the blocking investors control of the company. @kenhawkjuniper

HAVING A CORPORATE VC AS INVESTOR AND LARGEST CUSTOMER - JACOB BRATTING PEDERSEN - PARTNER, NORTHCAP

In my previous venture firm I was an investor in and on the board of directors of a Swedish software startup. We had a large Japanese corporation as the biggest customer responsible for around 50% of sales. As the technology of the startup was emerging as a new standard, the startup attracted the attention of the Japanese corporation's corporate venture arm, that saw a possible benefit from the value increase in the startup that was expected based on the revenue projections. As an existing shareholder we welcomed the idea of getting the corporate venture arm as an investor, as we saw it as a possibility of positioning the company to an exit to the Japanese corporation; contractually we made sure that the investment would not limit our chances of exiting the company to other parties.

The corporate VC made their investment. Following the investment there were ongoing commercial negotiations with the business unit of the Japanese corporation responsible for licensing the technology. They were being measured on how efficiently they could source components and software from all sub-suppliers. They were of course also very well aware of their negotiating power due to their size compared to the startup, and that they were responsible for a substantial part of the startup's revenue. The price pressure became significant, and a "fight" emerged between the corporate venture arm and the business operations of the corporation. They had very different agendas and incentive structures, and the startup ended up being a "plaything" between the units.

From a value generation perspective there is no doubt the Japanese corporation would have been better off not putting such a significant price pressure on the startup, as the revenue that was generated from the corporation drove a lot of the value creation in the startup, and the corporation's equity stake could increase significantly in value. But this is of course rarely the view on which corporations base their decisions. Commercial negotiations happen at total arm length.

My advice to entrepreneurs and financial VCs is not to pursue this constellation of having a corporate VC as investor, if the same corporation is also a significant customer of the investee.

Commercial validation from corporate VCs
As a financial VC it can indeed be beneficial to discuss possible syndication with corporate VCs. The advantage is that the corporate VC managers have direct access to the business units in their corporations, and can obtain information, not just on products that are on the market, but also future products, trends etc. that are being worked on in the business units. Hereby we can as a financial VC, get a validation of the future commercial possibilities for the startups' products, and take our investment decision on a much more informed basis. @NorthcapVC

HOW WE TURNED A BAD ROFO & ROFR INTO A WIN – ERIC ELFMAN, FOUNDER & CEO AT ONIT, INC., FOUNDER & CEO, DATACERT, INC.

I raised about $2m from UPS in 2000 because they wanted to get in the business of "digital packages" as well as physical packages. They wanted to sell secure email messages. Sounds silly now but pre-crash it made sense to them. Anyway, I offered them an early exit that would have quadrupled their money after the crash in very uncertain times and they said no. I was told by the head of the group at the time that UPS only exits investments in one of two ways: the company sells or fails...no in between. Thought it was silly but they eventually got a 10x return.

Raised almost $5m from a strategic that wanted to buy us but we weren't ready for it. I was naive and got bum legal advice and accepted a right of first offer and right of first refusal. I know, a story as old as time. A couple of years after the investment, and more attempts to buy us, they bought a competitor. Given that, I concluded having the ROFO & ROFR didn't seem appropriate. We lawyered up but came to the conclusion that suing would likely get dropped before discovery, where we were certain we would find impropriety. So we had to figure out a way to get them to sue us. (PS, our firm was Wilson Sonsini). We got really creative, created a holding company parent of our operating company and moved all of the assets and equity up. But we left agreements, including their ROFO and ROFR, in the operating company. So we could sell the parent without triggering the ROFO and ROFR. Now, doing so in reality would have been complex and probably not really work. But it was enough to get them to sue us. They almost immediately wanted to settle. The terms were dropped and they invested another $8m in us, and 7 years later acquired the entire business.

TRUECAR - VICTOR PASCUCCI III - FOUNDER & FORMER HEAD, USAA VENTURES AND HEAD OF CORPORATE DEVELOPMENT

Due to an ill received marketing campaign, TRUECar lost approximately 60% of its dealer customers in a 90-day period. Damage to the business was further compounded from a business development deal gone wrong with a large ISP causing the company to pay multi millions of dollars with no meaningful revenue in return. Additionally there was a sports sponsorship that did not provide the financial lift expected despite the significant cash outlay. Needless to say the company was in dire straits. As an investor, there could be no riskier time to provide capital. As a strategic, you could legitimately question the viability of the entire service. However, believing in the business, its strategic value to USAA and benefit to USAA members, USAA invested a much needed $10m bridge to stabilize the company and get it running right. Two years later, TRUECar IPO'd with one of the most successful public offerings of the year. The company reached a market cap of over $1.5bn. USAA members have saved over $5bn on new car purchases through the USAA/TRUECar partnership. @victorpascucci3

MEDICAL PERSPECTIVE WHERE DEALS INCREASINGLY REQUIRE A CORPORATE TO GET DONE AT ALL - PETER RULE - CHAIRMAN & CEO, OPTISCAN BIOMEDICAL, INC.

This next story comes from Peter Rule who has raised over $100m in funding from financial VCs and CVCs and sold his last company for approximately $220m. In his words:

Essentially, corporates are not viewing direct investment in ventures as an element of R&D. They are viewing it as a prelude to an acquisition at best. Thus, with the latter view, they expect to see something that impacts their business in the "here and now," with obvious exception, but this is the general case. So, it's a "guessing game" as to which corporate may or may not invest and when. The major exception is JJDC (Johnson & Johnson Development Corporation), but even they have the limitation of needing a division sponsor.

Compounding this is the corporate mentality of tyranny of the annual bonus, and the related tyranny of the near term stock price. Investing in a venture does not help either of those.

So, what would I advise an entrepreneur with a great, but not yet impactful business to the corporates? First, talk annually, at most, to them. More than that wastes everyone's time. Second, understand their needs, and reflect that "fit" in your conversations, asking openly, "have I got it right?" Third, understand that this is a long-term relationship process, one of building trust. It is not a sprint, more like a marathon. They want to see performance over time. It's the rare corporation in medical devices that will move quickly, or even predictably.

One is always in fund raising mode, realistically. It's just part of the job. OptiScan has raised over $100m and we are in the process of raising a large Series E round. The traditional venture capital model was not designed to carry companies like ours to the stage now required. The IPO markets simply require a much more mature company than in past years. So, one has to find many sources of capital. Corporates are part of the solution, but only a part. Traditional investors are also only a part. Private Equity funds are interested in today's late stage medical device company, but, again, those do not move quickly, and the larger ones can and often do take more than one year to follow you and make a decision.

I tell my team all the time: "would you mortgage your house and invest in our company? If you would, then you should expect new investors to join us. If not, why not, and what can we do to overcome that resistance?" It's a very interesting test. For those of us who have had success in the past, I think it's only reasonable for our investors to expect us to invest in our own ventures.

Romans' update: OptiScan closed a $29.45m Series E financing round in June 2016.

WHAT TO DO WHEN CVC MONEY COMES KNOCKING? - TOM NICHOLSON - CEO, NICHOLSON NY (ACQUIRED BY ICONMEDIALAB AB); CHAIRMAN & CEO, LBI INTERNATIONAL; FOUNDING MEMBER, ANGEL ROUND CAPITAL (ARC) FUND

What to do when CVC money comes knocking? We all know the pros and cons of corporate strategic money. As an early stage investor today in NYC I encounter the question frequently from the startups I meet. I faced it myself back in the earliest days of the Internet when the company I founded was riding the crest of that first wave - guiding the likes of IBM, News Corp, NBC, etc. on adapting to the opportunities of the new medium.

When I got the call, it was from the CVC arm of a $6bn advertising holding company that had just made a bundle on the first-ever Internet services firm to go public and they were now out shopping for their next deal. And that would be us. But as we learned in our early discussions this time it would be different. Now their objectives were entirely strategic rather than financial and we were to help their own agencies come up to speed on providing Internet related services to clients – and they wanted to own us outright. The valuation: $18m.

I said no. We'd been doing this for too many years. As the first digital agency in NYC we had our roots in the creative and technical challenges of inventing a medium well before the mania of the dotcom Kool-Aid days, and my staff was inspired by those green field challenges...not by doing car commercials. It was not clear to me that our future would be tied up with those Mad Men businesses selling the Kool-Aid and cars. But who could know for sure? It sure seemed headed that way when our first multi-million dollar client IBM started paying us $2m+ a year to handle their brand online.

So after turning down the buyout, I countered with a hedge, one that would give us a foot in the ad industry and a foot out, securing for us the opportunity to consider a full acquisition later. I would retain 80.1% of the company and accept a minority investment for 19.9% (accounting reasons) and importantly would stay in full control of our future. (Lesson 1).

Good thing. Within a few short months I was presented with a "terrific new plan" conjured in the back offices of our investor/partner. We would sell the rest of the company to them at a higher valuation than the original deal and they would roll us up together with three of their small internal groups starting to provide digital services. This would be the biggest thing ever to hit the industry! And last but not least, the son of one of their most powerful agency owners would be anointed to run the whole thing.

I thought again of those car commercials.

"What? You're turning down more money than you'll ever see in your lifetime!" retorted one of the lead deal architects. Things got a little warm. After all they were our major investor and sat on our board. I thought again of those commercials and held the ground.

Business continued to flourish along with the Internet and our people continued to be amazing at figuring out what it means to be a digital agency and how to craft awesome digital experiences. The creative energy of the time was beyond the beyond and many of those from the period have gone on to great things.

Our revenues and earnings continued to expand and sure enough soon a new suitor came knocking. But this time it was not corporate venture capital but a pure-play digital consultancy, already public in Europe and with all the right ingredients: a culture like our own, 100% focused on digital, an avenue for our clients into a dozen countries in Europe and Scandinavia, no presence in the U.S. and importantly they were already publicly traded so no disruptive road show if we, like our competitors, decided to go public which was our other primary option at the time. Finally, when I was offered a Board seat it meant as much control as one could expect in a full exit. We even negotiated a valuation that was at par with the public company's revenue multiples and when the acquisition was announced on the exchange the share price tripled over the next few weeks.

It was as they say, a win-win-win. We were positioned globally - the European-based company had its presence in the U.S. and most importantly from a CVC point of view our corporate investor not only had a 3x return on its investment but also a more significant strategic boost from this global play than an outright acquisition of our NYC-based firm would have provided. (Lesson 2)

Ok, that was then...well we're still knee deep inventing that new medium today but now it's about extending it into more facets of our lives and into more devices at all scales and everywhere. The fun continues. And new opportunities are being created that continue to shake up the established order.

For example, my first investment was a few years ago with a young entrepreneur who was looking to make art accessible "to anyone with an Internet connection." Crazy idea (Art.sy has raised $50.88m from VCs including Peter Thiel). As his first outside investor I completely cringed when the day came that he told me he was considering an investment from "strategic money" from one of the largest, most powerful gallery owners in the art world.

I thought about those car commercials. But as a minority investor now myself I remembered my lessons and sat back. And waited. Good thing I did.

PROVIDING A CEO OF THEIR OWN GAVE THEM THE BEST DUE DILIGENCE POSSIBLE - BART WÜRMAN - CEO, DDF VENTURES; FORMER CEO, AM PHARMA; FORMER CEO, LANTHIO PHARMA

This story comes from my old J.P. Morgan Healthcare Conference friend Bart Würman, a seasoned biotech CEO now turned VC.

When I was CEO of Lanthio I did a technology licensing deal with MorphoSys in Germany. They also invested in Lanthio as part of the €5m series A. A year later I was looking for further funding to develop our lead drug product up to Phase II Proof of Concept in fibrosis. MorphoSys were interested to continue funding, conditionally on providing a CEO of their own. The other investors agreed. Five months later they acquired Lanthio at a valuation of €30m. Providing a CEO of their own gave them the best due diligence possible and a very strong position to negotiate the acqui-sition. Cleverly done.

Bart was CEO of Dutch biotech AM Pharma when I met him for the first time. Pfizer paid $87.5 million for a stake in AM-Pharma along with an option to buy the company for $512.5m hinging on AM Pharma's suc-cessful completion of a Phase II study of a new treatment for acute kidney injury (AKI) related to sepsis.

THE CONCEPT OF TIME HAS DIFFERENT MEANINGS FOR CORPORATES AND STARTUPS - MORITZ VON PLATE - CEO, CASSANTEC AG

Moritz von Plate is one of my best friends, one of my roommates during MBA days. He listened to my war stories when I was raising funding from corporate Lucent Technologies and CVC Lucent Ventures when we were students together. Now I'm listening to his CVC war stories. Moritz was a senior exec at The Boston Consulting Group (BCG) before becoming an entrepreneur. In his words:

The concept of time has different meanings for corporates and startups. At my current company we recently went through a technical due diligence conducted by a CVC together with a business unit that had indicated an interest in collaborating with us. From the moment of our first interaction with the CVC a year had passed until the DD got underway. Then, after a smooth DD process, we received highly positive feedback about our technology and were told that an investment cum collaboration would receive serious consideration – earliest in six months from now.

In the meantime, a re-organization and a strategic review process would first have to be completed. While such longer processes are stan-dard business for a corporate, they are obviously impossible to accom-modate for a startup. The consequence for us is that we will continue building our business and raising capital independently. Having the pos-sibility of gaining a partner eventually is good to know, but we will not wait. Possibly, by the time the corporate is ready to take next steps, the opportunity will have passed for them.

THE CLASSIC CVC WAR STORY - ANDREW ROMANS

Here is a tale that has been repeated many times. A startup raises money from a corporate and the corporate's bureaucratic process to make the investment dragged on longer than with the financial VCs. So the startup and other VCs are spreading the news about how slow and difficult this CVC has been to work with, but they all have high hopes on the value they will get from the corporate. At least half the time the investment professionals at the CVC do not have the power to get the corporate BUs to do business with the startup. Just like a new US president may not have the mojo to get congress and the senate to pass her proposed legislative agenda, the heads of BUs do not report to the CVC and the promises don't always materialize as reality for the startup. And so the reputation of CVC gets worse.

The other half of the time the corporate becomes a customer and might in fact become the biggest customer of the startup. The corporate then decides that this is so strategic to them that they should buy the startup. From the perspective of the startup or financial VCs in the deal they might have ended up in play earlier than they ideally wanted to be in the sense that they were dealing with the M&A team when they really only wanted to deal with the CVC team, but unfortunately it's the same team or they are very closely linked.

Then after six months of exhaustive DD the corporate backs out of the deal and pulls back their revenue from the startup. This can be devastating for the startup that was probably dual tracking running two processes at the same time. Talking to the corporate about selling and also talking to VCs about investing, promising fast revenue growth and potential for a quick flip sale to the corporate. Then all of a sudden without warning the corporate backed out and does not want to buy them and with the revenue traction and blue chip customer disappearing this scares off the VCs. So now the startup is running out of cash.

In the Silicon Valley this is where you may find your tech team and sales team jump ship and walk across the street in Soma (South of Market part of San Francisco home to many startups) and take a job with another startup that just closed VC funding from Kleiner Perkins. With the startup being on the ropes the founders and existing financial VCs decide it's best to take the new much lower offer from the corporate to buy the startup on the cheap and get their money back 1x or even pennies on the dollar.

Some might argue that the corporate used CVC masterfully and played their cards quite well. The problem with this is that bad reputations spread and this inhibits other CVCs to access the best deal flow in the future.

Obviously, the CVCs cited in this book are working hard to turn this negative perception around, but I think it is important for corporates contemplating launching a new CVC or running a nascent one to understand this starting point of the reputation of many CVCs. Entrepreneurs should also go into the relationship with the CVC aware of this timeless tale. Of course, there are plenty of other stories that are pure success stories to balance this classic negative tale. This book aims to move the needle to mostly positive outcomes. I could also write a very long book of true stories where founders point out atrocities committed by financial VCs. Startups and early stage investing is a rollercoaster and everyone should buckle up and be ready for a bumpy ride and remain calm and ethical throughout the journey.

Seven

How to Get Funded by Corporate VCs

"We will either find a way or make one."

- Hannibal, 217 CE

WHAT SHOULD YOU KNOW WHEN CONSIDERING TAKING MONEY FROM A CORPORATE INVESTOR? - WILLIAM KILMER - FORMER HEAD, INTEL CAPITAL EMEA; OPERATING PARTNER, MERCATO PARTNERS; FOUNDER & CEO, PUBLIC ENGINES

I have the dubious distinction of being both a corporate strategic investor (former managing director at Intel Capital) and having run a company that took a corporate investment (Symantec). A lot has changed in the recent years in Corporate Venture Capital (CVC), the most of important of which is that corporate investors have matured tremendously in how and why they invest.

I think it's time to stop considering corporate investors as "dumb money." In fact, now that they have firmly been participating in such a large percentage of deals, let's stop comparing them to VCs at all. They are no longer an anomaly. Corporate Venture Capital (CVC) investors are just different. They are regular, active participants in venture investing that are as capable as VCs in helping you grow your organization, but they face the task of balancing both strategic and financial interests.

Setting that aside, it's time to face the facts that, in general, it's actually harder to get an investment from a strategic investor than it is a financial one. But in the end, you may get more value out of your strategic investor. Let me offer this as my rationale:

1) Your first filter with a corporate venture investor will always be strategic, instantly limiting the type of deals they invest in. You may be the next big thing, but if you don't fit strategically, you're not on their docket. Believe me, there were plenty of deals we wanted to do at Intel Capital that looked interesting financially, but we just couldn't come up with a strategic rationale.

2) A good corporate investor, just by nature of their brand, probably receives hundreds to thousands of investment pitches per year. They have choice and they do get smarter from all that deal flow.

3) A corporate investor will have more domain expertise than a typical VC to back them up in evaluating you. At Intel Capital, we had our pick of engineering, sales and marketing resources to check on every deal, as well as contacts with many customers and service providers to validate our investment hypothesis. Unless you are working with a theme-based VC, or an investor that is a former entrepreneur, they will not.

4) Most corporate investors are global in their reach, or at least their corporate parent is, so they have a vast number of investments they can choose from. If there is an alternative company doing what you are doing, they will not only compare you to them, they have the option to invest in them. Most VC will not have the ability to invest in your competitor in Mumbai.

5) A good corporate investor will be looking at you for strategic reasons so, if they are good, they will compare you to every other company doing the same thing and decide which is best to invest, even (or maybe especially) if that other company is in Mumbai.

6) Unlike financial VCs, the corporate entity behind the CVC investor has alternatives as to where to invest their money. Just ask any treasury department; someone, somewhere in the corporation

would just as soon invest that money elsewhere. They don't have to consider fund timing or fund dynamics like a VC; and yes, that does matter.

Supporting this is a general decline in the spray and pray strategy of former corporate investors. As shown by Intel Capital's recent plans to sell off some of its portfolio, corporations don't want to be saddled with too many investments and business units can't afford to be tied to external ventures that aren't going to help them reach a strategic objective. So, if you're seeking a corporate investment, you need to be on top of your game. You may also see strategic returns from that investment, in terms of their domain expertise, market access, and ability to accelerate the growth of your business.

So, what does an entrepreneur need to know when seeking an investment from a Corporate Venture Capital (CVC) investor? The best advice I can give anyone who is looking to raise money from a corporate venture investor is to stand in their shoes for a minute and be able to articulate the "why?" behind their investment: "Why would this corporate investor want to invest in me? I asked more than a handful of friends who are corporate investors from several different corporate venture groups to identify what they look for. I have included their feedback without attribution, mostly at their request.

Articulating the "why" goes beyond the superficial acknowledgement that you support a particular initiative or that you are being supported by a specific business unit. A simple method to understand this is to map out three things that will help you understand how you strategically "fit" with your potential corporate investor: Position, Priority, and Potential.

Corporate Position. First, you need to understand what the company's position is relative to the market you play in? Are they an incumbent leader, an attacker, or not even a player? What are their goals and strategic objectives? Are they taking an offensive position (going after a market), a defensive position (protecting what they have), or a neutral position (maybe they aren't even in the market)? Is this a big bet, large strategic initiative for them, or are they just dabbling? Are they just trying to get a foothold to learn something about the market, or your technology? Knowing what the corporate is trying to accomplish in the market regardless of their connection with you is the foundation for understanding your strategic value.

Corporate Priority. Second, you need to answer the question of what the corporate's priorities are relative to their position in the market. Understand what they need to accomplish to support their strategic initiatives. What pieces do they need from someone like you? Maybe they are looking to create a valuable option for the future. As one corporate investor put it, "Answering that question will tell you to whom you're the most valuable, who will be most motivated to help you succeed long-term, and help identify additional ways they may be able to help you accelerate your business plan."

Strategic Potential. Strategic potential refers to the fundamental elements of the relationship that you should be able to articulate is how you will help the corporate, and vice versa. As one corporate investor put it, "the most obvious things that come to mind are both related to potential synergies between the company and corporation: 'What can you do for me?' – 'What can I do for you?'" This should generally be articulated in a business agreement that accompanies the investment.

At Intel this was called the "Gives and Gets" of the deal and reflected the symbiotic nature of the investment. First you, as the CEO, need to understand what the corporate investor wants you to "give" them to make this relationship successful. Conversely, you need to ask what do you need to "get" (the corporate investor's "gives") from them for this to be a successful for you and them.

Don't be afraid to ask for your "gets" during the investment phase. As one CVC investor advised, "if the company is able to help the corporation but not the other way around I would probably not accept the investment as the entrepreneur." Your success should help their success, so articulate how they need to help you help them.

Finally, ensure that your corporate investor sees the financial clarity behind the investment. Don't assume any investor has the strategic clarity to throw away millions to support a business unit initiative. You would be wrong to consider them any less motivated by financial gain than any other financial VC. One investor noted to me that, "some companies have a misguided notion that corporate investors will pay more and do less than financial investors when really the exact opposite is true."

After you have been able to articulate and demonstrate strategic value, here are a few additional things to consider.

At the top of the list: don't fall into the trap of the CVC as lead investor. I have met too many companies that have one or more corporate ventures interested in investing, but no financial investors ready to step up. I recently spoke with one CEO that had three strategic investors seriously interested and no lead: this is a clear red flag. If you have existing investors, make sure they are comfortable and understand CVC investing.

Next, understand their process. VCs vary in how they approve deals, and many have a fairly loose process for deciding on an investment. Corporates, on the other hand, generally have a more rigid, defined process. I've talked to plenty of CEOs who thought they were much further along than in the corporates investment decision process than they actually are. If in doubt, ask the CVC what their process is and what approvals have been done/what remains to get them from "interested" to "approved for investment."

Also, consider the individual investing, not just the corporation. As one friend recommended, ask yourself, "Do you want this person potentially on your board? Can they actually add any value beyond simply connecting you to colleagues within their company? Do they have any pull in their company? Do they genuinely understand the challenges a startup faces?" Another CVC investor warned, "Too many CVCs simply don't have start up experience, don't know the day to day challenges of executing, managing the ups and downs of startup life, and have no network outside of their own company." Also, don't fall into the trap that they are always your advocate. You're not the one paying them.

Lastly, understand beforehand if the corporate investor usually asks for any special terms. Beware of CVC encumbrances, whether in the investment or an accompanying business deal, limiting your scope or the customers you might work with (competitors) or any rights that might affect your appeal or exit. Do your homework by calling CEOs or CFOs at some of their other investments.

A corporate can be a very valuable addition to your company if you position yourself correctly with the right investor and avoid some common pitfalls. @wkilmer

HOW TO APPROACH CVCS AND WIN - IGOR SHOIFOT - PARTNER, TMT INVESTMENTS; ADJUNCT PROFESSOR, UC BERKELEY, UC SAN FRANCISCO & NYU

CVC motivation and structure

Corporate venture capitalists are generally motivated by reasons different from those that motivate entrepreneurs and private VC firms, but not entirely different.

Much like traditional VC firms, CVCs want to bet on scalable successful products, which will be enjoyed by innumerable users and will bring an admirable return on investment. They equally understand the PR effect of a technological triumph and its remarkable reflection on the whole fund, or, in CVC case, the whole corporation.

Not unlike entrepreneurs, CVCs also understand the value of "cool tech for the sake of cool tech" - although not out of their sheer love of science and technology, but because that cool tech may benefit the corporation and enhance its products.

The unique motivation of CVCs, and the key to approaching them, is obviously their understanding of pitfalls and perils of disruptive innovation attempted within a framework of the corporation. The Innovator's Dilemma by Clayton Christensen is widely read in business schools and board rooms and depicts thoroughly how and why innovation within corporations is stifled by customers' and distributors' needs and motivations. Strategic value is what motivates CVC investments the most.

So, when approaching CVCs, the first step should obviously include research. Before you pitch a CVC, find out what are the corporation's strategic directions. A simple Google/LinkedIn/Twitter search should help. Find a way to talk with companies that the corporation has acquired, and, of course, with those in which its CVC unit has recently invested. This should give you a good sense of where their focus lies. Often, you would be surprised: corporations are sophisticated enough to search outside of their usual competitive advantage areas.

In many cases, CVCs would be interested not only in new technologies, but also in potential product/service line extensions, new business models, new markets and alternatives to their own products/services. Keep in mind that CVC motivations are defined by their reporting relationships within a corporation. Most CVCs report to the C-suite or to the Corporate Strategy/Development office. Some report directly to R&D or to Finance. In some industries (medical, pharmaceutical), and in some countries (Japan, South Korea) CVCs typically report to R&D.

It's important to understand these relationships in order to understand how to approach specific CVCs and what drives their searching, thinking and decision-making. Oh, and you can just ask them about it...

Approaching CVCs

Do not send your pitches to CVCs using online forms or online email addresses. With an even higher probability than at a private VC firm, these will end up in mail boxes of young associates and interns and will have rather slim chances for a serious consideration. Yes, these forms and email addresses are out there – but just don't waste time on them.

Find the right ways to talk with CVCs. It's not too complicated, although it does take a lot of time and effort.

Here is a quick list of ways to approach a CVC for entrepreneurs:

- Find and pitch CVCs at your industry events. They go there for a reason and that reason is – finding startups.

- Ask corporate workers that you meet to forward your pitch to their CVC units. They often meet the right people at corporate meetings and even cooperate with them on some internal projects. In most cases CVCs use company employees for screening deals and due diligence. Also the majority of CVCs won't invest unless a business unit within a corporation would "sponsor" the deal.
- Approach portfolio companies of a CVC (it's better if you actually meet them, but LinkedIn, AngelList and other networks also work), explain to them how and why you would be a great fit and ask them for an introduction. VCs love it when their successful entrepreneurs suggest new companies to them.
- Join online and offline groups, meetings, seminars, networks, conferences organized by a corporation whose CVC unit you want to pitch. Get involved. Help bring others. Pitch.
- Go through law firms representing CVCs in their deals. Investors listen to their lawyers.
- Other investors both VCs and angels are the leading source of a deal flow for CVCs. There is a greater risk adversity among CVCs than among traditional VCs or angels, so, they often prefer deals brought by other investors. Independent VCs are an especially valuable deal flow source for CVCs. Most CVCs do not invest alone, and many prefer not to be a lead investor. Ask investors that you know to connect you with the right CVC.
- If a journalist or a blogger has interviewed a CVC with whom you are looking to connect, ask the journalist for an introduction.

Last but not least: keep in mind that "search and empower" is only one of CVC modes while others whether you want it or not, are "search and copy" and even "search and destroy." Corporations are trying to identify not only what to bet on, but also innovation threats to their core business as early as possible and often their motivation is not in sync with those of startups and even of financial VCs. Plenty of horror stories are told about that by both investors (Fred Wilson of Union Square Ventures) and entrepreneurs (Charles Fergusson of Front Page) who have dealt with large corporations.

However, besides the obvious value of smart money, corporate VCs can provide startups with great sales and marketing channel access, help entrepreneurs with suppliers, customers, partners and even with engineering. Equally important, an analysis of CrunchBase shows that startups with CVC funding are three times more likely to be acquired than those with only private VC funding. In fact, almost every third CVC-funded company gets bought.

So the risk may be well worth it. After all, isn't entrepreneurship about risk-taking? @shoifot, @tmt_plc

HOW TO APPROACH A LARGE CORPORATE – THE DIFFERENCE FOR EUROPEAN VS US DOMICILED ENTREPRENEURS - FRÉDÉRIC ROMBAUT - FORMER MANAGING DIRECTOR & HEAD OF CORPORATE DEVELOPMENT INTERNATIONAL, CISCO SYSTEMS; FORMER FOUNDER & MANAGING DIRECTOR, QUALCOMM VENTURES EUROPE; FORMER APAX PARTNERS; COFOUNDER, BOUYGUES TELECOM; FOUNDER-IN-RESIDENCE, FOUNDERS FACTORY

Make no mistake, for a US-based entrepreneur, approaching a large tech corporate is relatively easy and possible joint go to market initiatives make them an obvious and ideal co-investor. For a European entrepreneur, located 5,500 miles away from the Silicon Valley, it's the exact opposite. Entrepreneurs are struggling to navigate the large corporates with their complex organizations and frequently changing strategies. They also struggle to communicate properly, because of the intercultural gap. I've spent a lot of time coaching entrepreneurs about how to make their pitch more effective and more straight to the point. The large corporates have little imagination during their interaction with entrepreneurs. Entrepreneurs must prepare in advance, be direct and explain clearly the value proposition, their differentiation, and what's in it for the corporate. The best technology, though, is rarely the best presented.

Lastly, VC funds are often reluctant to let the big corporates approach too closely, as they don't believe in, nor understand their value-add as an investor. It is fair to say that not all CVCs are able to keep their promise of adding value, but when they do, it is certainly one of the most powerful ways to accelerate the growth of a startup. Amusingly some VCs insist "never" [to take funding from a corporate], others say "always." I think the right decision must be based on a more rationale analysis and case by case basis.

One common mistake in dealing with a CVC is to believe it has a well-defined list of strategic goals, and that they have just to execute on that list by identifying investment or M&A targets. The reality is that there are many different forces at work within the corporate, and they are not necessarily aligned. For instance a CVC could very well be willing to invest and partner with a given startup, while Corporate R&D could be in a process to try to get a budget for a new, innovative and over-lapping project, whilst Engineering is late at developing its own alternative but trying to catch up. Strategic Partnership meanwhile is looking to partner with a more established and visible company. Sales might be trying to partner with another startup recommended by their customer. Corporate IP on its part could be licensing prudently with potential IP conflicts. Finance might well be pessimistic about the figures, and M&A busy conducting due diligence on your competitor. And at any time in the process, there may be an organizational change, with new leaders and changes in priorities. It is an art navigating this complexity in such a fast moving environment and that requires leadership, fast analytic skills and deep networking.

Note from Andrew Romans: Frédéric's contribution here highlights the need for what I call "back channeling." You can clearly see from Frédéric's description of the complexity of what reality looks like that to be effective in either raising CVC funding or getting your M&A transaction to the finish line one needs to have relationships in place where you can call someone on their mobile phone and get the truth of what's going on in this complex environment. Are you a stalking horse or are you on an actual path to get the funding or M&A outcome you seek? This requires back channeling. That requires relationships and a history of gives and gets doing favors for these people.

THE BEST WAY TO EMAIL A VC OR CVC WHEN SEEKING FUNDING – ANDREW ROMANS

Everyone will tell you the best way to approach a VC or angel is through a warm intro. Beyond the obvious, contacting their portfolio CEOs is a smart way to get the warm intro and do some DD on the VC to see if their existing CEOs like them. That said some of our CEOs are much harder for you to get through to than many busy VCs. If you ever get negative feedback ask the CEO if the VC funded their last round. The CEO may just be sore that the VC decided to hold back from putting good money in after bad or is waiting for the next key milestone breakthrough. That may be or not be the kind of investor you want in your syndicate. The key thing to understand is that VCs get a high volume of deal flow via email and they often have very little time to spend looking at email on a daily basis. VCs schedule a lot of pitch meetings and calls with founders and book their days and evenings with dinners and events. So when you send a VC your pitch via email I think it is critical to understand that the VC is most likely triaging deal flow email as if it's the emergency room tent in a war zone. The VC is trying to figure out as quickly as possible if this is an investment opportunity she should spend time on, forward to someone else on the team for more analysis or expert review or save the team time and pass on it quickly.

For me personally I hate it when the CEO sends a lot of information, but hides the company's stage. It is hard for me to review a long text cover email in big block paragraphs and a long slide deck and all the information I see appears to be about the vision of what the founder wants to do and I just can't for the life of me figure out what milestones have already been accomplished and understand this company's stage. Sometimes it is literally on page 42 where the founder mentions that the company is totally bootstrapped or has raised $10m from tier I VCs.

I like it when the entrepreneur tells me in bullet point format in the cover letter of the email a few key things such as:

- How they were referred to me (name of someone I might know that referred them to me, an event, TV, just found me on LinkedIn or read one of my books. It's all good, but it saves me time if I see that right at the top)
- Total funding to date, distinguished between non-founder outside capital and founder self-funding
- Any other investors I may have heard of including big name angels, VCs or corporates
- Current monthly and annual revenues
- Key milestones achieved and pending, showing the company's stage
- How much funding they seek to raise
- Where they are in the process of raising that funding
- Location of the HQ and team members

This is what I want to see before reviewing twenty slides of vision and pitch. It may be too much to ask for, but if the founder hides this info deep in the presentation or keeps it a secret I end up flipping through slides very quickly trying to find this information, checking Crunchbase and other online databases to determine the company's stage and whether it is remotely a fit with our investment strategy. If I get my key questions answered up front I can calmly go through the slides and natural flow of problem, solution, vision, pitch, etc.

When I see a really bad pitch I email the founder back and pass on the deal so that it does not take up more time from our team. A founder should never email more than one person at the same venture team. That's making more work for us. If the founder is really good at raising capital then it is less likely the company will run out of cash – the number one cause of death for startups. If I spend a few minutes trying to figure out the company's stage and can't find it, but it was sent by someone I know, I forward it to an Associate on our team to review and either bring back to one of the other members on our team or email the entrepreneur that we are a pass. Processing a high volume of deal flow is a real life challenge for every good VC. If you require additional time for the VC to find out the minimum amount of information they want to know you are making your case worse. Some entrepreneurs email me saying they will only share the deck in an in-person meeting. That does not give me enough information to know whether I want to take a meeting. Saying no to a meeting or conference call gives me more time to triage email. So I am keen to say no. Asking for a meeting and saying you will only present the deck in person and not share it up front is an automatic pass from me. You just made my day easy with more time for email.

When an entrepreneur asks me to sign a Non-Disclosure Agreement (NDA) before giving me any decent information to form the decision to take a meeting or not, I decline right away and advise them to stop asking for NDAs from VCs. I would not mind signing the NDA if I had more time, but it slows me down from triaging other deal flow and makes it harder for me to later raise capital for that startup from other VCs when I know they will send my fellow VCs the NDA and most VCs have a policy of not signing NDAs or don't want the torture of killing time with the NDA. I think it's good to get right to the point.

Eight

Corporate Venturing By the Numbers – Anand Sanwal & Jonathan Sherry, cofounders of CB Insights

"Success breeds complacency. Complacency breeds failure. Only the paranoid survive."

- ANDY GROVE

"Seek truth from facts" first appeared in the *Book of Han* and was later made famous when quoted by Mao Zedong and later Deng Xiaoping. Here in this book, we go direct to the source of the activity and provide insights from the key practitioners. This chapter lets the facts speak for themselves. Anand Sanwal and Jonathan Sherry at CB Insights were cool enough to share their quantitative research and league tables for you to understand corporate venturing by the data and facts.

More info at www.cbinsights.com.

The ` doubled from Q3'12 to Q3'15. A record 185 corporate VC firms completed an investment in Q3'15, representing a 31% year-on-year increase and a jump of 97% from the 94 firms making an investment in Q3'12.

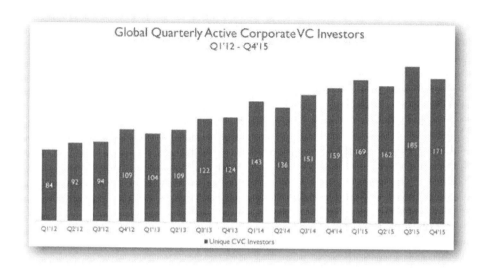

In 2015, 126 unique CVC arms participated in at least one seed VC round worldwide. That represents a fourfold increase from the 30 corporate VCs who completed such deals in 2011.

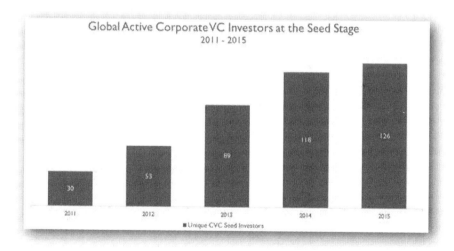

85 new corporate VC units globally made their first in investment in 2015, including notable names such as Twitter Ventures and Workday Ventures. This continues a steadily upward march in new participants since 2010.

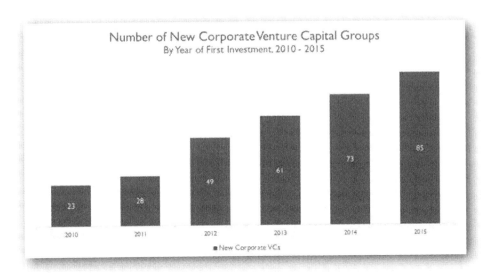

Number of New Corporate Venture Capital Groups
By Year of First Investment. 2010 - 2015

The most active corporate venture capital groups. Intel Capital led all CVCs in global activity, investing in more than 75 companies, roughly 18% more than second-place GV (Google Ventures). They have been aggressively investing abroad, with about 32% of their 2015 investments made in companies outside the US.

Rank	CVC Investor	Recent* New Investments			
1	intel capital	DataRobot	savioke	chargifi	LISNR
2	GV	ARMO BIOSCIENCES	pindrop	toast	UDACITY
3	QUALCOMM VENTURES	Housejoy	MindTickle	ATTUNE	CLOUDFLARE
4	salesforce ventures	bloomreach	FinanceFox	MapAnything	CARTODB
5	GE VENTURES	APX	Omni-ID	MORPHISEC	omada

2015 Most Active CVCs (by # of unique global company investments)

*Includes investments in 2016 YTD. Note Rubicon Venture Capital co-invested with Intel Capita into LISNR.

2015 saw corporate VC investors participate in $28.4bn of funding across 1,301 deals, topping 2014's record numbers. However, as overall venture activity slowed in Q4'15, corporates pulled back as well, with deal activity dropping to its lowest level since Q1'14.

North American startups took over half of the deals with CVC participation in each of the five quarters analyzed. However, North American deal share steadily dropped throughout 2015, with no. 2 Asia and no. 3 Europe both seeing upticks in deal share.

Note that some of these charts are difficult to understand in black and white. Please find a color version of this entire chapter here for download: http://www.slideshare.net/andrewromans.

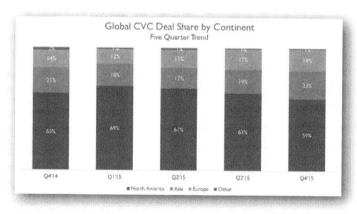

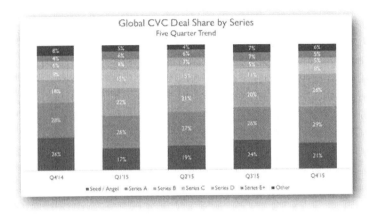

Q1'15 represented a 5-quarter low for early-stage (seed/Series A) CVC activity, with deals dropping to 43% while Series D+ rose to 14% of the total. However, by Q4'15 late-stage deals had pulled back to 10% of CVC deals, while early-stage deals rebounded to 50%.

Despite fluctuations in absolute share, the internet sector remained the top recipient of global CVC deals, taking 48% of them in Q4'15. Deal share to mobile & telecom startups topped the share for healthcare in 4 out of the past 5 quarters.

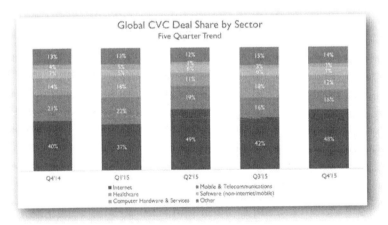

Beyond dedicated venture arms, corporations themselves are also funneling dollars directly to VC-backed startups. Led in activity by Chinese heavyweights like Tencent and Alibaba, corporates participated in 668 deals that represented $26.9bn of funding in 2015*.

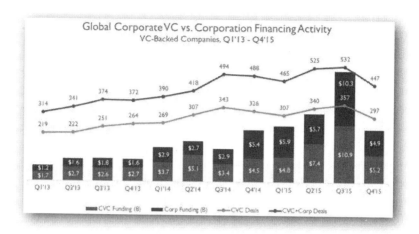

The most active corporate venture capital groups investing in the US. With a US-centric portfolio, GV traded places with global leader Intel Capital to claim the top spot here. Salesforce also swapped places with Qualcomm Ventures to place third.

2015 Most Active CVCs (by # of unique US company investments)

Rank	CVC Investor	Rank	CVC Investor
1	GV	6	GE VENTURES
2	intel capital	7	Bloomberg BETA
3	salesforce ventures	7	F·PRIME
4	QUALCOMM VENTURES	9	SAMSUNG VENTURE INVESTMENT
5	COMCAST VENTURES.	10	cisco Cisco Investments

Country Recaps: UK, China and India

CVCs took part in $1.7bn of investment across 41 deals to UK-based private companies in 2015, representing a sharp rise from 2011 (22 deals and $203M). Some of the year's largest deals include July's $460m Series H to O3B Networks and a $320m financing to Immunocore.

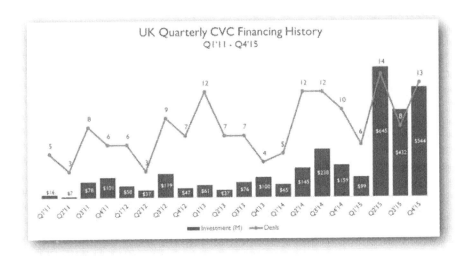

Corporate venture units participated in $6.2bn of financings across 66 deals in China, rising from just $910m and 57 deals in 2014. CVCs were prominent in megadeals, including an $850m Series E to Dianping in April and a $2bn Series F to Didi Kuaidi in July.

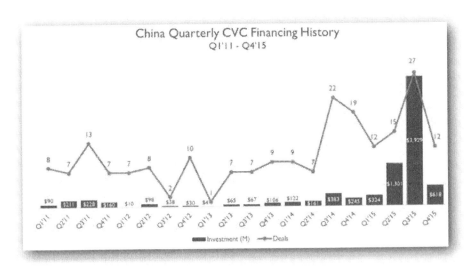

CVC activity receded in India in 2015, down from $443m and 29 deals in 2014 to $421m across 24 deals. Q3'15 was a strong quarter, with 10 deals, but funding was driven by a $100m round to home furnisher Pepperfry and a $90m round to doctor search portal Practo.

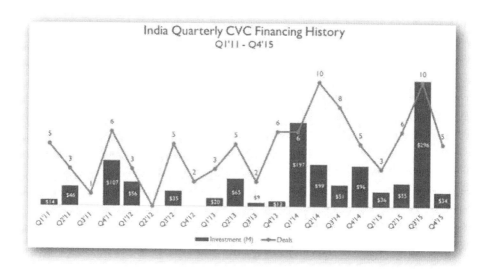

Qualcomm has been actively sourcing investments from outside the US, ranking in the top 5 investors in each of these markets since 2011. Intel was the most active in both China and India, while Bertelsmann's investment arms also make appearances.

Most Active CVCs in the UK 2011-2015		Most Active CVCs in China 2011-2015		Most Active CVCs in India 2011-2015	
Rank	CVC Investor	Rank	CVC Investor	Rank	CVC Investor
1	QUALCOMM VENTURES	1	intel capital	1	intel capital
2	SR·one	2	LEGEND CAPITAL 君联资本	2	QUALCOMM VENTURES
2	INGENIOUS VENTURES	3	BAI Bertelsmann Asia Investments 贝塔斯曼亚洲投资基金	3	BII Bertelsmann India Investments
4	Johnson-Johnson INNOVATION	4	QUALCOMM VENTURES	3	CISCO Cisco Investments
4	Unilever	5			

Corporate VCs participated in 806 deals representing $17.4 bn of funding to US-based companies in 2015. Funding dollars rose 33% in the year, but deal growth nearly flat-lined at just 2%. The Q4'15 year-end slowdown saw the fewest CVC-backed deals since Q4'13.

California takes over half of US CVC deals in 2015. Aside from a Q1'15 dip to below 50% share, the Golden State continued to dominate US CVC deal activity, securing 51% of US deals with CVC involvement in 2015 overall. New York edged out Massachusetts by a single deal to secure second place for the year.

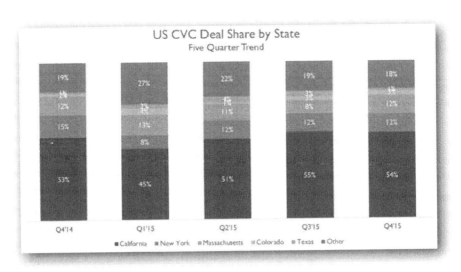

Series B activity only made up 17% of US CVC deals in Q4'14, but grew to 28% in Q4'15. Mid- stage (Series B and C) took a 38% share in that quarter. Apart from a peak in Q3'15, seed/angel activity took under 20% of deals done by CVC arms in the US in 2015.

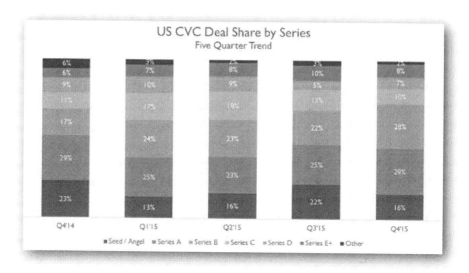

How does corporate venture capital measure up to the greater VC ecosystem?

CVCs participate in a fifth of all VC deals in 2015. Corporate venture firms participated in 19.3% of the 6,743 venture-backed financing rounds in 2015, compared to a participation rate of just 16.5% in 2013.

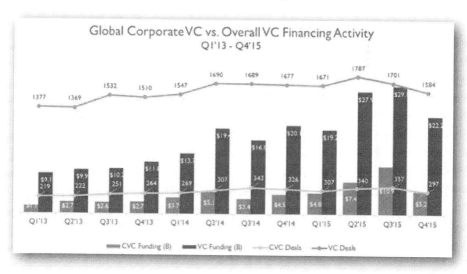

On a quarterly basis, CVC deal share topped out at 21% in Q3'15, which was the frothy peak for VC funding overall.

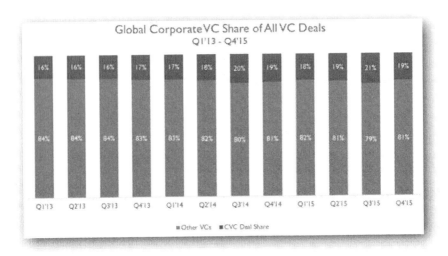

CVC deal sizes continue to outpace VC overall. Average deal size with CVC participation has topped $21m+ for 3 consecutive quarters, including a Q3'15 spike bolstered by monster deals to Didi Kuaidi and SoFi (among others).

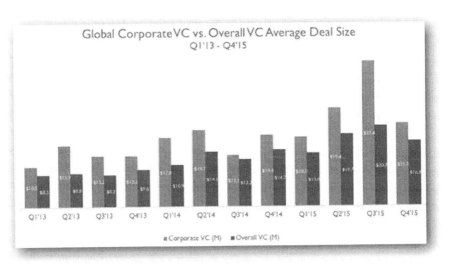

The average size of deals with CVC participation was larger than overall US VC deals, mirroring the global pattern. The average size of deals with CVC investors stayed under $16m throughout 2013, but was above $21m in final 3 quarters of 2015.

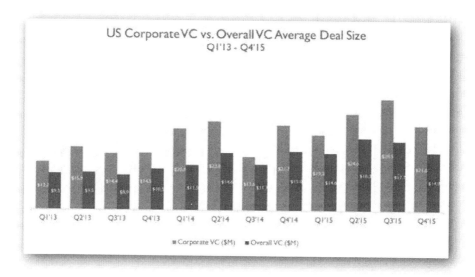

Since 2011, Kleiner Perkins, NEA, and Andreesen Horowitz have completed the most deals alongside a corporate venture arm.

Rank	Investor	Rank	Investor
1	Kleiner Perkins Caufield & Byers	11	True Ventures
2	New Enterprise Associates	12	Venrock
3	Andreessen Horowitz	13	Greylock Partners
4	SV Angel	13	Bessemer Venture Partners
5	First Round Capital	15	Sequoia Capital
6	500 Startups	16	DCM Ventures
7	Accel Partners	16	RRE Ventures
8	Atlas Venture*	18	OrbiMed Advisors
9	Draper Fisher Jurvetson	19	Norwest Venture Partners
9	Khosla Ventures	20	US Venture Partners

Top 20 VC Firms With Most Global CVC-Syndicated Deals 2011-2015

Intel Capital ranked first by number of tech exits for the third straight year. It had more than double the exits of second-place GV.

Top CVCs By Number of Global Tech Exits in 2015	
Rank	**CVC Investor**
1	(intel) capital
2	G/
3	QUALCOMM VENTURES
4	salesforce ventures
5	CISCO Cisco Investments

Comparing select tech CVCs

CVC Investor	Typical Number of Deals Per Year	Median Deal Size	Most Frequent Stage
(intel) capital	80-90	$12M	Series B
G/	70-90	$6M	Seed / Angel
QUALCOMM VENTURES	50-70	$10M	Series A
salesforce ventures	30-50	$8M	Series A
CISCO Cisco Investments	20-30	$15M	Series B / C

Comparing select healthcare CVCs

CVC Investor	Typical Number of Deals Per Year	Median Deal Size	Most Frequent Stage
venture funds	10-20	$20M	Series A / B
SR·one	10-20	$21M	Series A
Pfizer	1-10	$21M	Series A
LILLYVENTURES	1-10	$15M	Series A
Global Health Innovation	1-10	$10M	Series B

Comparing select media CVCs

CVC Investor	Typical Number of Deals Per Year	Median Deal Size	Most Frequent Stage
COMCAST VENTURES	20-30	$12M	Series B
BDMI	10-20	$4M	Seed / Angel
HEARST ventures	5-15	$14M	Series B
TimeWarner INVESTMENTS	1-10	$11M	Series B / C
axel springer digital ventures	1-10	$6M	Series C

Comparing select telecom CVCs

CVC Investor	Typical Number of Deals Per Year	Median Deal Size	Most Frequent Stage
T Venture	5-15	$10M	Series A
Verizon Ventures	5-15	$6M	Series A
innov8	5-10	$8M	Series A / B
Telefónica Ventures	1-10	$13M	Seed / Angel
TELUS	1-10	$9M	Series B

Comparing select fintech CVCs

CVC Investor	Typical Number of Deals Per Year	Median Deal Size	Most Frequent Stage
citi VENTURES	5-15	$21M	Series B
VENTURES	1-10	$15M	Series B
AXA Strategic Ventures	1-10	$2M	Seed / Angel
MassMutual VENTURES	1-10	$9M	Series A

100 Most Active Corporate Venture Capital Firms of 2015 (global)

100 Most Active CVCs of 2015 (by # of unique global company investments)			
1 - 25	**26 - 50**	**51 - 75**	**76 - 100**
Intel Capital	Alexa Fund	Bertelsmann Asia Investments	Unilever Ventures
Google Ventures	Citi Ventures	ITOCHU Technology Ventures	Swisscom Ventures
Qualcomm Ventures	Siemens Venture Capital	MS Ventures	Boxer Capital
Salesforce Ventures	Ping An Ventures	Mitsubishi UFJ Capital	WuXi Venture Fund
GE Ventures	DG Incubation	EMC Ventures	Presidio Ventures
Comcast Ventures	YJ Capital	Sanofi-Genzyme BioVentures	Reed Elsevier Ventures
Samsung Ventures	SMBC Venture Capital	Kaiser Permanente Ventures	Shea Ventures
F-Prime Capital	Lilly Ventures	Technicolor Ventures	Motorola Solutions Venture Capital
Bloomberg Beta	Mitsui & Co. Global Investment	Kickstart Ventures	3M New Ventures
Cisco Investments	Merck Global Health Innovation Fund	Axista Digital Innovation Fund	Nissay Capital
SR One	TIM Ventures	Zaffre Investments	CAA Ventures
Legend Capital	Roche Venture Fund	Investor Growth Capital	West Tech Ventures
Novartis Venture Funds	Robert Bosch Venture Capital	MassMutual Ventures	Time Warner Investments
GREE Ventures	Fosun Kinzon Capital	Deutsche Telekom Strategic Investments	Evonik Venture Capital
Recruit Strategic Partners	Eircom Digital Boost Initiative	McKesson Ventures	Santander InnoVentures
Bertelsmann Digital Media Investments	AXA Strategic Ventures	Ascension Ventures	Broadway Video Ventures
Verizon Ventures	American Express Ventures	Hewlett-Packard Ventures	STC Ventures
Hearst Ventures	Dentsu Digital Holdings	Baxter Ventures	Autodesk Spark Innovation Fund
Novo Ventures	Tengelmann Ventures	Monsanto Growth Ventures	Caixa Capital
Google Capital	Rakuten Ventures	Simon Venture Group	B2rive Ventures
Johnson & Johnson Innovation	BioMed Ventures	Advance Vixeid Partners	CHV Capital
CyberAgent Ventures	Takeda Ventures	Syngenta Ventures	Vorwerk Direct Selling Ventures
Pfizer Venture Investments	SingTel Innov8	NTT DoCoMo Ventures	Lazarus Israel Opportunity Fund
Renren Lianhe Holdings	BlueCross BlueShield Venture Partners	Transamerica Ventures	Infosys Innovation Fund
In-Q-Tel	Orange Digital Ventures	UPS Strategic Enterprise Fund	Telstra Ventures

100 Most Active Corporate Venture Capital Firms of 2015 (US)

100 Most Active CVCs of 2015 (by # of unique US company investments)			
1 - 25	**26 - 50**	**51 - 75**	**76 - 100**
Google Ventures	Alexa Fund	Takeda Ventures	Rakuten Ventures
Intel Capital	Renren Lianhe Holdings	DG Incubation	Axel Springer Digital Ventures
Salesforce Ventures	Johnson & Johnson Innovation	Time Warner Investments	Twitter Ventures
Qualcomm Ventures	Mitsui & Co. Global Investment	Presidio Ventures	Cornerstone Innovation Fund
Comcast Ventures	AXA Strategic Ventures	CAA Ventures	Wipro Ventures
GE Ventures	BlueCross BlueShield Venture Partners	GREE Ventures	GM Ventures
Bloomberg Beta	Roche Venture Fund	Dentsu Ventures	E.ON Venture Partners
F-Prime Capital	Simon Venture Group	MRL Ventures	Boxer Capital
Samsung Ventures	Sanofi-Genzyme BioVentures	Transamerica Ventures	Baidu Innovation Fund
Cisco Investments	Technicolor Ventures	CME Ventures	Santander InnoVentures
Novartis Venture Funds	Advance Vixeid Partners	Fosun Kinzon Capital	Motorola Solutions Venture Capital
SR One	American Express Ventures	SingTel Innov8	NTT DoCoMo Ventures
Bertelsmann Digital Media Investments	UPS Strategic Enterprise Fund	Robert Bosch Venture Capital	Biella Venture Partners
Verizon Ventures	Investor Growth Capital	Syngenta Ventures	Microsoft Ventures
Hearst Ventures	Ascension Ventures	MedImmune Ventures	Wells Fargo Startup Accelerator
Citi Ventures	Kaiser Permanente Ventures	Autodesk Spark Innovation Fund	Crawley Ventures
Google Capital	McKesson Ventures	Monsanto Growth Ventures	WME Ventures
Novo Ventures	MassMutual Ventures	Amgen Ventures	Ping An Ventures
Pfizer Venture Investments	Zaffre Investments	Brace Pharma Capital	Constellation Technology Ventures
In-Q-Tel	Broadway Video Ventures	CHV Capital	Reed Elsevier Ventures
Merck Global Health Innovation Fund	Baxter Ventures	Fletcher Spaght Ventures	3M New Ventures
Lilly Ventures	Hewlett-Packard Ventures	Workday Ventures	Gibraltar Ventures
Recruit Strategic Partners	WuXi Venture Fund	Rex Health Ventures	Orfin Ventures
Siemens Venture Capital	Shea Ventures	Capital One Ventures	Tyco Ventures
BioMed Ventures	Orange Digital Ventures	Dell Ventures	ICG Ventures

The Future of CVC – Recommendations and Conclusions for the Best Corporate Venturing Programs

"I think that my leadership style is to get people to fear staying in place, to fear not changing."

- Louis V. Gerstner, Jr.

I started this book with this quote from The Rolling Stones.

"You can't always get what you want
    But if you try sometimes,
        well you might find…
            You get what you need."

One can study corporate venturing, learn from the successes and mistakes and come up with an optimal strategy. In the end, however, the political environment or corporate culture may not allow this optimal strategy to become a reality. Getting some CVC program going is better than nothing at all and one must respect what is possible or realistic and what is not. Maybe it's just what you need, after all.

Each corporate should tailor its own strategy, but I think all would benefit from some of the same things. First, draw up a list of key objectives, why you are creating a CVC and what you hope to achieve. For example, is it more important to use CVC as a tool to feed your M&A group and generate multi-billion dollar revenue streams, or is it more important to bring outside innovation into your internal product development? Chapter 1 of this book has a comprehensive list of reasons to operate a CVC. I advise all corporates to write down their own list and prioritize these goals and objectives. Then all other decisions on how to structure the CVC can flow from there. Get your list approved by the CEO and board of directors so you have top level buy-in from the start and this list will enable you to defend all of your remaining decisions on how to structure and operate the CVC.

Draft a list of your corporate assets that can be leveraged to add value to startups and complement the value to the startups from the financial VCs. Microsoft and IBM are unique examples of companies that have tons of technology they can offer to startups for free or at cost ranging from software to cloud computing services that compete with AWS. They also have customers in all corners of the globe ranging from small to huge – commercial to government – that they can introduce to startups. Every corporate has its own unique set of value adds they can bring to startups beyond dollars to invest. Make a list of what you can bring to the table and incorporate that into your strategy. This is right in line with taking an audit of your unique resources and capabilities, comparing that with your competitors and setting strategy in this context. CVC strategy should be the same.

The next step is to get true allocation for a specific amount of capital for the program. In an ideal world this would be set for at least ten years, but in the world of corporates living quarter to quarter that is unlikely. I think you should fight for a 10-year vehicle, but expect you may need to compromise to get going. I would suggest most corporates consider a budget of $25m to $100m per year for at least the next three to five years, but they should in fact be thinking fifty years and CVC should be a profit center generating earnings within ten years and act as an evergreen self-sustaining program. When done properly it should never be canceled.

It's hard to give this as advice, but try to get the CEO and CFO super fired up that this is the right thing to do and, like Intel, CVC will remain a pillar of the company's strategy forever. Try to get the most powerful people in the organization personally involved and secure a long-term twenty-year commitment to CVC for all the reasons in Chapter 1 of this book. Do not dock the CVC program in one business unit like R&D. Establish a committee of business unit (BU) heads across the entire company and find a way to involve them. CVC is pointless if there is no transfer of knowhow from the startups to the BUs and pointless again if the BUs are not doing anything to help the startups. People involved with the launch or ongoing management of a CVC beyond the CEO and CFO often include the head of corporate development and head of strategy. Again, each corporate needs to tailor their unique CVC strategy, but to the outside world at least pretend that corp dev is very separate from CVC. I believe corp dev and CVC are both full time jobs. Trying to do one of them part time will not get the same good results of allowing one person to focus on one of these only and manage separate and focused teams.

Consider a calendar of events or other ways to formalize interaction among the heads of many BUs and the CVC. I think it is of particular interest to keep high connectivity between the CVC and the head of HR. I would recommend semi-annual events with heads of every BU. Stage beauty contests where you have demo days of the existing portfolio companies and suggest a few prospective investments to create this interaction. This will generate internal deal flow from the BUs to the CVC, as well as foster partnerships between the BUs and innovative startups.

Success in business all comes down to execution and execution all comes down to the competence and teamwork of the individual people. It's all about the right people. The CVC should have a mix of veteran VCs and inside corporate employees that have strong mojo and internal networks within the corporate to get things done. The head of corporate development along with the head of strategy teamed up with a team of senior and junior outside financial VCs could be the dream team. Another way of considering the dream team would be one internal person that was the right hand man of the CEO and has huge influence over the CEO combined with a very successful outside financial VC. Then staff the team from there. In my view you must hire a financial VC from the outside that has the complex skills, relationships with other VCs, lawyers and other ecosystem networks and deal flow. Pure internal teams fail for many reasons. The challenge here is most successful financial VCs will not leave a thriving 2&20 VC practice to become an employee of a large corporate lowering their compensation and freedom to operate. This is a dilemma. Good luck recruiting the good ones and not the bad ones! I'd add that it's important to have some folks on the team that enjoy going to three networking events per night and really get out there. That often translates to a few young folks on the team.

Compensation issues have historically been one of the reasons CVCs fail, perform poorly or are simply viewed negatively by many entrepreneurs. Poor compensation prevents CVC teams from working together long enough to establish subliminal communication and learning how to work together. Most CVCs earn less than financial VCs and so many CVCs are job-hunting from their first day as a corporate VC. One of the main criteria for investing in a financial VC is how long the GPs have known each other and how loyal they will remain to each other. Each fund is viewed as a ten-year vehicle and it may be the following fund or next fund following that one that will truly deliver breakaway out-sized returns. The best VC teams stay together for twenty to thirty years. The average duration for an individual CVC's stay at a CVC is very short, and the average duration of a CVC itself before being discontinued only recently increased to five years.

I believe that the CVC investment professionals should share in some form of financial upside with the good outcome of their entire portfolio and should be punished for failure. I would not advocate deal-by-deal carry but fund wide carry. This is simple enough to do for CVCs even if they invest off the balance sheet. I also think these professionals should have part of their bonus tied to strategic value, which is harder to measure, but some effort should be made for both. If your CVC team makes less money working at the CVC than at a financial VC then you should expect the good ones to leave and the bad ones to stay. So bite the bullet and pay them enough to stop them from leaving and have the guts to fire the bad ones. I also think that corporates should reward employees throughout the organization for good collaboration with the CVC and portfolio companies. Provide a financial incentive to middle managers throughout the organization tacking on something to their bonus for a successful partnership with portfolio companies and encourage the entire company to support the CVC which will lead your company to become more innovative and dynamic like an Apple, which I believe has always behaved like one big internal VC fund.

These key issues can be largely fixed via compensation. The obvious goal is that these CVCs should be of equal quality to the financial VCs. They are not, in general, the same quality today. This should change. You get what you pay for.

I recommend that the CVC practice begin by investing into financial VC funds as the first step. It makes sense to launch a Fund of Funds (FoF) investment program to immediately achieve your Chapter 1 goals, learn how venture capital works and to access highly filtered deal flow for direct investing via your CVC brand. It is important that your first few investments are good ones and that you get up and running with a respectable investment pace. Founders and other VCs rank you by the quality of the deals you have invested in and they pay attention to your investment pace. When founders see that you invested in Facebook, Google, SalesForce, Twitter, etc. they view you as hot and they want to be funded by you. If they see you made three investments in your first year that were super strategic, but not of interest to founders and VCs, your direct deal flow pipeline is likely to suffer. Three in one year sends a signal that you are NOT active. Why should a founder or VC take the time to meet with you and show you a deal if their mathematical probability of getting funded by you is 365 days divided by 3 new investments? Many CVCs fail to get deals done in the first year and founders don't want to waste time meeting a CVC that has a reputation for being slow. One tip is to use an outside law firm for the first year to get the right advice and not rely on your in-house legal counsel that may slow things down in your first critical year. Dividends in a term sheet mean something completely different than what your internal legal team may understand. Go with a law firm that is very active doing corporate securities work for venture financings. After a year you can bring this in-house once your in-house counsel is up to speed and can move quickly to get deals done.

Review deal flow from these financial VCs in which you have invested, learn the sophisticated skill set for VC and begin to invest directly into some of these companies where your corporate can do business with the startup and this will launch your CVC brand. Over time increase the direct investment pace. This will build a strong brand and a successful and sustainable CVC practice. There is a lot of talk about strategic vs financial goals when investing. All investments should pass the test of looking very financially successful at the time you invest and no investment should be made that does not appear to be strategic within the investment framework set for the CVC. At Rubicon, if we can't add value we don't invest. The same should be true for you. Every investment should meet the test of "gives and gets" as well as financial.

Consider investing in one VC fund where your corporate owns 25% to 50% of the fund to have a major position in that fund, but the fund can operate independently, providing your corporate with access to deals that would never accept funding from a CVC run by your corporate. Telefónica Ventures recently seeded a new fund with $200m as the only investor, but open to that fund raising another $200m from non-Telefónica LPs.

Try to get these VCs you invest in to accept an executive from your corporate on loan for one year periods to get more optics, transfer innovation and knowhow from the startups and learn the VC skill set. Eventually rotate employees between the corporate, the financial VCs and your CVC group. Opportunities will present themselves to invest in early stage companies via the FoF investments and close relationships with those GPs providing cautious guidance. All of these VCs have legacy portfolio companies and some should be good candidates to do business with your corporate and take direct investment from your CVC. FoF enables you to hit the ground roaring at 100 MPH and avoid much of the learning curve of mistakes. Imagine investing in 5 VCs and each has an existing legacy portfolio of at least 20 operating companies. That gives you a set of over 100 funded startups to track where you should have inside information and access. Now you are an insider.

When advising a corporate recently, I advised them to establish a $100m budget per year for a Fund of Funds (FoF) investment program and invest into five VC funds in the San Francisco / Silicon Valley, two VC funds in New York, two in China, one in London and one in Tel Aviv. List key technologies and topics you wish to invest in and make sure these financial VCs have good coverage of those topics. Get in writing from the general partners of the VC fund how information will be shared with your corporate. Take a ten-year plus long-term view and commit not to cancel the budget for the CVC for at least ten years by which time it should be profitable and self-sustaining.

The FoF investments should begin to return capital over a two to five year period and should be understood to be a profit center making the program financially sustainable. FoF is the best way to access high quality deal flow, convince CEOs to take investment directly from your CVC and develop the complex VC skill set on a deal-by-deal basis for your direct investing program. Most leading CVCs started with FoF: Cisco, Verizon, Teléfonica, SAP, Novell and many others.

FoF is a mature business. You will need advice on FoF portfolio construction and investment pace. When getting into the top VC funds you must demonstrate a twenty-year commitment. GPs want LPs that will re-up and invest in their next three to four funds at a minimum. Showing a one-year budget will scare off the best VCs.

I think it's OK to plan on two years of pure FoF investing and then shift into direct investing, but hopefully you will find financially sound strategic investments earlier.

Many CVCs make the mistake of investing into later stage startups that are backed by tier I VCs, have already achieved solid product market fit, are able to scale globally and leverage your business units to achieve global scale. These later stage companies are theoretically a few years closer to an exit compared to seed deals. If you feel obligated to put points on the board for the longevity of your program, investing in 100%

seed stage deals puts you at a disadvantage. Many adopt a bar bell strategy with a mix of later stage and early stage investments to balance the timeline of cash returns from exits. Seed stage investing will produce more startup failures. Keep in mind, the cost of failure at a CVC can be high depending on the culture.

In recent years CVCs have launched accelerators and / or started making seed investments. Some like SalesForce Ventures have been very successful with this strategy. Investing in the later stage deals attaches your name to some big name successes; by contrast, investing in early stage companies separates you from the negative view the industry has of CVCs as only investing in late stage. Both have their merits. I advise not to let this core part of the business be an accident. Establish a well thought out portfolio construction strategy that clearly states how many investments you will make, over what period of time, with a specified amount of capital. Be clear on the stage and range of check size and be clear on your follow on investment strategy, target ownership percentage for each startup and number of companies and total investments per year or three-year cycle.

All of these decisions should be made with consideration of your list of goals and objectives. Do you want to spread the smallest check possible into the widest set of startups like the original SalesForce Ventures did; or do you want to operate like Rubicon pushing most of the fund dollars into the winners of a wide portfolio and make as much money as possible? SaleForce Ventures today is writing huge checks into later stage deals alongside Fidelity. That works for them, but my advice again is to tie all decisions to your list of goals.

I think the best for most new CVCs is a mix of these two strategies. Get into enough deals to access the strategic information and goals, but double down making larger investments when the financial gain is clear to make the program self-sustaining and profitable. Especially when your corporate is delivering rapid revenue growth for the startup and you know you can make a lot of money quickly, why would you not?

Some CVCs being formed these days are set up very much like financial VCs. Many VCs invest with a rule that each investment needs to have the potential to return at least 25% or 33% or 100% of their fund. For most CVCs investing off the balance sheet, I do not think they need to operate this way. I advise accepting smaller ownership percentages to access the best deals and innovation, learn quickly from financial VCs why these are good investment opportunities and establish a reputation of getting into the most competitive deals. If you insist on large ownership percentages you will fail to get into the most competitive deals or you will be forced to lead deals before you are ready.

I think most CVCs make the mistake of investing in VC funds or direct investments into startups tied too closely to their perceived core and peripheral businesses. Innovation and disruption have happened and will happen in places and ways no one can predict and so the sector focus should be opened more broadly than your CEO thinks it should. If you are a telecom company and think you should only invest in telecom startups you are wrong. Look at Verizon buying Yahoo!'s internet assets. Maybe Verizon Ventures should have been investing in an internet portfolio all along? Many CVCs get a shopping list from their CEO on which sectors and topics to invest in. I view this as a mistake.

The most effective crystal ball belongs to the VC with the best deal flow and network to evaluate it. Clearly Microsoft knew that ubiquitous Internet with faster edge speeds of the fixed and mobile web would threaten their monopoly of PC operating systems and Microsoft Office applications as well as their position in the enterprise server market; so for Microsoft CVC, investing into anything connected to the internet made sense. Look at their acquisition of LinkedIn. Would investing in Reid Hoffman's LinkedIn been on their narrowly defined shopping list? For a large taxi company it was less obvious that they would be radically disrupted by Uber on smartphones. Blockbuster knew everything about video streaming via set top boxes and web streaming yet failed to react to Netflix quickly enough and went bankrupt. The automotive industry is aware that driverless connected cars and new models of ride sharing will change the types of cars people want to drive or ride in, who will purchase them and who will service them. Everything will change inside, outside and all around the automobile. Your industry may be less obvious than automotive, but I can say CVC is a must have to protect from disruption for every large business. For most corporates I can say with 100% certainty that your core and peripheral businesses will transform with significant change and no one can predict what that change will be. CVC is about offense and defense. Therefore I advise to make a "shopping list", but open it up radically.

It is good to have some areas of focus, but no restrictions. Internal innovation is full of restrictions. Don't go and limit your CVC program, which is designed to find innovation outside of the company. A focus on transformational companies will bring you more than following a strict shopping list. The conclusion from this analysis is to maintain a sector agnostic investment approach that adopts investment themes to focus the team on an annual basis. Each year have an off-site meeting with the CVC and Executive Committee to adopt core investment themes for the year. Build your shopping list around these themes. Plan to invest at least 25% of your fund dollars outside of your shopping list or investment themes.

Many CVCs have an Executive Committee that needs to approve any investment. Sometimes the CVC has the freedom to make investments below a certain size without the approval of the Executive Committee and other times they need it. The obvious disadvantage of an Executive Committee is that it slows down and in some cases paralyzes the CVC from getting deals done. By the time the Executive Committee approves a deal the startup may have completed the round or been sold and the CVC missed out. Word gets out about this and I think all CVCs suffer from this view that CVCs are too slow and therefore a waste of time to meet with at all. There is however an advantage to having an Executive Committee populated by important execs like the CEO, CFO, Head of Strategy, Head of R&D, Head of Product, Head of Sales, etc. After the deal is done and the CVC team is struggling to get the head of a BU to do business with the startup, they can point to the fact that this has the support of these important people and the BU middle manager should stop fearing damage to her or his career and take a risk and do business with the startup. I once advised a large corporate to form a five person Executive Committee for their CVC and have that committee report to the CEO. I advised in this specific case to populate the Executive Committee with the CFO, Head of Strategy, Head of R&D, Head of Sales and an outside board member that is an experienced VC. Head of Corporate Development and Head of HR are also good candidates, but in many cases corp dev may be purposely kept far away from the CVC or it may be the same person. I like to keep them separate. Of course, if the CEO is interested, truly available and responsive, she or he would make a great addition to the Executive Committee.

Sometimes it makes sense to put dollar values on the decision making process. For example a CVC might choose to allow the CVC team to make investments under $2m quickly without any Executive Committee oversight. Investments between $2m and $20m require approval of the Executive Committee. Investments above $20m require approval of the corporate development team. I'm just throwing out some numbers here. All of this needs to be tailored to the unique corporate and its goals.

After a few years when the CVC becomes more fluent in getting deals done, the CEO and CFO should start to trust the team more and approve deals without taking the time to look at these relatively very small check sizes and partnerships between the corporate and the portfolio of start-ups, it is best to terminate the Executive Committee and give the CVC full autonomy to make decisions and get deals done at its own pace within its annual or 10-year investment budget. GV (Google Ventures) has a one person Executive Committee – Bill Maris. He is the CEO of GV and makes the final call for each investment. A GV partner must lead the deal and get the support of Mr. Maris. That's it.

Most CVCs face the question of where to locate their physical CVC team. Here are the main options for most.

1) One office in Silicon Valley
2) Offices in Silicon Valley, New York, London, Tel Aviv and China
3) More global with additional offices in Mumbai, Sao Paolo, Paris, Berlin, Moscow and more.

The map of Silicon Valley is changing. Just like the startup scene in Germany moved from Munich to Berlin and the startup scene in London moved from Mayfair to Shoreditch, here many startups have been moving north from Silicon Valley into San Francisco. Today San Francisco is officially part of the Silicon Valley. You can't expect a founder to borrow a car to drive down from SF to meet a VC on Sand Hill Road in Menlo Park for a late seed round. You can expect them to do that when they are seeking their $10m Series A, but the VC that's in SF and Palo Alto will meet more founders. I think the ideal is to have an office in SF and one in Palo Alto if you want the best coverage of the Silicon Valley. GV is located in their Mountain View HQ, but also has an office in SF.

Clearly the San Francisco Bay Area/Silicon Valley is the Hollywood of the technology world that attracts the most talent and is home to the most evolved startup–venture ecosystem. If you simply look at the number of tech companies that can buy a venture-backed startup, most of those are in the Silicon Valley: Google, Facebook, Oracle, VMware, etc. The list is endless. With every acquisition a new solar system of startups is born. These founders and early employees run off with cash in their pockets and confidence to found new companies and get funded by angel investors that they worked with at their last company. Every M&A creates a new population of angels and startups. This is happening everywhere from Stockholm to Shenzhen, but nowhere is it happening with such volume and frequency as the Silicon Valley. I think all CVCs should have part of their team living here so they can be at all the networking events in the evening and breakfast meetings throughout the week and even find deals on a Saturday when taking their kids to soccer practice.

CVCs must decide if they will be structured as investing off the balance sheet of the corporate or set up with a GP-LP structure. Most CVCs use the first structure. I personally think the GP-LP structure is better, because the rest of the community will take you more seriously and your investing team is more likely to stay in place. It is more likely the fund will last for a full ten-year term rather than become a statistical CVC with a five-year life span before being discontinued. This also has the best chance to attract and retain a high quality team in a competitive market.

That said I would not lose too much time pushing for this as most senior execs at corporates making these decisions may be a bit uncomfortable with CVC employees making more money than they do. They should look up the compensation of winning NCAA football coaches relative to the salaries of their college presidents!

Corporates that generate revenue in specific currencies and jurisdictions may want to take advantage of tax laws and investment schemes for venture capital and benefit by committing that capital to local VC funds or their own separately structured CVC. If you have revenue in China this may be the perfect opportunity to invest in an RMB Chinese VC fund. The same goes for the UK or EU.

To access the earliest innovation at nascent startups, assign employees as mentors to top accelerator programs in key technology corridors in the US, Europe, Israel and China. You may find it makes sense to launch a branded accelerator with a partner like TechStars or build your own, but I think an easy first step is just to put some employees part time as mentors to a few good accelerator programs in key geographies and areas of focus. Start to attend demo days of the most relevant accelerators. Launching an accelerator is a big endeavor. There are probably too many already in the SF Bay Area. I worry most have negative unit economics. The time delay to exits and commercial viability is even longer than venture. I suspect you'll have adverse selection with negative deal flow. I'm not really a fan of most corporates starting accelerators.

All deals must be both financial and strategic. Don't make an investment without both. To sell CVC internally look at how much you spend annually on R&D and position CVC to be zero cost R&D after five to ten years and then an evergreen profit center that achieves R&D externally and effectively brings that into the corporation. Maintain patience and persistence. If you look at VC from an LP's perspective you should invest into VC every year. You will have good cycles and bad ones. If you are in it every year you will statistically come out better than the stock market, PE or any other asset class.[32] If you make one LP investment you might have entered at the top of the market and it will look like Los Angeles vintage 2000 – a real loser. Historically corporates enter the VC asset class at the top of the market and abandon at the bottom. Keep a steady and measured investment pace with an eye on the long-term goals that take time. Don't invest too much at the height of the market and don't invest too little at the bottom. History has taught us that the best returns are made investing during economic downturns.

CVC should be active at every large corporate in one form or another, the CVC should never be discontinued. It's good to learn from the mistakes and successes of others, but the best way to learn CVC or VC is to make investments ... then make more investments!

---

32 If FINRA or the SEC is reading this, I am just saying what I think. Of course I cannot guarantee financial outcomes. This is just what I would "expect".

Afterword – Andrew Romans

"Brevity is the soul of wit."

Wᴵʟʟᴵᴀᴍ Sʜᴀᴋᴇsᴩᴇᴀʀᴇ

Rubicon **Venture Capital** is an early stage financial VC fund with offices in San Francisco and New York City, focused on backing consumer and enterprise technology companies in the internet, software and connected hardware verticals at Late Seed, Series A and B stages. We are backed by a diverse set of value added LP investors including accredited angels, family offices, corporates and institutional LPs located worldwide. We invest in startups from our fund and then we enable our LPs to co-invest with our fund via our sidecar funds at Seed, A and B financings. We continue to invest in our portfolio companies all the way to exit via our sidecar funds providing our LPs with access to select late stage investment opportunities.

www.rubicon.vc

If you have a story or case study that you think would add to this book's insights, please send it to me:

Andrew@rubicon.vc

If you are an investor seeking to learn more about investing into VC funds, feel free to contact me directly as we are happy to introduce LPs to our VC friends around the world.

If you are an entrepreneur, we are always looking for great startups to invest in. Please visit our web site to learn more about us, check this book's earlier section on "The Best Way to Email a VC or CVC When Seeking Funding"… then fire away.

If you are interested in hosting or sponsoring a book tour event or publishing my book in another language, please get in touch. I am keen to take these corporate venturing insights from this book format into workshops, master classes, keynotes and speaking directly with players in our ecosystem. You can find planned and past events here:

http://rubicon.vc/our-events
http://andrewromans.eventbrite.com

For other stuff you can reach us at
info@rubicon.vc.
You can find more of my writing here:

http://rubicon.vc/blog/
http://amazon.com/author/romans
https://www.linkedin.com/in/romans
https://twitter.com/romansventures

Also by the Author
The Entrepreneurial Bible to Venture Capital, Inside Secrets from the Leaders in the Startup Game

- Published by:
    McGraw Hill (English)
    Machinery Industry Press (Chinese)
    Alpina (Russian)

    English: http://amzn.com/0071830359
    Chinese: http://goo.gl/XNOkHY
    Russian: http://www.alpinabook.ru/catalogue/2401616/

- Available from Amazon, Apple, and many book stores

- Read a free chapter on M&A containing interviews with directors of corporate development from Facebook, Yahoo!, Google and others:
    http://rubicon.vc/free-ma-chapter-from-my-book-which-way-to-the-exit-2/ or shorter URL: http://goo.gl/9Kp25l

About the Author

Andrew Romans is a General Partner at Rubicon Venture Capital, an early stage VC firm with offices in San Francisco and New York City. Andrew is based in Silicon Valley with 23 years' experience as a venture capitalist, founder of VC-backed tech ventures, an investment banker advising startups and VCs on fundraising and M&A and angel investor. Romans also advises corporates on the formation and management of CVC programs. Andrew was the founder of The Global TeleExchange (The GTX), where he raised $50m from VCs and corporates including Lucent Technologies and Lucent Ventures and built a team of 90. Andrew was also a Managing Partner at Georgetown Venture Partners (GVP), a venture capital focused boutique investment bank in London active in Europe, the US and Israel and Georgetown Angels, a global angel investment group. He was General Partner of The Founders Club, focused on secondaries & equity exchange VC funds where Romans recruited 42 VCs and CVCs from the US, Europe and Israel to the advisory board. He was Managing Director of EMEA at VC-backed Sentito Networks (acquired by Verso Technologies). He also managed enterprise software sales at VC-backed Motive Communications (NASDAQ IPO) opening new markets in France, Benelux, Scandinavia and Ireland. He opened new markets and acted as country manager for fiber optic cable manufacturing and turn-key project construction company Dura-Line in the UK, Austria, Czech & Slovak Republics, Slovenia, Croatia and Bosnia-Herzegovina. He began his career in 1993 working in the UNIX computing industry at Pencom

Systems in New York, Silicon Valley and Austin. Andrew is a frequent venture capital guest speaker on TV shows including CNBC, MSNBC and ABC as well as Chinese, European and Russian TV. He was born in Japan, lived in Europe for 15 years, is fluent in English, German and French and conversant in Slovak. He completed high school at Ecole Active Bilingue (EAB) in Paris, holds a BA from the University of Vermont and an MBA in finance from Georgetown University, completed on scholarship. Andrew resides in Silicon Valley with his wife and two sons and leads the Rubicon office in San Francisco.

Acknowledgments

I would like to thank all of the contributors to this book for their generosity and wisdom. Pay it forward and giving to the ecosystem is the mantra of the startup world. Members of the ecosystem helping each other is our religion. So I thank everyone for his or her contributions to the book. I'd also like to thank those that contributed but do not appear, due either to their corporate or my editors. I thank you my reader for using this book to make something happen for you or someone else.

As with my first book, I would like to thank my mother, Lyn Adams, and my stepfather, John Cusick, for flying into California on angels' wings to help me edit this book. Both were involved with corporate development, tech startups and CVC working as expat country managers for AT&T and NYNEX in Japan, Taiwan and Europe in the 1980s and 1990s. Big thanks to all you other early readers that suggested edits, corrections and advice. A special thanks to Mat Kaliski, investment associate at Rubicon Venture Capital, who read and proof read the entire book in one day when asked. You rose to the occasion. Thanks! Just like a startup, a book requires investing, experimenting, A/B testing, time and hard decisions. Thanks to Paul Harvey Douglas, also widely known as PHD or as my kids like to call him, "The godfather of Chelsea," for introducing me to a cool London artist that created true works of art for possible book cover designs. I loved those unique drawings and artwork, but in the end went with the same artist and book cover designer for "The Entrepreneurial

Bible to Venture Capital." Thanks to my brother John Romans, CEO of Biomedix, for coming up with the idea for that final cover design.

Carrying insight and information from an inherently finite book to the big real world can make lots of good stuff happen. I'm totally game for a few book tour events and CVC workshops anywhere my passport will take me. Thanks in advance to everyone that offers to organize or sponsor such an event for *Masters of Corporate Venture Capital*.

I enjoyed meeting everyone and learning so much about corporate venture capital myself. I hope to continue to meet lots of corporates and find new ways to create partnerships among our startups and your huge companies. Let's get to work mastering this together!

Be bold, go far, stay long.

Andrew

San Francisco

Index

Made in the USA
San Bernardino, CA
21 February 2017